LEVELING THE PLAYING FIELD

Sports and Entertainment
Steven A. Riess, *Series Editor*

LEVELING THE PLAYING FIELD

THE STORY OF THE SYRACUSE 8

David Marc

FOREWORD BY JIM BROWN

Syracuse University Press

For a listing of books published and distributed by Syracuse University Press,
visit www.SyracuseUniversityPress.syr.edu.

ISBN: 978-0-8156-1030-4 (cloth)   978-0-8156-5255-7 (e-book)

Library of Congress Cataloging-in-Publication Data
Marc, David.
Leveling the playing field : the story of the Syracuse 8 / David Marc ;
foreword by Jim Brown. — First Edition.
pages cm. — (Sports and Entertainment)
Includes bibliographical references and index.
ISBN 978-0-8156-1030-4 (cloth : alk. paper) — ISBN 978-0-8156-5255-7 (e-book)
1. Syracuse University—Football—History. 2. Syracuse Orange (Football team)—
History. 3. Racism in sports—New York (State)—Syracuse—History. 4. Discrimination
in sports—New York (State)—Syracuse—History. 5. African American football players—
New York (State)—Syracuse—History. 6. African American football players—
Interviews. 7. Civil rights movements—United States—History—20th century.
I. Title. II. Title: Story of the Syracuse Eight.
GV958.S9M37 2015
796.332089—dc23   2015016596

Contents

Illustrations

Tables

Foreword

In 1970, I answered the call of a group of young African American men at Syracuse University, and traveled to Syracuse to see if I could be of help in resolving a situation that threatened their future as athletes. I went with the intention of being a conservative, moderating force. My original goal was to help them reconcile with the coach—my old coach—so they could get on with their careers. But these young men showed me they had something more than that in mind. While their courage was obvious, it was their wisdom that impressed me most deeply. They were young men, but they were wise men. They had the foresight and the ability not only to stand up for themselves but to outline their principles in terms that would live in history and benefit future generations. How bright can young men be? Just have a look at their resumes today, and you will see academic accomplishments and graduate degrees and career achievements that demonstrate that the men who became known as the Syracuse Eight had a far more realistic grasp of who they were and what they were capable of doing than those who ignored, reviled, or opposed them.

I think of the Syracuse Eight and I cannot help but also think of the young men who are now making millions of dollars playing sports, and their histrionics and their endless exhibitions of individuality, displaying so little sense of being part of any community. The Syracuse Eight took action and risks on behalf of themselves in a way that was designed to benefit others. Did they succeed? Look at the things they were asking for in 1970: an end to race discrimination in assigning player positions, an end to race discrimination in academic support for student athletes, medical care that prioritized the health of the athletes above patching them up for the next game, and a diverse coaching staff capable of relating to the needs of all the team members. As punishment for demanding conditions that are now taken for granted by student athletes entering any collegiate sports program in the nation, they were denied their careers as athletes. This is what was done to Muhammad Ali when he was stripped of the heavyweight boxing championship for standing up for his right to protest the Vietnam War. This is what was done to Nelson Mandela when he was denied his place among his people and thrown in prison for twenty years.

If you have the privilege, as I have had, to talk to members of the Syracuse Eight, you will hear no sense of bitterness or revenge in their voices as they recount their stories. Instead, you are impressed by a humbleness and a humility that grow out of their appreciation of what they were able to accomplish for others. It is my personal hope that some of those "others" will read this book, know the names of their benefactors, and be influenced to follow in their footsteps.

Jim Brown

Acknowledgments

We offer our thanks to the people who made this book possible:

Nancy Cantor, former chancellor of Syracuse University, whose compassion and courage moved a university to acknowledge a past wrong and make it right.

Anonymous, whose pivotal financial support was truly a gift from the heart.

Larry Martin and Angela Robinson, whose understanding of the power of healing in the development of institutions provided a guiding spirit. Without Larry Martin's compassion, the story of the Syracuse Eight would have passed into history without a whimper.

Art Monk, member of the College and NFL Halls of Fame, three-time Super Bowl Champion, and Syracuse University Trustee. He is a humble man who embraces the wisdom of understanding and truth. He believes that everything is God's time, and it is this spiritual conviction that shows us his humanity. He will always be respected by the Syracuse Eight for his activism and commitment to seek truth and fairness for all people. The Syracuse Eight family will always be grateful for his moral purpose and that he has joined us while on this journey.

Douglas Biklen and Victoria Kohl, Dean and Assistant Dean, respectively, of the Syracuse University School of Education, who recognized the story of the Syracuse Eight as a missing chapter in the history of American education.

Jerry Beck, who freely shared his research expertise.

We also offer our thanks to the people who made it possible for the Syracuse Eight to get through the difficulties they endured as student athletes:

Dr. Charles V. Willie, Professor of Sociology. The first African American professor at Syracuse University, Charles V. Willie is the author of some twenty-five books. He taught at Syracuse from 1950 to 1974 before leaving to join the faculty of Harvard University, where he served as Charles Elliot Professor of Education. Dr. Willie engaged in behind-the-scenes negotiations with the administration to ensure that the Syracuse Eight were treated fairly and that the issues they raised were taken seriously.

Dr. John L. Johnson, Professor of Education; later Provost and Director of Minority Affairs at Syracuse University. John L. Johnson served as a faculty representative on the Athletic Policy Board and as a member of the SU Athletic Investigating Committee and the Syracuse Eight Recognition Committee. He ensured the athletic scholarships held by the Syracuse Eight would be honored, securing a written agreement to that effect with Chancellor John E. Corbally.

Dr. Allen R. Sullivan, a graduate student in the Syracuse University School of Education during the late 1960s. He earned a master's degree in 1966 and a doctorate in 1970. According to Bucky McGill, "Dr. Sullivan served us by providing the Syracuse Eight with leadership, advice, and strategies regarding our relationships with the administration and the press."

Reverend Dr. George Moody, who served as Director of the Martin Luther King On-Campus Elementary School, where the Syracuse

Eight were invited to hold many of their meetings. Dr. Moody was an influential adviser and advocate who provided the Eight with ideas and strategies on how to deal with the administration, press, and coaching staff.

Prologue

On any given day between orientation and commencement, chances are that an institution of higher learning somewhere in the United States is conferring honors upon one or more of its alumni. Captains of industry, maestros of the arts, scientists crossing thresholds, politicians ranging from elected officials to persecuted dissidents, and other contenders for a spot in the starting lineup of history make the trip back to the alma mater for these affairs. They turn off their handheld devices, shake off their day-to-day cynicism, and do their best to feel the love for a few hours during which they can do no wrong. The ceremonies are, by definition, old school. Professors bask in their proximity to visiting warriors from the Real World. Where wine is permitted, it may come in jugs or boxes. Students spear white and orange cheese cubes with toothpicks. The go-getters among them muster assets for networking opportunities.

Convinced that a lifetime of academic hitchhiking had shown me all four corners of that envelope, I was not fully prepared for the alumni event I attended at Syracuse University on the afternoon of October 21, 2006. For one thing, during the obligatory milling-about period, I noticed that civilians seemed to outnumber students and faculty, even though no media personalities or computer-age industrialists were scheduled for honors. Visitors are easy to spot on a college campus. They dress up a tick, as if for business or religion, a sign of respect that marks them as tourists in the citadel of casual skepticism. What's more, I spotted several notable out-of-town alumni celebrities, people rarely seen at campus events honoring others. They apparently had flown in just for this.

Without fanfare, the chancellor entered the lecture hall through a door down front near the podium, accompanied by the honorees. The group appeared to be, by broad American definition, successful middle-class citizens: an insurance executive from Chicago, a telecommunication systems consultant from Buffalo; a teacher who works with emotionally disturbed children in St. Paul; an instructional coach for teachers in the Massachusetts juvenile justice system; an official of the Virginia juvenile justice system; a Michigan public housing administrator; a Boston real estate attorney; and a Connecticut state development officer. All were African Americans who had attended Syracuse University during the late 1960s. Several had graduate degrees. They were large, impressive men, who looked like they might have played football back in the day. In fact, they had all been standout athletes in high school who had their pick of athletic scholarships. All of them had been offered and had accepted football scholarships in Syracuse University's Division I football program.

And then a funny thing happened on the way to the American dream.

In the spring of 1970, they presented their college football coach with a list of grievances. When he responded by turning a deaf ear, they walked away from spring practice. The petitioners were then summarily dropped from the team, as if being punished for a prank that could not be tolerated. Just like that, they found themselves removed from the red carpet and told to stand over there with the others. It didn't stop at that. Several of these athletes were good bets for the NFL, and any one of them might have made the most of a tryout, but they discovered they had been effectively blacklisted from professional football. They had engaged in a collective act of protest, and it had changed each of their lives profoundly. One of them—his whereabouts unknown that day—had never recovered from the shock. Now, some thirty-five years after things had gone wrong, the survivors had been invited back inside and asked to sit in a place of honor.

The chancellor, who had been a student at Sarah Lawrence when all this happened, apologized to them on behalf of the university, and awarded them alumni medals for the courage they showed in standing by their convictions. Like other Americans who stood up for their rights, they had been reviled and scorned, but their efforts had not been in vain. They had forced the university to reevaluate itself, and the conditions they protested had long ago been redressed at Syracuse and at other colleges around the country. Each of the honorees, known collectively as the Syracuse Eight, was introduced to a thunderous standing ovation. Long-buried emotions rushed to the surface. Some people cried. Diane Weathers, a classmate of the Syracuse Eight who became a reporter for *Newsweek* and then editor-in-chief of *Essence* magazine, told me that for years after graduating she avoided visiting the university or even driving through the city of Syracuse, in fear of stirring up painful reminders of this and related incidents. Bitter memories surely lingered, but the day belonged to forgiveness and reconciliation. An unlikely group was shedding a tear at dear old alma mater.

Of the tributes offered to the Syracuse Eight that day, one stands out for its ferocity and grace. The speaker was Jim Brown, Syracuse University class of 1957, arguably the greatest athlete of the twentieth century.

"You see these guys," he said, gesturing in the direction of the Syracuse Eight. "When they were just kids, they were looking at the possibility of playing pro football and getting a piece of all the money and fame that comes with that. But they were being treated badly and unfairly and they would not overlook it. They *demanded* change— change for themselves and change for those who would follow them. Now let me ask you something. In the past thirty years or so we've had all these NFL and NBA multimillionaires strutting around on TV and showing off their houses and their cars and their jewelry and everything else they've got. Tell me something: Can anyone in this room name a single one of them who has had the courage to stand up for what's right? To take a risk and do what these men did when they were just students in college?"

He pointed at the honored guests: Greg Allen, Richard Bulls, Dana Harrell, John Lobon, Clarence McGill, Alif Muhammad,

Duane Walker, and Ron Womack. (John Godbolt, also honored that day, was not in attendance.)

After a long moment of palpable straining for an answer, the audience's silence became deafening. Jim Brown had brought heroism into focus, and everyone in the house knew exactly what the Syracuse Eight were being honored for, and how fully they deserved it.

David Marc
Syracuse, New York
September 6, 2012

PART ONE

Injuries

1

A Context for Action

During the 1960s, the converging influences of the civil rights struggle, the Vietnam War, and youth culture found their way into every aspect of American popular culture—including sports. Long hair, traditionally taboo for male athletes at every level of competition from the schoolyard to the pros, sprouted among the crew cuts. Marching bands added Motown and Beatles tunes to the John Philip Sousa standards in their halftime shows. The American Basketball Association, launched in 1967, adopted a multicolor ball as regulation equipment. Beneath these surface decorations, seismic shifts were transforming the substance of American sports, and most of the energy driving change was emanating from African American athletes.

Cassius Clay remade himself into Muhammad Ali, denouncing the war in Vietnam and refusing to fight in it. Despite all efforts, in the ring and out, to remove him from boxing, Ali stood fast as the central figure in the sport, ultimately reigning as heavyweight champion on his own terms. Jim Brown of the Cleveland Browns, who never missed a game in nine seasons as the National Football League's greatest running back, startled the sports world by walking away from pro football while he still had two good legs to become Hollywood's first African American action-picture movie star. Tennis ace Arthur Ashe, the first black member of the U.S. Davis Cup team, turned pro in 1968 and promptly won the U.S. Open. He applied for a visa to play in South Africa, knowing it would be denied by the apartheid regime despite his victory in a Grand Slam event. Having created an ideal media occasion, Ashe used it to call for South

3

Africa's exclusion from world tennis competition. When Curt Flood was traded away by the St. Louis Cardinals without his knowledge or consent, he took on Major League Baseball, Congress, and the Supreme Court rather than be forced to work for an employer not of his choosing. "I do not feel I am a piece of property to be bought and sold, irrespective of my wishes," Flood wrote, invoking the specter of slavery in a 1969 open letter to baseball commissioner Bowie Kuhn. Flood's act of leadership initiated a series of events that ended baseball's exemption from U.S. antitrust laws, and major league ballplayers of all races have been millionaires ever since. Among these and the many acts of protest that shook up the sports world during the 1960s, one remains a milestone at the vanishing point where gesture becomes substance. Following his record-breaking gold medal time in the 200-meter sprint at the 1968 Olympics in Mexico City, Tommy Smith assumed his place on the podium for the victory ceremony alongside bronze medalist John Carlos. Instead of putting their hands to their hearts, each lifted a clenched fist in a black glove— the "black power salute"—while the "The Star-Spangled Banner" played, Old Glory flapped in the breeze, and millions of television viewers watched.[1] African American athletes were taking charge of their lives, and the implications of their actions were changing the rules of the games for everyone.

In Ithaca, New York, at a place less visible to the public eye, Harry Edwards, a Cornell University graduate student, was embarking on a lifelong scholarly enterprise that would have an effect on the sports world eventually rivaling that of any star in a uniform. A 6-foot 8-inch, 245-pound student athlete from hard-times East St. Louis, Illinois, Edwards went west to Fresno City College, broke a California junior college record in the discus throw, and transferred to San Jose State University, where he played intercollegiate basketball and football. He was of one of approximately seventy black students (about half of them on athletic scholarships) at a state campus serving some 24,000 students. After graduating, Edwards turned down tryout invitations from the Minnesota Vikings (NFL) and San Diego Chargers (AFL) to accept a Woodrow Wilson Fellowship in pursuit of an Ivy League doctorate. Applying the skills of a professional social scientist to the lessons of personal experience, Edwards dedicated himself to debunking the popular belief in the 1960s that sports in the United States had evolved from the bad old days of Jim Crow baseball and great-white-hope boxing into an abundant and benevolent source of opportunity for people of color.

Edwards first gained national attention as head of the Olympic Project for Human Rights (OPHR), an organization founded to persuade African American athletes to boycott the 1968 Mexico City games. OPHR announced a variety of demands, ranging from issues of the moment, such as the exclusion of white-ruled South Africa and Rhodesia (now Zimbabwe), to the ousting of Avery Brundage, whose hefty resume as a member of the U.S. and International Olympic committees included promotion of Nazi Germany as host of the 1936 games. In the long view, Edwards believed, a boycott by black athletes would underscore the central role African Americans played in spectator sports, and an uproar around their absence would help shift public attention to the more pressing matters threatening black people. "For years we have participated in the Olympic Games, carrying the United States on our backs with our victories—and race relations are now worse than ever," Edwards told the *New York Times*. "It's time for black people to stand up as men and women and refuse to be utilized as performing animals for a little extra dog food."[2]

Only a few athletes of Olympic caliber responded to the call, and most of them were college basketball players who could look forward to lucrative careers in the NBA, whether or not they participated in the Olympics.[3] Kareem Abdul-Jabbar (known then as Lew Alcindor), was probably the biggest name to publicly sympathize with the boycott. A UCLA junior during the 1967–68 academic year, Abdul-Jabbar was the dominant player on the dominant team in college basketball. His absence from the Olympic trials in Denver that spring made headlines.[4] But otherwise, Edwards had little success in convincing elite athletes to risk what they assumed was a gateway—perhaps their only gateway—to personal fame and professional opportunity. For track-and-field hopefuls and others in "nonprofessional" sports, an Olympic medal or even selection for the U.S. team could spell the difference between continuing to compete after college under sponsorship of an athletic club or, after a life of striving for perfection at the top, an abrupt end to their dreams with little to show for all their hard work. To complicate Edwards's task further, several prominent African Americans, including past Olympic gold medalists Jesse Owens and Rafer Johnson, issued public statements opposing the boycott as a self-defeating tactic. As it became clear to Edwards that an effective boycott of Mexico City could not be organized, he urged participating athletes to put their moments in the media spotlight to good use by making bold statements highlighting the plight of black people. The silent protest of Tommy Smith and John Carlos survives in media storage as the tangible result of that effort.[5]

Edwards's attempts to convince black athletes to withhold their talents were not limited to the Olympics. After completing graduate work at Cornell, he returned to San Jose State as a part-time instructor and assistant football coach. Wielding the authority of his position, Edwards urged players to consider sitting out the season with the aim of creating a public platform to air their own grievances concerning race-based mistreatment and, in the process, gain publicity for national and international issues of concern to black people. Although few members of the San Jose State team had realistic hopes of finding careers in pro football—less than 1 percent of college football players ever become pros—most reacted as the Olympic hopefuls had reacted to the OPHR boycott campaign. They had invested too much of their self-worth in football, and as slim a possibility as an NFL contract might be, it was a dream too dazzling to ignore.[6]

Edwards did manage to convince some San Jose State players to participate in isolated actions. Before the start of the 1967 season, several agreed to stand with him in a demonstration designed to disrupt the home opener against the University of Texas-El Paso, a state university that fielded an all-white team. When the planned protest became public knowledge, it galvanized Klan members, neo-Nazis, and garden-variety white supremacists, on campus and off, who were chomping at the bit for a violent confrontation with demonstrators in front of television cameras. Fearing a riot, school officials cancelled the game. This had the twin effects of burying the demonstration's intentions deep inside a media feeding frenzy, and generating public anger at "extremists on both sides" for causing the game to be called off. San Jose State then played out the balance of its schedule without incident.

In 1968, Edwards called for a boycott of a road game in Provo, Utah, with Brigham Young University, a school affiliated with the Church of Jesus Christ of Latter-Day Saints. The Mormon Church was widely viewed by African Americans as a racist institution, a reputation that owed much to a ban, lifted in 1978, on black clergy instituted by BYU's namesake. Tony Jackson, San Jose State's starting defensive end and president of the campus's Black Athletes Federation, was among those who participated in the BYU boycott.[7] "Those were tough times," recalled Jackson, who went on to a distinguished career as a military officer, rising to the rank of major general in the U.S. Marine Corps. "We were criticized by some for doing too little and by others for doing too much in combining race and politics with sport. I was the public face for the black athletes. At 19 years old, that was a challenge for me."[8] In terms of advancing Edwards's long-range goal of raising awareness of the pivotal role played by African American athletes, the protest lost much of its force when San Jose State managed to defeat BYU despite the absence of the boycotting players.[9]

Another attempt was made by African American student athletes to protest Mormon racial policy during the 1969 football season. This time a different tactic was used. Fourteen members of the University of Wyoming team decided among themselves that they would play in a scheduled home game against BYU, but would wear black armbands to voice their disapproval of the race policies followed by the university and the LDS Church. They informed head coach Lloyd Eaton of their intention on the Tuesday before Saturday's game in Laramie. Eaton's response came at a team meeting that Friday: "The coach requested that the group be seated in the bleachers at the field house. In the presence of two assistant coaches, Eaton called the Blacks 'rabble-rousers' who could no longer be supported by taxpayer money. He told them they could go back on 'Negro relief.' Repeatedly he told the athletes to 'shut up' and suggested that if they had not come to Wyoming, 'they would be out on the streets hustling.'"[10]

According to former Wyoming Attorney General James E. Barrett, who represented the state in litigation stemming from the incident, "The meeting ended after Coach Eaton, convinced that the fourteen were insistent on wearing the black armbands during the football game, notified the fourteen that they were no longer members of the football squad."[11] The players sued for reinstatement, but their suit was dismissed in federal court. Three of the fourteen players separated themselves from further legal action and were permitted to return to the team the following year. Clarence "Bucky" McGill, a member of the group of Syracuse University football players who became known as the Syracuse Eight, notes a bizarre connection between the Wyoming and Syracuse protests, which occurred less than a year apart: "The two main schools that recruited me were Wyoming and Syracuse. It looks like no matter which one I chose or how well I performed, I wasn't going to be playing out my full eligibility."[12]

After his experiences with the 1968 Olympics and the San Jose football program, Harry Edwards had become disillusioned by the overwhelming reluctance of black amateur athletes to join him in building a boycott movement. But Edwards found other ways to push for social change in the sports world and never flagged in his commitment. Over time, he refocused his efforts on professional sports, where he met with success in helping to create new career opportunities for African Americans in coaching, front office administration, and franchise ownership.[13] Edwards began moving in that direction after leaving San Jose for Berkeley to take a full-time position on the University of California sociology faculty in 1970.

That same year, about an hour's drive from the Cornell campus where Edwards had articulated many of his ideas about the complex relationships among sport, race, and politics in American culture, a group of African American student athletes at Syracuse University was independently deciding to embrace the very tactic Edwards was abandoning. They would articulate a series of grievances and organize one of the only such collective protests in the history of American collegiate sports. Although their number varied, a headline proclaimed them "the Syracuse Eight"—and it stuck.

Coming from a variety of working- and middle-class backgrounds, all had tasted early glory as high school stars and all had demonstrated the required capacities for focused concentration in athletics, academics, and the balancing of the two. Up until this point in their lives, things had pretty much fallen into place as promised. They were recruited, in some cases enticed, by big-name universities to come to college. They had achieved a mythic state, an American dream life whose image continues to float like an advertising blimp above inner-city schoolyards and rural playing fields across the country. They were scholarship students in an NCAA Division I program in a money sport. The cost? All they had to do was play the game right.

They weren't the first to follow this path. William Henry Clay Lewis and William Tecumseh Sherman Jackson, members of Amherst College's class of 1892, are believed to be the first nonwhites to have played intercollegiate football as members of a racially integrated team. A limited number of majority-white schools outside the South began recruiting African American student athletes in the early twentieth century. Among those who had gotten their educations playing ball with university athletic programs were such leadership figures as the renowned performer and political activist Paul Robeson and baseball Hall-of-Famer Jackie Robinson, whose dazzling career stats will never be as impressive as the courage he displayed in breaking Major League Baseball's boycott of black players. But as Paul Robeson, Jackie Robinson, and others among a chosen few discovered after arriving on campus, they would be put through more than just college by their athletic scholarships.

Paul Robeson, a Phi Beta Kappa student at Rutgers in the early 1920s, and the first African American selected for an All-American football team, sustained multiple injuries in practices at the hands of teammates opposed to his presence. Jackie Robinson lettered in four sports at UCLA, meeting a year-round schedule that left him short of graduation credits at the end of his senior year. When his athletic eligibility expired, he was forced to quit school, without a degree, for financial reasons. Gregory George, the first black All-American basketball player, captained Columbia University to its first two Eastern (now Ivy) League titles in 1930 and 1931. Like many scholarship athletes before him at Columbia, including Lou Gehrig, George needed to supplement his scholarship by working. He could have had his pick of jobs on campus but chose instead to work as a redcap baggage porter in Pennsylvania Station.[14] "He used to say how all the hard work and lifting helped him stay in shape," according to his teammate, Lou Bender. "But years later he admitted to me that he went down there to work because it was a chance to get away from feeling like he was under a microscope."[15] Willie Thrower's dilemma as a black student athlete at a white university was less subtle. He routinely received death threats while quarterbacking Michigan State to an undefeated season and the national collegiate championship in 1952.[16]

The administrators of historically white universities that offered athletic scholarships to African Americans generally believed they had met or exceeded the obligations of enlightened institutions by granting opportunities to deserving individuals, paying little or no attention to the consequences of thrusting talented young people into unfamiliar environments fraught with psychological and physical dangers. As for the student athletes, they tended to suffer the indignities they encountered in silence, protecting their educational opportunities as means to greater ends in their lives. This was as true of those who became activist-heroes as it was of the members of the San Jose State football team that Harry Edwards could not rally to political action.

There is no denying that before World War II, athletic scholarships to "white" universities functioned as a rare and precious conduit into higher education for exceptional African Americans who otherwise might not have been able to attend college at all. Take the example of Jerome H. "Brud" Holland. One of thirteen children, Holland was born and raised in Auburn, New York, a small Finger Lakes town that otherwise appears on the map of African American history as the home of Harriet Tubman, chief engineer of the Underground Railroad. Holland was an excellent student at Auburn High School, and news of his football achievements was regularly relayed to the Cornell University coaching staff by Holland's father, a campus groundskeeper. Admitted to Cornell with an athletic scholarship in 1935, Holland continued to demonstrate his academic abilities as a straight-A student. As starting offensive end for the Big Red football team, he was twice selected as a first-team All-American, despite the refusal of newspapers in segregation states to even mention him in their sports pages. Graduating in the Depression year of 1939, he did not have the option of playing professional football; blacks were barred from the National Football League by an informal agreement among franchise owners that lasted from 1933 until 1946. That closed door did not hold Holland back from turning elsewhere with his talents. He stayed at Cornell as an assistant football coach while studying for a master's degree, and then earned a doctorate in sociology at the University of Pennsylvania. His Ivy League education complete, Holland applied his expertise to the needs of historically black colleges. A distinguished teaching career at Lincoln University in Pennsylvania led to his appointment as president of Delaware State College (now University) in Dover, where he oversaw the school's return to accreditation, which it had lost four years before his arrival.[17] Holland then served as president of Hampton Institute (now Hampton University) in Virginia from 1960 to 1970. Some of the other lines on Holland's resume include U.S. ambassador to Sweden; national executive director of the American Red Cross; and member of the board of directors of the New York Stock Exchange (the first African American so appointed). The recipient of more than twenty honorary doctorates, Holland remained a supporter of Cornell University throughout his life. A campus dormitory for international students bears his name.

Among the indignities Holland was spared while playing Big Red football was the forced benching of African American players, a "courtesy" shown by integrated teams from the North when they played on the road in segregation states. The Cornell football schedule never sent the team south of Philadelphia while Holland was a student (1935–39). But Wilmeth Sidat-Singh, who lettered in both basketball and football at Syracuse University during those same years, was not so lucky. The Orange didn't go South too far or too often, but when they crossed the Mason-Dixon Line to face football or basketball rivals in Maryland (including the U.S. Naval Academy at Annapolis), African American students were barred from playing, and in some cases barred from attending games.

Dating back to Wilmeth Sidat-Singh's days as a star high school basketball player in New York City, some sports writers and many fans took it for granted that a kid named "Sidat-Singh" was either born in India or was of South Asian descent. Neither was the case; his parents were both African Americans. Elias Webb was a pharmacist in Washington, DC, who died shortly after Wilmeth was born; several years later, Pauline Webb married Samuel Sidat-Singh, a medical student at Howard University who had emigrated from India. Samuel Sidat-Singh formally adopted his wife's son in 1924 and gave the child his name. The family then moved to New York City, where Dr. Sidat-Singh set up a general medical practice on the ground floor of his brownstone home on West 135th Street in Harlem.

At DeWitt Clinton High School in the Bronx, Wilmeth Sidat-Singh had led the basketball team to a New York City championship as a junior and was named to the all-city team as a senior. He graduated with a college preparatory degree in 1935 but received only one scholarship offer—from Syracuse University. The particulars of why Syracuse, alone, saw fit to approach him are not known.[18] What can be said with certainty is that the historical traditions of the school and the region supported racially integrated education, a legacy of Central New York's years as a hotbed of antislavery activism before the Civil War. Syracuse University was founded in 1870 by staunch Methodist abolitionists, some of whom risked jail in the

1850s by harboring fugitive slaves on the escape route to Canada. In his inaugural speech to the faculty, Rev. Dr. Jesse T. Peck, founding chair of the Syracuse University Board of Trustees, told the professors, "The laws under which you will do your work say, 'the conditions of admission shall be equal to all persons . . . there shall be no invidious discriminations here against woman or persons of any nation or color."[19] A decade after classes began, Syracuse alumni were overwhelmingly white, but they also included African American men and women, as well as international students from Latin America who were recruited for Syracuse by Methodist missionaries. Dr. Sarah Loguen Fraser, the fourth African American woman to become a physician in the United States, was an 1876 Syracuse graduate. The university's ability to live up fully to the egalitarian mandate of its founders waxed and waned during the early twentieth century, but in the 1930s, when the Syracuse athletic department offered a basketball scholarship to a nonwhite student from a Bronx public school, tradition and policy supported it, no law stood against it, and no organized opposition was voiced by faculty or alumni. The same cannot be said of many or most American universities at that time.

A zoology major at Syracuse, Sidat-Singh was described in a student magazine as "more interested in a sheepskin than a pigskin"; that is, a serious student who seemed to be following the footsteps of both his biological and adoptive fathers into the medical professions.[20] Recruited for basketball, he tried out for the football team at the urging of lacrosse coach Roy D. Simmons Sr., who spotted the 6-foot, 190-pound freshman playing an intramural game and was impressed by the strength and accuracy of his passing arm. By fall of his sophomore year, Sidat-Singh was leading Syracuse's single-wing offense, playing a position roughly analogous to a present-day T-formation quarterback. Fans attending Syracuse–Cornell games during the late 1930s witnessed the unusual spectacle of two racially integrated college teams on the field, a long-deferred fulfillment of a vision from Central New York's abolitionist past. Those fans were treated to a particularly exciting afternoon of football in

1938 when Sidat-Singh threw three touchdown passes during the final nine minutes, giving Syracuse a spectacular 19–17 victory over favored Cornell. The famed sportswriter Grantland Rice, attending the game to scout Cornell's postseason bowl prospects, devoted his column instead to singing the praises of Sidat-Singh, comparing him to Sammy Baugh and Sid Luckman, the greatest passing quarterbacks of the day. Rice was moved to write a poem, which concluded with these lines:

> in Ithaca now the sad boys ring their change on a bitter theme—
> "Did you see that thing? That's Sidat-Singh—the Syracuse
>   walking dream."[21]

If the Cornell–Syracuse football games of the late 1930s are highlights in the pre–World War II history of U.S. student athletics, the 1937 Syracuse–Maryland football game is a lowlight. Oscar "Ossie" Solem, Syracuse's new head coach in 1937, faced the difficult job of replacing Vic Hanson, a local high school star and Orange alum who had captained teams in three sports and played minor league baseball for the Yankees before returning to Syracuse to take charge of the football team. For Solem, a stranger from the Midwest hoping to make a good impression, Wilmeth Sidat-Singh did indeed arrive at spring practice like a "walking dream": a walk-on football player who could rifle 30-yard passes right on the numbers or, when faced with blitzing linebackers, chew up yards like a halfback. Solem constructed a classic single-wing offense around Sidat-Singh that summer, and the Orange surprised everyone with September victories over regional rivals Clarkson, St. Lawrence, and Cornell in its first three games. But the upcoming Maryland game presented Coach Solem with a problem he could not solve with his playbook. It was a road game scheduled to be played at Baltimore's old Municipal Stadium, and athletic director Lew Andreas informed Solem that he would have to bench his premier player because of a custom, or "gentlemen's agreement," banning "Negroes" from playing on the same football field as whites.[22]

Solem learned about the myth that had grown up among (white) New York City basketball fans that the light-complexioned Sidat-Singh was a "Hindu," a term for South Asians then commonly used by Americans. Several old newspaper stories referring to Sidat-Singh as a "Hindu" were circulated to the Baltimore press. Any plan to hide his race would likely have worked had it not been for investigative reporting by Sam Lacy, who broke the story of the Syracuse ace's real identity just days before the game, hoping it would help to expose the absurd pettiness of segregation.[23] Maryland officials, already fighting efforts to reintegrate the state university (which had briefly admitted African Americans during the late nineteenth century), wasted no time in demanding that Sidat-Singh be excluded from the game.[24]

Marty Glickman, who would later become the play-by-play radio voice of four New York City pro sports teams, was a member the Syracuse football team in 1937. He was also Sidat-Singh's roommate. A Jew and an African American, the two were assigned special accommodations in the basement of the men's gym. In his autobiography, *The Fastest Kid on the Block*, Glickman recalls the locker-room announcement that Sidat-Singh was to be excluded from the Maryland game: "There was shocked silence. I sat there, alongside Wil, and said to myself, 'If Wil doesn't play, I don't play.'"[25] If anyone should have been prepared to take a stand for Sidat-Singh, it was Glickman. Just fourteen months earlier, he was benched by U.S. track coaches Dean Cromwell and Lawson Robertson at the Berlin Olympics after Adolph Hitler let it be known that he didn't want Jews competing at the games. But Glickman did not speak up or act on Sidat-Singh's behalf, nor did any other member of the team or coaching staff. According to Marjorie Glickman, who had heard her husband rehash the event innumerable times over the years, "Marty thought people would say, 'There goes that *Jewboy* causing trouble again.' So he decided to play."[26] Glickman's rationale for failing to protest or to boycott the game is strikingly similar to the explanations offered thirty years later by the players who said no to Harry Edwards at San Jose State. Underneath the big-jocks-on-campus bravado, student athletes were powerless amateurs who were "pay-ing" for their educations with their athletic skills, and they were not prepared to risk their scholarships—and the brightest visions of their own futures—over a question of right and wrong. The Syracuse offense was powerless in every way that Saturday; the Orange was shut out, 13–0.[27] A year later, the home-and-home series resumed up north and, led by Sidat-Singh, the Orange got revenge, beating Maryland in a 53–0 route. "We got even," Glickman wrote, "but . . . it wasn't like standing up and saying, 'If Wil doesn't play, I don't play.' I have regretted my silence ever since."[28] The incident held an extra measure of personal pain for Sidat-Singh; his relatives from nearby Washington had made plans to attend the game. His aunt, Adelaide Webb Henley, was among them. "Wilmeth was just sit-ting there, with his head down, so embarrassed and humiliated," she recalled to a reporter some sixty-five years later.[29]

Sidat-Singh faced one more challenge to his right to play football for Syracuse University. During the 1938 season, a few weeks after the triumphant victory over Maryland, the Orange were scheduled to host Duke University for the first-ever football match-up between the two schools. Much to the surprise of just about everyone, includ-ing Coach Solem, Lew Andreas announced that Wilmeth Sidat-Singh would not be eligible to play in that game. Two years earlier, when Syracuse and Duke arranged the 1938–39 home-and-home series, Andreas, who had just become athletic director, had signed a contract with his counterpart at Duke agreeing that no black player could participate in any game, regardless of location.[30] (There had been no such contract with Maryland.) But Sidat-Singh had become quite a star for the Orange since then, and he had been the game hero in two big wins that season: the fourth-quarter comeback triumph over Cornell and the revenge trouncing of Maryland. When he made a big play, the marching band struck up "It Don't Mean a Thing If It Ain't Got that Swing," a popular Duke Ellington tune, and the pep squad led fans in singing a parody, "It Don't Mean a Thing If It Ain't Got Sidat-Singh."

Students, alumni, fans, and others, not all of whom held progressive views on race issues, expressed varying degrees of disappointment and/or outrage; all agreed that without the home team's
offensive powerhouse, Syracuse hardly stood a chance against Duke,
the best defensive team in the country that year. Andreas told the
press that he was forced to abide by the contract and his hands were
tied. The crisis was defused by an unlikely source. On October 29,
1938, Duke head coach Wallace Wade sent a telegram to the Syracuse athletic department: "Duke will raise no objection to Sidat-
Singh playing in the game of November 12."[31]

A sports brief in the *New York Times* on October 22 announced
that Wade had given Syracuse "permission" to play the "crack Negro
back" despite the contract, signed by both parties, which contained
a clause forbidding Sidat-Singh from playing against the Blue Devils. Wade is quoted as saying "We don't want to penalize Syracuse
by forbidding them to use Sidat-Singh."[32] But Wade was not acting
on any principle but self-interest. Duke was ranked ninth and Syracuse tenth in the national Associated Press poll for the last week of
October, 1938. Hoping for Duke's first-ever Rose Bowl invitation,
the Blue Devils needed a "clean" victory over the Orange to get it.
Wade feared that a win based on the forced benching of Syracuse's
star player would be viewed as tainted—perhaps seen as worse than
a loss—in the eyes of the publicity-consciousness Pasadena invitation
committee.[33]

Although Sidat-Singh was spared the humiliation of being banned
from playing on his home field, and the university was spared the dis-
grace of complicity, the outcome was not a happy one. The Orange
could do nothing to penetrate Duke's legendary 1938 defense. The
Orange was shut out—as was every other opponent the Blue Devils
faced during the regular season. Duke got its invitation to the Rose
Bowl and, on New Year's Day, 1939, seemed on its way to a perfect
season of ten shutouts when USC scored a touchdown in the final
minutes for a 7–3 Trojan victory. Those were the only points scored
on Duke for the entire season.

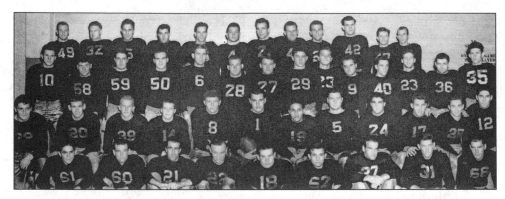

1. The 1938 Syracuse University football team pictured in the 1939 *Onondagan*. Wilmeth Sidat-Singh, no. 19, second row, seventh from the left. Marty Glickman, no. 25, second row, second from the right. Hugh "Duffy" Daugherty, top row, sixth from the left. Photograph Collection, University Archives, Syracuse University Libraries.

Any public impression that Duke had invited Sidat-Singh to take the field in Syracuse as an act of leadership in racial moderation was dispelled by an incident that occurred during the lead-up to the Rose Bowl. Duke offered Rose Bowl tickets at face value to white hometown season ticket holders in Durham but did not extend that courtesy to the fans who sat in the "Colored Only" section of Duke Stadium. In its coverage of that story, the *Carolina Times*, an African American newspaper, reported that a Duke official said the university would sell tickets to the Japanese before it would sell them to blacks, using vernacular language in his comment. To end the uproar that ensued in the national press, Duke officials came up with 140 tickets for the black faithful, even though university officials had previously announced their tickets were completely sold out.[34]

In the spring of 1939, the two leading college football players in Central New York, Brud Holland and Wilmeth Sidat-Singh, both received bachelor's degrees. Because they were African Americans, neither had the option of playing professional football.[35] Holland, who seemed to have set himself a steady course for a career as a scholar and educator, may not have cared to. But Sidat-Singh, after earning his degree in zoology, did not pursue admission to medical or pharmacy school, as his family had hoped; instead he seemed determined to become a professional athlete. Even at the level of talent he had demonstrated, this was a remote possibility for an African American in 1939. Basketball, his one best chance, had not yet established itself as a viable commercial game. It had no mythic national identity like professional baseball, nor had it developed a brand name on the order of the National Football League or National Hockey League, both of which were founded in the twentieth century and had managed to survive the Great Depression as going concerns.

Although basketball had not yet made it as a professional sport, the popularity of the game was growing in the late 1930s, especially in the snowbelt states of the Northeast and Midwest.[36] Pro teams known as barnstormers traveled from town to town taking on all comers in return for most of the gate and whatever betting action could be found among opposing players and local fans. Successful barnstorming teams sometimes could be persuaded to join regional pro leagues for a season or two if there was money to be made, but when the pickings got thin or if league rules proved unfavorable to their style of play, they just as easily dropped out and went independent again. Touring in two or three automobiles, barnstorming teams, many with big-city home bases, took on local factory teams or played against impromptu teams composed of former high school or college players from the area, whose names could help fill the seats. As in other pro sports of the era, teams were typically all-black or all-white. The New York Renaissance, or the "Harlem Rens" as they were known, were widely acknowledged as the greatest of all-black professional teams known as "the black fives"; the Celtics (or the "Original Celtics" as they liked to be called to distinguish themselves from imitators) owned a reputation as the top white team. But barnstorming, by its nature, is not governable by official regulations. Games were played in school gyms, armories, and union halls, and received minimal newspaper coverage, if they were reported on at all. Radio was already the most popular mass medium in America, but basketball was thought to be too fast-moving and complicated to be described over the air. In this primitive media environment, local conditions ruled when it came to race. Outside of the South, it was not unusual to have all-white and all-black teams play each other, and it was not unheard of for a black player to show up on a white team, or vice versa, especially when injuries or better offers from elsewhere left teams suddenly shorthanded on game day.

In November 1939, six months after Sidat-Singh had graduated from Syracuse University, the Syracuse Reds, a recently formed barnstorming team made up of former college basketball players, announced they had signed Sidat-Singh and that he would be in their starting lineup. It thus became one of the few professional basketball teams of the era with a racially integrated roster.[37] Even though just about every sports fan in upstate New York knew that Sidat-Singh was an African American because of the hubbub surrounding his banishment from the Syracuse–Maryland football game two years earlier, a team picture of the Reds appeared in the *Syracuse Herald* under the headline, "Hindu Ace Aids Syracuse Title Quest."

It is possible that the Reds were hedging their bets by keeping the myth of the "Hindu" basketball star alive, and that the newspaper was sympathetic to the city's new team. The Reds had started the 1939–40 basketball season as a franchise in the New York State Professional League, but dropped that affiliation a few weeks into the season in favor of barnstorming. They truly took on all comers, defeating both the all-white Celtics on December 1 at the high school gym in Watertown, New York, and the all-black Chicago Crusaders on December 30 at the Jefferson Street armory in downtown Syracuse. These victories by an integrated team made the Reds a sudden topic of conversation in the barnstorming basketball world. Sidat-Singh scored a team-high 14 points in the Reds' 40–37 win over the Celtics, and Dutch Dehnert, one of the Celtic greats, told New York City reporters that the Syracuse "Hindu" was one of the best young players he had seen.

A year later, Sidat-Singh was playing for the Harlem Rens. A great sports career seemed in the making, but it was not to be. Sidat-Singh enlisted in the army after Pearl Harbor, and was accepted into

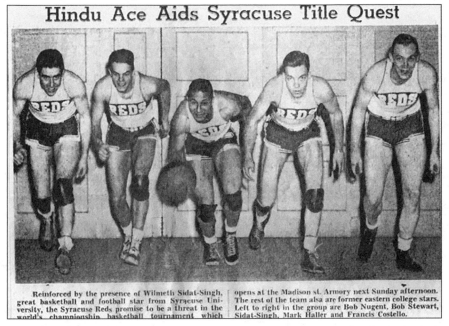

Hindu Ace Aids Syracuse Title Quest

Reinforced by the presence of Wilmeth Sidat-Singh, great basketball and football star from Syracuse University, the Syracuse Reds promise to be a threat in the world's championship basketball tournament which opens at the Madison st. Armory next Sunday afternoon. The rest of the team also are former eastern college stars. Left to right in the group are Bob Nugent, Bob Stewart, Sidat-Singh, Mark Haller and Francis Costello.

2. The Syracuse Reds professional basketball quintet, ca. 1939, with Wilmeth Sidat-Singh third from left.

flight school as a member of the Tuskegee Airmen, the only African American unit in the segregated U.S. Army Air Force. Shortly after earning his pilot's wings, Lt. Wilmeth Sidat-Singh died when his P-47 went down in Lake Huron with a failed engine during a training mission. He was just twenty-five years old.

2

Progress and Its Myths

When the World War II ended, the professional sports opportunities that had been denied to Brud Holland, Wilmeth Sidat-Singh, and other African Americans of their generation began to materialize. The NFL announced an end to its thirteen-year ban on black players in 1946. While publicists and many sportswriters emphasized that the league had seen the light because no team was about to refuse a place to any deserving American who had fought for his country, less was said about the fact that a rival pro league, the All-America Football Conference (AAFC), was launched that year with no race restrictions, official or unofficial. Paul Brown, owner, general manager, and coach of the AAFC's Cleveland Browns, signed Bill Willis, a defensive lineman he had coached at Ohio State before the war, and Marion Motley, a fullback he had coached during the war at the Great Lakes Naval Station. Willis and Motley played for the Browns on opening day 1946, breaking the pro football ban on African Americans. The NFL, in effect, was doing what it had to do to keep up with the competition.

At the same time, basketball was beginning to take form as a major professional sport. Danny Biasone, owner of the Syracuse Reds, the barnstorming team that Sidat-Singh had played for, purchased a franchise in the National Basketball League (NBL) in 1946. With postwar anticommunist rhetoric gearing up, Biasone acceded to the wishes of other NBL owners (including such corporate franchise holders as General Electric, Firestone, and Goodyear) and rechristened the Reds with a name that had a more patriotic ring: the Syracuse Nationals.[1]

The NBL had permitted African American players during wartime, when players were scarce, but with the war over and basketball players returning from military service en masse, no one was quite sure what league policy might be. Lester Harrison, owner-coach of the neighboring Rochester Royals, forced the issue by signing William "Dolly" King, a member of the Harlem Rens who had played on integrated teams for Long Island University during the 1930s. NBL commissioner Ward "Piggy" Lambert, who had coached black student athletes at Purdue, approved the contract, opening the door for other teams to sign black players. According to Harrison, lodging was a serious obstacle faced by black pro basketball players during the late 1940s. Indiana, which had three pro franchises in two leagues during the period, presented persistent problems, although segregation had no legal status there. "It was unheard of that a colored player be registered in a 'white' hotel in Indianapolis, Fort Wayne, or Anderson, and the only housing for colored players in those cities were the colored YMCAs," Harrison recalled. When the Claypool Hotel in Indianapolis refused to serve dinner to Dolly King in the main dining room with the rest of the team, the Royals walked out and ordered up room service, with King as their guest. The Claypool apparently had no problem with that.[2]

The NBL was the setting for another kind of racial integration, although some interpreted it as a new form of segregation with a twist: After Dolly King joined the Royals, Pop Gates, another established star with the Rens, signed with the Tri-Cities Blackhawks in Rock Island, Illinois. While African Americans generally welcomed the integration of professional sports as a harbinger of things to come, Gates's former teammates were furious that he had jumped ship, and fans of the Rens and other "black fives" feared the destruction of their teams and of the game as it had developed in black America. After a year in the league, Gates saw an opportunity to make things right with his teammates and took a bold step: He arranged for the Rens to replace a moribund NBL franchise in the middle of the 1948–49 season. After twenty-five years in Harlem, the team moved to Ohio and became the Dayton Rens, with Gates serving as a player-coach.

In 1949, the NBL merged with its rival, the Basketball Association of America (BAA), and thus the National Basketball Association—the NBA—was born. But the BAA had been an all-white league, and under the terms of the merger, the NBA came into existence as a segregated, whites-only enterprise. Seven existing NBL franchises were invited to join the new league, but the Dayton Rens were not one of them. In fact, all of the black players in the NBL suddenly found themselves out of a job.

With the birth of the NBA, Syracuse had the first—and only—bona fide major league sports team in its history. One of the Nationals' early stars was Earl Lloyd, who had become the first African American to play in the NBA when he stepped onto the hardwood as a member of the original Washington Capitals on October 31, 1950.[3] But two things happened during Lloyd's rookie season that put his pro basketball career in limbo: he was called up by the draft for basic training, and while he was in uniform the Caps folded, leaving him without a team when he returned. Biasone signed Lloyd in 1952, as his hitch was up. Lloyd started at forward for the Nats for six seasons, including 1955–56, the year Syracuse won the NBA championship. Lloyd's career with the Nats overlapped with Jim Brown's college career with the Orange, giving African Americans a prominent place in the sports pages during the greatest sports era that fans in Central New York State had ever experienced. "Syracuse, for me, was definitely the right place at the right time," Lloyd wrote in his 2010 autobiography.[4]

The 1950s was a sports-mad decade in Syracuse, and although African Americans helped put Syracuse on the national sports map with pro basketball (1955) and college football (1959) national titles, there was not a trace of Wilmeth Sidat-Singh to be found anywhere in town—including the campus—despite the fact that he had played both sports in Syracuse. As a student athlete in the late 1930s, he had given Orange football fans some of the most thrilling moments they had ever seen, and he had led the basketball team through its great 1938–39 season. As a pro athlete, he helped the Syracuse Reds upset the Original Celtics and beat other well-known barnstorming teams. As a wartime pilot, he had made the ultimate sacrifice. The historian Thomas G. Brown, who has documented a long history of slights, insults, and insensitivities in his studies of race and sports in America, was nonetheless astounded when he traveled to Syracuse in 2003 and learned there was no memorial to Sidat-Singh anywhere in the city. "Certainly, his talent is on a par with an Ernie Davis or a Jim Brown—and there's nothing to honor the guy *who made it possible* for them to have fantastic careers?" Smith said.[5] That sad omission would finally be addressed in 2005, when the Syracuse University athletic department retired Sidat-Singh's jersey in a ceremony at the Carrier Dome.

Sidat-Singh's football heroics during the late 1930s had been the last glory days that Syracuse sports fans would experience for quite some time. World War II drained college football of its most basic resource: fit young men. Many schools cancelled at least one season during the war and took the time-out to rethink their participation in the sport. Some dropped football completely and forever, while others placed stricter limits on their programs by raising admission criteria, granting fewer scholarships, and rearranging their schedules to play only opponents who would do the same.[6] Syracuse, which cancelled its 1943 season, declined to make changes in its program, even though its two closest traditional regional rivals, Colgate and Cornell, opted for stricter academic standards. The Orange had been playing intercollegiate football since 1890, and while never quite achieving the status of a national power, the team had been a consistent winner, suffering just six losing seasons between 1890 and 1942, and only three in the twentieth century. So when Syracuse resumed play in 1944, fans were shocked to find that the bottom had fallen out of the program. Syracuse registered six consecutive losing seasons under four head coaches from 1944 to 1949. While there is nothing unusual about scapegoating coaches when a program falls into disarray, Syracuse lost a pair of college football's greatest coaches, Clarence "Biggie" Munn and Duffy Daugherty, to Michigan State in 1947. Both were white, but the issue that caused their departure was race.

3. Wilmeth Sidat-Singh played varsity basketball and football at SU, graduating in 1939. A second lieutenant and fighter pilot in the U.S. Air Force, he was killed during a training mission in 1942 at the age of twenty-five. Portrait Collection, University Archives, Syracuse University Libraries.

Following the disastrous 1945 season, in which the Orange went 1–6 and were outscored 38–106, Ossie Solem was replaced by Biggie Munn, who was signed away from the University of Michigan, where he had served as line coach. In Munn's first (and only) season as Syracuse head coach, he made tremendous strides toward rebuilding the Orange, improving the team's record to 4–5 in 1946 and narrowing its scoring gap to 146–158. A native of rural Minnesota, Munn had been at Ann Arbor when the University of Michigan began an effort to recruit black student athletes from the Detroit area. He had personally mentored Julius Franks, an offensive guard who in 1942 became the Wolverines' first black All-American.[7] Taking over as head coach in Syracuse, Munn surmised that the best chance for turning the Orange football program around was to actively recruit black talent from nearby northeastern metropolises, especially New York City, where NYU had dropped football and Columbia, like Cornell, had taken itself out of top-rank contention by signing the Ivy Group Agreement of 1945. Munn's strategy did not sit well with Syracuse athletic director Lew Andreas. According to Marty Glickman, "Andreas was a bigot. On a few occasions he commented to me that 'jigs didn't have any guts when the chips were down.'"[8] In his account of the 1937 Maryland fiasco, Glickman notes that Andreas raised no protest at all to Maryland's demand that Sidat-Singh be barred from the game.

The 1946 football season ended with Syracuse fans encouraged by the progress Munn had made with the team in less than a year as head coach. But when Michigan State offered Munn the head coaching job in East Lansing, Andreas made no attempt to persuade Munn to stay or to lobby administrators to come up with a competitive counteroffer. Munn's departure amounted to a double loss for Syracuse because when he left, he took his line coach, Duffy Daugherty (a Syracuse alum), with him. The pair built Michigan State's team into a national power for the next quarter century, winning three NCAA championships between them. During Munn's seven seasons as head football coach, the Spartans had a record of 45–8–2, including a perfect 9–0 national championship season in 1952 with Willie Thrower, an African American, as the team's starting quarterback. When Munn was promoted to athletic director in 1953, Daugherty succeeded him as head football coach, remaining at the helm for nineteen years and winning two more national championships. Meanwhile, back in Syracuse, Andreas replaced Munn with Reaves "Ribs" Baysinger, who had been coaching the Syracuse freshman team. Baysinger proved on several occasions that he did not share Andreas's views, but neither did he have a plan for recruiting Syracuse students from Harlem and Bedford-Stuyvesant. The Orange returned to their tailspin under Baysinger, winning just four games during the two seasons following Munn's departure.

Andreas was a dominant figure in shaping Syracuse athletics for forty years, doing duty, and at times double duty, as head basketball coach (1924–50), head football coach (1927–29), and athletic director (1937–64). Sean Kirst, a columnist for the *Syracuse Post-Standard* and the city's unofficial historian, recounts other incidents in which Andreas put his vision of a "white" Syracuse University ahead of the interests of the institution, its teams, and its student athletes. For example, in his role as head basketball coach, Andreas did not have to be asked to bench Sidat-Singh, nor did he even care to announce the reason for it when the Orange played Navy at Annapolis in 1939. "The daily newspapers in Syracuse never bothered to explain why Sidat-Singh was absent . . . noting only that coach Lew Andreas 'revamped' his lineup," Kirst wrote.[9] Certainly an explanation was called for; Sidat-Singh had started all twelve games up to that point and was Syracuse's leading scorer. The sportswriters did not explore the reason for the change, perhaps because athletic directors control access to the locker room and have sway over player interviews.

If it seems mysterious that someone with Andreas's apparent views on race is responsible for bringing the first African American player to Syracuse's basketball team, consider this: It appears that Andreas had believed that the high school basketball star from the Bronx was, as the New York City newspapers had described him, a "Hindu." When Sidat-Singh arrived on campus, Andreas attempted to cover up his "blunder" by perpetuating the myth of Sidat-Singh, the "Hindu." Duffy Daugherty, who played football for Syracuse during the late 1930s, recalls that the football players were instructed always to refer to Sidat-Singh as a "Hindu" when speaking to the press (although everyone on the team knew he was African American), and that Sidat-Singh was repeatedly instructed to list his nationality as "Hindu" on any forms he was required to fill out.[10] According to James R. Coates Jr., who wrote a master's thesis at the University of Maryland on the exclusion of Sidat-Singh from the

1937 Syracuse–Maryland football game, Andreas went so far as to have Sidat-Singh make appearances before the press wearing "Hindu garments and head dress [supplied] by publicity agents of Syracuse University."[11] The local press corps dutifully referred to him in print as either "Sidat-Singh the East Indian" or "Sidat-Singh the Hindu" until the Maryland controversy exposed the truth.

That embarrassing public show aside, it is clear that Sidat-Singh got short shrift from Andreas in their player-coach relationship. Although a scholarship player, he started in just three basketball games during his sophomore year, scoring 10 points for the season. He remained a scrub as a junior, never appearing in the starting lineup and scoring just 20 for the season. By his senior year, the former high school basketball star had become Syracuse's most celebrated football player, and that notoriety appears to have forced Andreas to allow Sidat-Singh to play the sport that had earned him his scholarship. He had not forgotten how to play the game. Starting in sixteen of Syracuse's eighteen regular-season games in 1938–39 (and getting floor time in all but the Navy game), Sidat-Singh set a Syracuse season scoring record with 146 points. His memorable performances include 18 points in a victory over archrival Penn State; 17 points in a 57–22 rout of Fordham in the Bronx; and 20 points in a 49–38 drubbing of the University of Pennsylvania. If those scoring figures seem less than dramatic by current standards, it is worth remembering they were achieved without the help of the three-point field goal or the shot clock, neither of which would become part of college basketball for decades. Possessions of two or more minutes were not unusual in college basketball, especially for a team that had a big lead in the second half, such as Syracuse had in the three games mentioned above.

Despite the success, renown, and honor in two sports that Sidat-Singh brought to the athletic department and the university, it was not until 1951—twelve years after his graduation and seven years after his death—that another African American student got a chance to play for the Orange basketball team. The late 1940s had been successful years for Coach Andreas's all-white Syracuse basketball squads; the Orange made it to the National Invitational Tournament for the first time in 1945 and was asked back again in 1949. But in every part of the nation except the South, the number of black students enrolling at predominantly white colleges was growing incrementally during the postwar decade, aided by G.I. Bill education benefits and encouraged by high-profile civil rights breakthroughs, such as the racial integrations of U.S. armed forces and of Major League Baseball. In 1947, the same year that Jackie Robinson took the field for the Brooklyn Dodgers, one college coach played an important role in ending segregation on the basketball court. John Wooden, who would later guide UCLA to ten NCAA championships, was athletic director and head basketball coach at Indiana State University, Terre Haute. When his team was invited to play in a postseason tournament, Wooden refused participation because one of his players, Clarence Walker, was black, and the National Association of Intercollegiate Basketball (NAIB) expressly banned nonwhites from its tournament.[12] As a result of Wooden's protest and others that followed, the NAIB dropped that rule in 1948. Wooden's Indiana State Sycamores made the tournament again, and Clarence Walker was the first to break the color line.[13] The NAIB eventually expanded into the range of college sports and became the National Association of Intercollegiate Athletics (NAIA), whose membership today includes many traditionally black colleges.

As black student athletes began to appear in greater numbers—and achieve greater prominence—in intercollegiate competition, pressure increased on Andreas to make sure Syracuse shared in the emerging talent pool. Syracuse alumni in Central and Western New York State were especially enthusiastic about recruiting Ronnie Kilpatrick, a 6-foot 4-inch forward at Madison High School in nearby Rochester who was touted in local media as perhaps the best shooter and the best rebounder ever to come out of the city. In the spring of 1950, after more than twenty-five years as head basketball coach, Andreas stepped down, keeping his position as athletic director (which he had held in tandem with it since 1937). In his continuing capacity as athletic director, Andreas named his assistant and protégé, Marcel "Marc" Guley, to succeed him in the basketball program as "interim coach." Guley, a Czech immigrant who had played basketball under Andreas and captained the 1936 team, stayed on the job for twelve years, all of them with his old coach as his boss. Emma Guley, Marc's wife, worked for Andreas as well, serving as an administrative assistant in the athletic department office.

Canisius, St. Bonaventure, and Niagara—three Western New York Catholic schools that were all collegiate basketball powers at this time—did their best to recruit Kilpatrick, but he chose an offer from Syracuse. According to Mel Besdin, captain of the Syracuse basketball team during the early 1950s, there was friction between coach and player from the start. "Guley kept his distance from players, but he generally got along with most of them," Besdin says. "It was a different story with Ronnie. They were always at odds over one thing or another. Looking back, I don't remember Guley having that kind of problem relationship with any of the white players."[14]

One account of this tension alleges that in a Syracuse–St. John's matchup at Madison Square Garden, Guley took Kilpatrick out of the game with just a few minutes left in the half. Instead of taking a seat on the bench, Kilpatrick went directly to the locker room, violating a team rule. Guley treated the matter as a serious offense, speaking openly of cutting Kilpatrick from the team. Guley purportedly put Kilpatrick's future to a vote among the players; Kilpatrick's teammates, all of them white, voted to keep him.

Despite his conflicts with Guley, Kilpatrick made impressive progress on the basketball court. Playing forward or center, as needed, he averaged more than 16 points per game as a junior, matching the output of Besdin. About two-thirds of the way through the 1953–54 basketball season (Kilpatrick's senior year), his basketball career came to an abrupt—and somewhat mysterious—end. After excelling as the team's high scorer during the first dozen games of the season, Kilpatrick did not appear on February 2, 1954, for a home game against Niagara. The following day, the athletic department announced Kilpatrick had been dropped from the squad for "disciplinary reasons." No further details were offered. The *Syracuse*

Post-Standard ran a brief item parroting the official line ("for disciplinary reasons") and devoting the rest of its article to a review of Kilpatrick's career for the Orange, presenting it as over, fait accompli.[15] The next day, the story took on added dimension in an article headlined "Kilpatrick Quits School." Offering no new information about what had precipitated his dismissal or his decision to leave school in the middle of the semester, the piece only referred to Kilpatrick's rush to the locker room in Madison Square Garden, an incident that had occurred more than a year earlier. No mention is made of the fact that by "quitting school," Kilpatrick was giving up a student draft deferment and, in effect, sending himself off to fight in the Korean War. The *Syracuse Herald-Journal* had even less to say than the *Post-Standard*, trivializing the loss of one of the team's best players by limiting its coverage to a single line in a sportswriter's column: "Kilpatrick departed the Orange basketball squad after a disagreement with coach Marc Guley."[16] The nature of the "disagreement" is not mentioned. The Orange went 3–4 without Kilpatrick, ending the season with a disappointing record of 10–9.

As for Kilpatrick, after serving in the military, he returned to Rochester, worked as a community organizer, and won election to the Monroe County Board of Supervisors in 1965. He completed his bachelor's degree at the University of Rochester (without the benefit of an athletic scholarship) and then earned a law degree at John Marshall University in Atlanta. A 1980 University of Rochester alumni publication noted that Kilpatrick was a faculty member at Atlanta (now Clark Atlanta) University, serving as chair of the doctoral program in educational administration, and that he had recently received the Distinguished Alumni Award from his high school.

Manny Breland, the third African American student to play basketball for Syracuse, enrolled in 1952 and joined the varsity in 1953–54, the year Kilpatrick left the program. Breland cannot pinpoint a particular incident that caused Kilpatrick's departure. "Ronnie had his moods and liked to do things his way," Breland says. "I remember one time we were coming back on the train from New York after a bad loss. Guley called a practice for the next morning. Nobody was happy about it, but Ronnie didn't show up. I don't know why. He could have needed the sleep or maybe he was behind in his classes. But Guley didn't try to find out anything. It was just, 'Do what you're told . . . or else.' You don't treat people that way. I can tell you from personal experience that Guley just didn't have any use for black people; same thing with Andreas." Breland was a student at Syracuse Central High School when he had his first encounter with Andreas. "Ken Beagle, my coach, had played for Andreas back in the thirties, and he told Andreas that I was taking college prep courses, and that he thought I should have a basketball scholarship to SU. Coach Beagle told me that Andreas just laughed and said, 'Oh, I don't think Syracuse University is ready to have a Negro basketball player.'"[17] But Beagle was persistent in his advocacy.

Andreas had used his position to foster a culture of exclusion, and when that became impossible in the 1950s, it appears he settled for a culture of tokenism. He seemed not to welcome nonwhite students, but rather to tolerate their presence for only as long as he had to. From Wilmeth Sidat-Singh to Ronnie Kilpatrick to Jim Brown, African American students were evidently seen as second-class citizens, no matter how significant their contributions or achievements. When Andreas retired in 1964, after more than forty years in the Syracuse athletic department, he left behind an all-white coaching staff that was still heavily influenced by his policies.

It was against this institutional backdrop that the Syracuse Eight arrived as freshmen in 1967 and 1968 on a campus that had become immersed in sweeping cultural shifts associated with the nation's civil rights movement and accustomed to the student-led protests that were emblematic of the decade. During this time, the university's football program had been bolstered by its image as the triumphant training ground of Ernie Davis, a reputation that drew African American applicants like Floyd Little, the team's star running back in 1965 and 1966. Given the country's evolving social climate and the Syracuse football program's reputation, African American players on the 1969 football team had good reason to believe that athletic administrators might be open to hiring a black coach. Instead, the players were confronted with the day-to-day realities of an environment Andreas had built over the course of decades. By 1969, they were ready to pose a public challenge to the all-white coaching staff.

"We asked for a black coach in 1969 and they said, 'Oh sure, we'll get you a black coach for spring practice,'" Alif Muhammad of the Syracuse Eight recalls. "That spring, Floyd Little came to Syracuse, and while he was in town he comes down to practice a couple of times and then leaves. Later on, we found out that he was in Syracuse that week to get his taxes done by a friend. But the next time we asked, 'Hey, what about the black coach you promised?' we find out that our black coach had already been here—and gone. It was Floyd Little showing up at those practices."[18]

Greg Allen, who had joined with other students advocating for a Black Studies Center on campus, remembers being excited by the possibility of working with Little until an unexpected encounter changed his mind. "Floyd pulled me aside and told me he wanted to talk," says Allen, who would later become spokesperson for the Syracuse Eight. "We sat down in the locker room and he said that the coaches thought I really had promise, but I needed to be careful about who I was hanging around with. He said they were concerned about me getting too involved in campus politics and all the 'black stuff.' I told him it wasn't anything that would interfere with my playing or my focus on football. He then said he was just passing along the message." Later that day, Allen met with the others and told them about what happened. "We all knew we'd been deceived," Allen says.[19] Perhaps no single issue did more to poison the relationship between the coaching staff and the players who walked out of spring practice in 1970 than the response to their request for a black assistant coach.

This anxiety about the personal lives of the black players on the team extended beyond involvement in campus political groups to more personal matters. Coaching staff reminded the players of the story of Avatus Stone, Allen says, portraying Stone as a "ladies' man" who dated white women.[20] Stone, a star high school athlete from Washington, DC, had joined the university's varsity squad in

1950. Despite a stellar athletic career with SU, he was ostracized by the coaching staff at that time for allegedly dating white co-eds, and labeled a troublemaker. Two days before the opening game in 1952, Stone tore the ligaments in his right knee and missed the entire football season. Syracuse University records show that Stone remained on campus during his senior year and, apparently using the time to catch up on his schoolwork, received a bachelor of arts degree in May 1953. The painful stereotype that was built up around him would nonetheless endure to plague black athletes at Syracuse for decades. Greg Allen arrived on campus as a freshman more than fifteen years after Avatus Stone received his degree. "Believe it or not," he says, "they were still telling me, 'Don't be like Avatus Stone! Don't be like Avatus Stone!'"

David Johnson, an offensive tackle on the 1968 team, says he received the Avatus Stone warning as well. In spring 1966, Johnson says, he was admonished by the offensive line coach for dating a "mixed-race" student. He then learned from the woman that she too had been paid a visit by a member of the coaching staff who warned her not to see Johnson. "The coaches told us not to date white women, mixed-race women, or even black women from prominent families (which included all black women who were college students). It appeared the only black women who we could date were local women whose families lived in Syracuse," Johnson says. "That didn't leave much room for a social life."[21] That summer, he married his high school sweetheart from Montclair, New Jersey. Marriage appeared to be one of the few arrangements acceptable under the rules laid down by the football program; Larry Csonka, the team's star (white) running back had gotten married during his senior year. But when Johnson informed the coaches that he had been wed, they did not offer congratulations; instead, Johnson recalls, they angrily threatened to take away his scholarship due to his "personal behavior." Johnson knew that under the terms of his scholarship he had the right to be married. Unfazed by what struck him as an empty threat, he requested that the amount allotted in his scholarship for dormitory room and board be applied to the rental of an off-campus apartment, where he intended to live with his wife. He was told it was out of the question. So Johnson consulted his constitutional law professor, Michael Sawyer, whom he considered a mentor. Johnson says that after reading the terms of the scholarship and other relevant documents, Sawyer advised him that the athletic department was obliged to respect both his marriage and choice of dwellings, with only one qualification: Johnson would have to pay any difference in price between a dorm room and the apartment he rented. "It cost me about $20 a month extra to live with my wife," Johnson says.

Despite the interest the coaching staff appears to have taken in the African American players' private lives, less attention seems to have been paid to their academic pursuits. Members of the Syracuse Eight argued that they were denied access to qualified academic advisors. Allen R. Sullivan, a doctoral candidate in psychology at Syracuse during the late 1960s, had graduated from the same Cambridge, Massachusetts, high school as Alif Muhammad, and he took an interest in following the younger man's progress. "I would pop in on him from time to time to see how he was doing," says Sullivan, a career educator who would later serve as executive director of student development and student advocacy for the Dallas Independent School District. "At the end of his first semester, I said to him, 'Okay, let's see your report card.' I was completely shocked. Here was this student who was a National Merit Scholarship finalist and had close to a perfect score on his SATs. I look at his grades and I see they have him taking courses on swimming and golf and so on. So I ask him, 'Who the hell is your advisor?' and he tells me it's the assistant football coach. I say, 'No, I mean your *academic* advisor.' Same answer—the assistant football coach."[22]

Blaming what he saw as Andreas's prejudice for many of Syracuse's athletic problems, Marty Glickman went so far as to conclude that "Syracuse didn't blossom as a national power in football and basketball until Andreas left."[23] While a case can be made that Andreas's departure as athletic director was absolutely necessary for Syracuse basketball to earn its place in the national spotlight, Glickman seems to be making an ethical rather than fact-based sports judgment in regard to Orange football, and in doing that, he fails to address the paradox of Syracuse football that confronted the Syracuse Eight: Andreas's alleged biases notwithstanding, it was during his continuing tenure as athletic director that Ben Schwartzwalder was hired and Syracuse football rose from its postwar status as a withered regional power to a national contender whose African American stars played a prominent role in the team's success.

Institutions, as Ralph Waldo Emerson noted, are the lengthened shadows of the people who shape them and run them, and there were other influential figures in the Syracuse athletic department whose efforts served to counterbalance Andreas. Roy D. Simmons Sr., the longtime head coach of the men's lacrosse and boxing teams, was an effective advocate for African American student athletes throughout his forty-five-year career in the Syracuse athletic department. It was Simmons who in 1928 recruited Ted Graham, a letter winner in boxing and track, and one of the first black athletes to represent Syracuse in intercollegiate competition. It was Simmons who spotted Sidat-Singh playing intramural football in 1936 and urged the freshman basketball player to try out for football. It was Simmons, as freshman football coach in 1947, who gave Bernie Custis, an African American student, a fair opportunity to win the first-string freshman quarterback job, which led to Custis breaking a national race taboo as Syracuse varsity quarterback. And it was Simmons, who during his forty-two years (1928–70) as head coach of the men's lacrosse team, became a mentor to Jim Brown, providing a caring alternative to the callousness and hostility that Brown had to face elsewhere among his coaches.[24] Oren Lyons Jr., Brown's teammate and the All-American goalie on Syracuse's 1957 undefeated lacrosse squad, describes Roy Simmons Sr. as "one of the few [coaches] who treated black athletes fairly."[25] Former NFL star Joe Ehrmann, a football teammate of the Syracuse Eight who also played lacrosse under Roy Simmons Jr., admired both father and son as coaches who took full responsibility for their positions and transformed the lives of their students. "Roy Senior took Jim's side when it deserved to be taken within the athletic department; he defended Jim when the faculty and staff unduly criticized him, and he often convinced Jim not to leave, despite the racist attacks he was experiencing," Ehrmann recalls.[26] "Roy Junior sat at the table and watched Roy Senior become a trusted advisor to Brown, to Ernie Davis, to John Mackey and others at crucial moments in their lives. He learned from his dad."[27]

Among Syracuse alumni, there probably was no one more active in fighting to secure the advantages of racial diversity in the Syracuse athletic department than Dr. Meyer "Sol" Bloom. Born to emigrant Jewish parents in the Catskill Mountain village of Ellenville, Bloom attended high school in Norwich, New York, an hour southeast of the university. He enrolled in Syracuse in 1909 and was among its first basketball stars, captaining the team during his junior year. He earned a second varsity letter in track and field as a pole vaulter, although he had no previous experience in that sport. "Dad was quite an athlete," recalls his son, Dr. David Bloom. "He decided to learn how to pole vault when he found out he could get his meals at a special training table they had for the track-and-field team. Money was tight, and he just decided to put his mind to mastering it."[28] Sol Bloom received his MD degree in 1916 from the Syracuse University College of Medicine (now SUNY Upstate Medical University), and after serving in World War I, he established a lifelong practice in the Binghamton area. Bloom never lost his love of sports. For decades he volunteered as a high school basketball and football referee, and he was never shy about sending tips to Syracuse coaches concerning talented prospects he observed. He was also a founding member of the Anti-Defamation League and an outspoken supporter of racially integrated education (as classroom diversity was known during much of the twentieth century).[29] Bloom made a point of highlighting promising African American athletes in his informal scouting reports and, if given the go-ahead, he acted as a recruiter on behalf of the university. It has never been clear as to how Wilmeth Sidat-Singh managed to receive a basketball scholarship to Syracuse at a time when head basketball coach Lew Andreas made no secret of his opposition to admitting black students to the program, but there is some speculation that Bloom played a part in bringing Sidat-Singh to Syracuse in 1935 by using the "Hindu" ruse to get past Andreas.[30]

Sol Bloom endowed a scholarship for Binghamton area residents attending Syracuse University, but his contributions to diversity and athletics would likely be forgotten if not for the recollections shared by some of the African American alumni whose athletic scholarships he facilitated. William Haskins Jr., a track star and running back for Binghamton's high school football team in the mid-1940s, broke two New York State high school sprinting records, but he did not know it until he was in college because his high school coaches had not bothered to tell him. Bloom, who kept a close eye on Binghamton-area high school sports, was well aware of Haskins's prowess. "Sol Bloom recruited me for Syracuse," Haskins explains. "Nobody in my family had ever gone to college, and my mother had her doubts about how I would get along up there." Her maternal fears were not unfounded. Haskins recalls arriving on campus in the fall of 1948 with directions to a student residence and a letter of introduction. "This big guy—a football player—answers the door and he looks me right in the eye and says, 'Nobody told me anything about any niggers living here.' He slammed the door right in my face."[31] Fortunately, Tony Fialco, who had played for a rival high school in the Binghamton area, was anticipating Haskins's arrival. Hearing the commotion, Fialco came rushing to greet Haskins and show him to the room they would share. The hostile encounter in his first moments on campus was not enough to scare Haskins away. In addition to playing halfback for the football team, he won letters in track and gymnastics. After graduating from Syracuse in 1952, he went on to earn a master's degree in sociology from Columbia University and held leadership positions in such organizations as the Urban League and the (national) Boys Club, before retiring.

Horace W. Morris (1928–83) of Burlington, New Jersey—another Bloom recruit—arrived on campus in 1946 as the first nonwhite admitted to Syracuse with a football scholarship. Morris, who served as director of the New York Urban League during the 1970s, offered a picture of the strangely ambivalent world awaiting a black student athlete at a "white" university during the immediate postwar period, a year before Jackie Robinson took the field for the Brooklyn Dodgers:

> The Syracuse football team was traveling on the New York Central Railroad for a road game in New York City against Columbia. The players assumed they were heading for Grand Central Station on their way to the Henry Hudson Hotel, where they usually stayed on their trips to play Downstate opponents. But as the train approached a suburban station in Westchester County, the coaches suddenly announced to the team that they were about to get off. A Syracuse alum had made an arrangement with Lew Andreas for the team to stay, gratis, at his country club, which was otherwise unoccupied that November weekend. There was just one thing: the club was "restricted"; no blacks allowed. Coach Baysinger was not about to send one of his players off to a Manhattan hotel on his own, so he remained with Morris on the Manhattan-bound train, planning to share a room with him. When the players learned what had happened, several expressed outrage and threatened to sit out the game if Morris was not permitted to bunk with the team. An assistant coach telephoned Baysinger at the Henry Hudson Hotel and apprised him of the situation. Baysinger told Morris to pack his gear, and the two caught a train back to Westchester. The entire team spent the night at the country club, apparently without consequence.[32]

3

The Rise of Syracuse Football

In 1949, Lew Andreas hired his fourth head football coach in six years: Floyd Burdette "Ben" Schwartzwalder. A successful high school coach in his native West Virginia before World War II, Schwartzwalder had a distinguished military career as an officer in the Eighty-Second Airborne Division, winning seven battlefield medals in France, serving as the military governor of Essen in the Allied occupation of Germany, and rising to the rank of major. In 1946, he took over as head football coach at Muhlenberg College in Allentown, Pennsylvania, where he compiled a three-year record of 25–5. Some Syracuse alumni worried that with so little collegiate experience, and all of it at a school with just two thousand students, the thirty-eight-year-old Schwartzwalder lacked the experience necessary to resurrect an ailing big-time football program. For his part, Schwartzwalder expressed some reluctance to take the job, calling Syracuse "a graveyard for football coaches."[1] Despite some controversy about the decision on both sides, the hire went forward and Schwartzwalder began his twenty-four-year career in Syracuse.

Mirroring Biggie Munn's debut at Syracuse, Schwartzwalder achieved quick results, improving a 1–8 record to 4–5, and like Munn, he received offers to go elsewhere. But this time Andreas stuck by his hire, and Syracuse's fortunes steadily improved. In 1950, the Orange broke its six-year losing streak, the longest in team history, finishing even at 5–5, and the following year, at long last, the team posted a winning season at 5–4. The turnaround was complete when they improved to 7–2 in 1952 and won the Lambert Trophy, awarded annually to the top-ranked Eastern independent

41

team. What's more, Syracuse received an invitation to play in the Orange Bowl in Miami on New Year's Day 1953. This was a monumental achievement for long-suffering Syracuse football fans. The team's only previous opportunity for postseason play had been a 1915 invitation from the Rose Bowl committee, which university officials politely turned down, citing the costs of a cross-country trip during winter intercession. Despite a 61–6 drubbing in the Orange Bowl at the hands of Alabama (led by quarterback Bart Starr), Schwartzwalder had succeeded in bringing Syracuse football back from the dead—and then some. The team would not suffer another losing season for twenty years.

Syracuse's Orange Bowl appearance cast a national spotlight on the university and on Schwartzwalder, ushering in an era of unprecedented success for the football program. But there is a racial footnote to the 1953 Orange Bowl game that links the boom years to the virtually forgotten era of Wilmeth Sidat-Singh, the team's lone African American player during the 1930s. Avatus Stone, a versatile athlete who broke records for interceptions at Syracuse, had missed the entire regular season in 1952 due to a leg injury, but by December he had healed sufficiently to rejoin the team for the Orange Bowl game.[2] With several key players ailing, Schwartzwalder certainly could have used Stone for the big game in Miami, and there was no Jim Crow law or "gentlemen's agreement" preventing Stone from playing in it. Three years earlier, with an eye toward Syracuse's growing tourism industry, city officials had created a special exclusion from local segregation laws for the Orange Bowl game. But Stone, the only black player on the team, was not reactivated. That said, Syracuse's "liberal" reputation on race still managed to become a front-page issue in the lead-up to the Orange Bowl.

University of Alabama President John M. Gallalee, as was his custom when Alabama faced athletic opponents from outside "the Confederacy," had his staff assemble a comprehensive file of press clips and public relations material concerning the Syracuse football team. It was commonly known that Syracuse was a racially integrated institution and that it had fielded racially integrated football teams. With the game only weeks away, Gallalee's research produced a preseason team photo that included Avatus Stone. Dramatic posturing typical of the post-Reconstruction/pre-civil-rights-law South followed with Gallalee's announcement to the press that he had instructed head coach Red Drew to take the Crimson Tide back to the locker room if even one "Nigra" in a Syracuse uniform set foot on the field in Miami.[3] There is no way of knowing whether Schwartzwalder, a young coach facing the most important game of his career, wanted to fight the Alabama ultimatum or not. To make matters worse, Andreas, who had consistently accommodated segregationists throughout his career, issued no public statement about Stone's injury. He was satisfied to let the public believe that Syracuse was supporting Alabama's demand for a segregated game.

What if Syracuse had responded to Alabama's threat by announcing the Orange *would* reactivate Avatus Stone? The game was scheduled to be televised by CBS to the thirty or so cities across the country that had television stations at this time. Would Miami officials have cancelled the Orange Bowl and taken the financial bath and the bad publicity, or would they have found an opponent willing to play Syracuse under the rules? At the very least, the registering of a protest by Andreas would have put a different slant on Alabama's lopsided victory over a Syracuse team not permitted to field all its players. The following year, Orange Bowl officials made a decisive statement on racial integration by signing a long-term agreement with the (then) Big Eight Conference to automatically invite its annual champion to the game, knowing full well that Nebraska and Oklahoma, the two perennial conference powers, had racially integrated football programs.

The issue of conforming to local segregation laws in postseason play came up later in the decade for another Upstate New York college football team, and the response was very different. In 1958, the University of Buffalo, with a longer football history than Syracuse, finished the season with an 8–1 record and received its first-ever postseason invitation, a chance to play East Texas State in the Tangerine Bowl at Orlando, Florida. The university accepted the invitation, but a few days later, word came from Orlando placing a condition on the school's participation. Buffalo's two African American players, Willie Evans and Mike Wilson, were declared ineligible to play because the stadium was operated by the local public school district, which was not permitted by local law to host "mixed race" sporting events. Buffalo head coach Dick Offenhamer called a team meeting at which the squad voted unanimously to refuse to participate in the game. "They insulted two of our teammates, and we were going to hit them back between the ears by refusing to go," quarterback Joe Oliverio says.[4] Members of the 1958 Buffalo team were later honored for their decision at a fiftieth anniversary event held in Orlando in conjunction with a (regular season) Central Florida University–University of Buffalo football game. The Buffalo alumni appeared to have no regrets. Many expressed gratitude to Coach Offenhamer and athletic director Jim Steele for giving them the opportunity to make a show of support for their teammates. "I think now looking back, if we had given in, caved in, gone to the game and won the game, we would have never had the camaraderie we have now. We would have always felt we let our buddies down," says Phil Bamford, an offensive lineman for the 1958 team.[5]

Syracuse's blowout loss in the 1953 Orange Bowl game may have seemed little more than an unpleasant detail to many Syracuse fans. The football program was on the move, and that's what counted. The university administration, silent on the subject of postseason play since its 1915 snub of the Rose Bowl Committee, had chartered an airplane to fly the team, the coaches, and the families of the coaches from Syracuse to Miami for the game. Even Chancellor William Tolley, not known as an advocate of big-time college football, got into the spirit of the occasion. Introducing Coach Schwartzwalder from the podium at the Orange Bowl Kickoff Luncheon, he joked, "Earlier [Syracuse] coaches were out to build character rather than just win football games. There was a time when we regarded the making of a first down as a great moral victory."[6] Tolley had reluctantly increased the number of football scholarships at Syracuse from twelve to sixteen at Schwartzwalder's request in 1951, but the Chancellor made no attempt to resist an avalanche of alumni support for an increase to twenty-one scholarships in 1953.[7] From then on, the number rose to keep pace with the most successful programs in the country. After waiting more than seventy years for its first postseason game, Syracuse became a bowl-game regular, making three more appearances in the next seven years.

By 1959, strong alumni and fan support for Schwartzwalder had spiraled in the direction of worship as Syracuse sailed through an undefeated season. The 1959 team was not merely good; it was a dominant powerhouse in every way. The offense led the nation, averaging 39 points a game, with 451 total yards, including 314 on the ground. The defense was perhaps more effective, limiting opponents to an average of 96 total yards per game—including just 19 yards rushing! This perfect storm of a football team made landfall in Dallas, and on New Year's Day 1960 Syracuse University's racially integrated team, including such prominent African American stars as Ernie Davis and Art Baker, beat the all-white University of Texas Longhorns in the Cotton Bowl. Voted "Number One" in the AP and Coaches polls, Syracuse had its first national collegiate football championship. No Division I team with a New York address has done that since; none have even come close.[8]

The coach showed no signs of hostility toward black players during these glory days; in fact, the public and the football world found good reason to place him on the progressive end of the spectrum in the context of his times and profession. Whether it was Schwartzwalder's intention or not, the African American players he coached at Syracuse from the late 1940s to the early 1960s brought down longstanding racial barriers in college football, even as some universities were still pondering the merits of integrating their sports teams, or in some cases, their classrooms.

Those who know the history of college football associate Schwartzwalder with the great African American running backs who came out of Syracuse during the first two decades of his tenure: Jim Brown, Ernie Davis, Jim Nance, and Floyd Little. In the glare of their achievements, it is all but forgotten that Schwartzwalder was among

Table 1
1959 Syracuse Football Schedule

Game	Date	Opponent	Venue	Score (Syr–Opponent)
1	Sep. 26	Kansas	Syracuse, NY	35–21
2	Oct. 3	Maryland	Syracuse, NY	29–0
3	Oct. 10	Navy	Norfolk, VA	32–6
4	Oct. 17	Holy Cross	Syracuse, NY	42–6
5	Oct. 24	West Virginia	Syracuse, NY	44–0
6	Oct. 31	Pittsburgh	Pittsburgh, PA	35–0
7	Nov. 7	(7) Penn State	University Park, PA	20–18
8	Nov. 14	Colgate	Syracuse, NY	71–0
9	Nov. 21	Boston Univ.	Boston, MA	46–0
10	Dec. 5	(17) UCLA	Los Angeles, CA	36–8
11	Jan. 1, 1960	(4) Texas	Syracuse, NY	23–14

the first head coaches in NCAA history to field teams led by African American quarterbacks. During the 1940s, "prevailing wisdom" had held that blacks could not play the position, with one of two reasons usually cited: out-and-out racists said they lacked the intelligence to make the necessary strategic decisions; the more moderate explanation was that white men would not allow themselves to be led by a black man, no matter what his athletic capabilities. Schwartzwalder apparently subscribed to neither analysis, putting two black quarterbacks on the field for Syracuse while Harry Truman was still in the White House.

The first was Bernie Custis. Biggie Munn, either personally or through a representative (possibly Sol Bloom), had recruited Custis, a quarterback and track star at John Bartram High School in Philadelphia. But by the time Custis arrived on campus for the fall semester in 1947, Munn had already departed for East Lansing. With Roy Simmons Sr. coaching freshman football that year, Custis was given a chance to compete, and he won the starting quarterback job on the freshman squad. He advanced to the varsity in 1948 and Simmons, sensitive to the problems Custis might face, switched jobs to become varsity backfield coach. Head coach Ribs Baysinger, duly impressed by the sophomore's passing and scrambling abilities, made Custis starting quarterback for the Orange.

Although the event received no special attention from the local or national press, when Custis took the snap from center on opening day 1948, he ended the "whites-only" era of quarterbacks at predominantly white colleges as surely as Jackie Robinson integrated Major League Baseball. The Orange beat Niagara 13–9 in that game; however, their fortunes went nowhere but down all season and they finished with a 1–8 record. Despite this, the Syracuse quarterback made a favorable impression. Dubbed Bernie "The Arm" Custis by the press, he was named quarterback of the 1948 "All-East" college team, a remarkable honor in the face of his team's abysmal season. Schwartzwalder was impressed as well. When he took over from Baysinger in 1949, he could have easily dumped Custis based on the 1–8 season—had he been so inclined. Instead, Schwartzwalder stood by Custis as his starting quarterback. He wasn't sorry. Custis passed for 1,121 yards in 1949, setting a school record. In his three seasons as quarterback, Custis completed a total of 196 passes for 2,617 yards. More than a half century later, Custis remains in the record books among the top ten Orange quarterbacks in career completions. Later a successful college football coach, Custis always appreciated Schwartzwalder's coaching style, saying that Ben " . . . brought a winning attitude that we had never known . . . in the Baysinger regime."[9] Were the feelings mutually positive? Generally speaking, Schwartzwalder was not given to lavishing praise upon his players, but in a 1950 letter to his mentor, Carl Schott, concerning the loss of another player, Schwartzwalder clearly recognizes and appreciates the contribution Custis was making to his team: "This will be a serious loss, as Bill [Wetzel] was next to Custis in value to our squad."[10]

Schwartzwalder's respect for Custis presents a sharp contrast to the disrespect and hostility casually shown by others toward the student athlete during the same period. For example, during his senior year, Custis accepted an invitation to play in the East-West Shrine

Game, an annual postseason all-star game played at the old Cow Palace stadium in San Francisco. But after the university responded to a request for a publicity photo of Custis, the Shrine committee rescinded its invitation in a brief note to him, without so much as offering an explanation.[11] Custis's roommate, Al Davis, offered to travel to San Francisco and demand reinstatement at the threat of a law suit, but Custis declined. Davis eventually made his way to the Bay Area as coach and then owner of the Oakland Raiders.[12]

Custis was an eleventh round pick of the Cleveland Browns in the 1951 NFL draft. His selection was not surprising, as head coach Paul Brown had continually shown leadership in signing black players. But Cleveland, which had been absorbed into the NFL after the collapse of the All-America Football Conference, had won the NFL championship in 1950, and Browns quarterback Otto Graham was at the peak of a Hall-of-Fame career. Paul Brown told Custis that his best chance of making the team was to try out for an open position in the pass defense. When Custis made it clear that he would rather contend for the backup quarterback slot, Brown spoke frankly: He believed the NFL wasn't ready to accept a black quarterback, and the best chance Custis might have for a future as a pro quarterback was to join a Canadian team that would let him show the football world what he could do.[13] Although there had never been a black quarterback in Canadian pro ball, Custis took Brown's advice, signing with the Hamilton Tiger-Cats. In the second of his historical "firsts," Custis broke the color barrier for quarterbacks in North American pro football on opening day, August 29, 1951, leading the Tiger-Cats to a 37–6 rout of Montreal. He went on to win a place on the All-Star team in his rookie season. In a career cut short by injury, Custis played four seasons of pro ball in Canada, mostly as a running back, and was a member of the Hamilton team that captured the Grey Cup championship in 1953. But the most remarkable part of his career began after he hung up his cleats. Custis earned a master's degree in education at Niagara University and taught in Hamilton area schools, eventually becoming principal of Dundas High School. During these years, he also became a successful football coach in the

Canadian Junior League, which led, eventually, to a new career as a Canadian college football coach. As head coach at Sheridan College, he took the team to six consecutive conference championships (1973–78), and at McMaster University he won the Frank Tyndall Trophy as national "coach of the year" for 1982. Custis was inducted into the Canadian Football Hall of Fame in 1998.

During Custis's first winning season as a college quarterback—and the initial season of Schwartzwalder's quarter century as head football coach—three other African American football players had enrolled in Syracuse University. All three were offensive players, no doubt encouraged by the breakthrough Custis had made at Syracuse. Two of the three played freshman ball but could not keep up their grades and did not return to school as sophomores: Donald Willis, a wide receiver, and Jim Vance, a fullback. Avatus Stone was another story.

Stone was a quarterback who came to Syracuse from Armstrong High School in Washington, one of four "colored" high schools in the segregated District of Columbia public school system. Although Armstrong was officially designated a manual training school, its alumni included many students who went on to college and the professions, as well as such world-class musicians as Duke Ellington and Billy Eckstine.

When Stone began playing football for Syracuse, Custis was still quarterback, so Stone's position on the field was in jeopardy except as a substitute as needed. But artificial barriers could not keep him off the field. Stone possessed a remarkable variety of athletic talents, and Schwartzwalder made use of every one of them. Stone started on defense as strong safety and was first-string punter on special teams. When Custis was sidelined, Stone either substituted for him at quarterback or was sent in as a running back. Although Stone played just two seasons for the varsity, his name still appears in the Syracuse record books. As a pass defender, he is tied for the most interceptions in a game (three) and he remains fourth on the all-time list in career interceptions (twelve). He kicked a 68-yard punt that stood for decades.

Nationwide in 1950, there were just three African Americans who played even one down at quarterback for predominantly white teams, and two of them—Custis and Stone—were on Schwartzwalder's Syracuse roster. Remarkably, this national distinction did not emerge much in the Syracuse sports pages nor did it seem to be on the mind of Ben Schwartzwalder. Commenting on a Syracuse loss to John Carroll University, a reporter for the *Syracuse Post-Standard* noted, "Avatus Stone, brilliant Orange safety man and star punter, filled in well for Custis last week, but he doesn't have Custis's experience and ball-handling abilities, and it is this latter feature that probably spelled doom for [Syracuse]." When the reporter asked about Custis's expected return to the lineup for the upcoming game against archrival Colgate, Coach Schwartzwalder replied: "Having Bernie back in there next week should give the rest of the boys some much-needed confidence."[14]

The loss to John Carroll notwithstanding, Stone did manage some impressive performances during his rare appearances at quarterback. In 1951, for example, he threw for three touchdowns against Fordham and received this writeup in *Jet* magazine: "Avatus Stone, one of the few Negroes quarterbacking for major mixed teams, was the key player in Syracuse's 33 to 20 win over Fordham. He clinched his team's first win over the Rams in history by completing a 43-yard pass play in the final eight minutes of the game. The junior from Washington D.C. passed for two other tallies on plays of 69 and 61 yards. He completed 9 of 20 passing attempts."[15] If Stone's off-the-bench performance is any indication of the quarterback he might have been for Syracuse if allowed a fair chance to compete, his football career and Schwartzwalder's all-time win-loss record could have been better.

As noted earlier, Stone missed the entire 1952 football season, his senior year, because of a leg injury. But his established record as a college punter (a 39.8-yard career average) impressed the Chicago Cardinals, who selected him in the 1953 NFL draft. Stone chose, instead, to follow Custis's example, and headed north, signing with the Ottawa Rough Riders. In four seasons with Ottawa, he demonstrated the same remarkable versatility he had shown in Syracuse as a running back, long safety, punter *and* punt returner. Hitting peak performance in 1955, Stone won the Jeff Russel Memorial Trophy as top player in the East Division. A torn knee ligament the following season—the same injury that had kept him out during his final year at Syracuse—cut his pro career short. After several comeback attempts, including an appearance in the NFL for a single play (he kicked a 28-yard punt for the Baltimore Colts), Stone gave up pro football and went into the printing business in the Washington, DC, area.

If other African American sports stars—Wilmeth Sidat-Singh, Ronnie Kilpatrick, and Bernie Custis—were buried and forgotten by the Andreas athletic department, the same cannot be said of Avatus Stone. But Stone was not remembered for his brilliance on the football field. Like many college football stars, Stone had a more-than-lively social life on campus, which some admired as the exercise of youthful free spirit and others disparaged as the irresponsible behavior of an amoral womanizer. Apparently Stone's key offense was dating white women, a "crime" compounded by his adamant refusal to make any secret of it.[16]

Joseph Lampe, who became chairman of the Syracuse University Board of Trustees a half century later, roomed with Stone for a time as an undergraduate. He paints a somewhat different picture. "You have to understand, Stoney was from a different kind of background than most of the black athletes who had come to Syracuse at that point," Lampe says. "He was from an affluent family that owned apartment houses all over DC. He rode around town in a brand new Buick convertible. He was a fraternity brother in Pi Lambda Phi and, well, let's not forget, he was on the football team. Were women interested in him? They certainly were, and most of the women on campus were white. I don't mind telling you that I got more than one date just because I was his roommate. He was a great guy and didn't deserve to be called a 'woman-chaser.' If anything, the women chased him." Lampe notes that after Stone's pro football career in Canada, he returned to the Washington area and became a family man with a successful business. "He owned a security printing company," Lampe adds. "His clients included the national lottery of Brazil."[17] In 1966, Stone was appointed by President Lyndon Johnson to head an effort at increasing the number of African American volunteers serving in the Peace Corps.

William Haskins, who also roomed with Stone, is somewhat less sympathetic in his account. "Back in his days as a college student, Avatus Stone didn't mind making trouble for himself or for anybody else," says Haskins. "I remember one time he called me from a phone booth telling me he's got himself barricaded in there, with a bunch of guys out to get him. He asked me to drive downtown and save him. It wasn't the only time he wanted a favor like that. I did it, but I wasn't happy about it."[18]

If the accounts of two roommates tend to pull in opposite directions, the last word on Stone can go to the writer John A. Williams. Born in Jackson, Mississippi, Williams grew up in Syracuse and was among the few members of the local African American community during this period to attend the university, earning both bachelor's and master's degrees in English during the early 1950s. The author of more than twenty books, including several novels set in the city, Williams includes a remembrance of Avatus Stone in "Syracuse, the Old Home Town," an article intended for *Holiday* magazine in 1964: "I knew many of the Negro athletes [at Syracuse University]. One day I went with one, a quarterback, to his job downtown. We drove in his new convertible. His job consisted of brushing off the pool table in a private club with a whisk broom. When I was a graduate student, I happened on this same athlete in the library, who was then a senior scheduled for graduation. He asked me to instruct him on how to check a book out of the library."[19]

Were Stone's off-the-gridiron exploits more extreme than those of similarly inclined white student athletes in the early 1950s—or today? Did he take a more blasé attitude toward his studies than similarly inclined undergraduates, then or now? Probably not. Nonetheless, "Don't be like Avatus Stone!" became a mantra of "friendly" advice that was chanted by white coaches in the faces of black student athletes for decades. Jim Brown has said he recalls hearing the line ad nauseam when he came to campus in 1953. Greg Allen and Alif Muhammad of the Syracuse Eight say they both remember getting the exact same advice when they arrived on campus fourteen years after Brown.

Stone might well have been the last African American student athlete at Syracuse for a very long time if not for the efforts of Kenneth D. Molloy, a Manhasset, Long Island, attorney and later a judge of the New York State Supreme Court. Molloy, a 1940 Syracuse graduate, campaigned tirelessly for the admission of a Manhasset High School student, Jim Brown. Why Brown had any trouble at all getting admitted to Syracuse is difficult to comprehend. Brown's grades were well within admission standards and, if extracurricular activities counted for something—and they often do—Brown also happened to be the greatest high school athlete in the history of New York State, excelling at lacrosse, football, track and field, basketball, and baseball (his little-known pitching record at Manhasset included two no-hitters). Recruited by dozens of colleges, Brown was also looking at a $150,000 signing bonus from the New York Yankees. Molloy urged him to resist all suitors and to set his sights on Syracuse.

A two-time All-American lacrosse player, Molloy had earned both his bachelor's and law degrees at Syracuse, serving as a lacrosse assistant coach while in law school. His intense love of the game, of coach Roy Simmons Sr., and of the university had convinced him of a grand scenario: Jim Brown was going to be the greatest lacrosse player of all time, the superstar who would elevate the ancient Native American game into a popular American sport on the level of football and baseball, and Simmons was the best coach—technically, spiritually, and intellectually—to guide Brown and lacrosse to that destiny.

When Syracuse inexplicably rejected Brown's application for admission, Molloy refused to take no for an answer. He appealed the decision directly to Chancellor William Tolley, bringing Manhasset School Superintendent Raymond Collins to the meeting to personally attest to Brown's academic competence. Tolley reversed the rejection, although he apparently was moved to do so by reasons other than correcting an injustice. In his 1989 memoir, *At the Fountain of Youth*, the chancellor recalled admitting Brown as a favor to Nassau County Executive Holly Paterson, a Long Island politician who wielded political clout in Albany, affecting several issues dear to the chancellor's heart.[20] But while Tolley could open the school door for Brown, dispersing athletic scholarships was another story; that was the province of the athletic director, Andreas. Not all the Syracuse coaches agreed with Andreas's decision not to offer Brown financial support, but those who did not agree with the head coach were powerless. Roy Simmons Sr., who had learned about Brown's situation from Molloy, made an attempt to enlist Schwartzwalder's help in an effort to change Andreas's mind. But the man who had coached college football's first black quarterback was not prepared to oppose his boss. According to Roy Simmons Jr., Schwartzwalder's reply to Simmons Sr. was abrupt and to the point: "Not interested. He's colored."[21] And so Jim Brown enrolled in college without an athletic scholarship of any kind. Many people believed for decades that Molloy had managed to secure a lacrosse scholarship for Brown. But that was not the case. At Judge Molloy's funeral in 1999, Ken Molloy Jr. set the record straight. "There was no scholarship," he told the mourners during his eulogy. "He just passed the hat around Manhasset and got enough money to send Jim to Syracuse."[22]

The unlikely story of how Syracuse University, in 1953, had to be forced into accepting the greatest high school athlete in the country occurs at the chronological and spiritual center of the history of black student athletes at Syracuse University from the admission of Wilmeth Sidat-Singh (1935) to the political action of the Syracuse Eight (1970).

Jim Brown began his college sports career as a walk-on in four sports: football, basketball, lacrosse, and track and field. As is usually the case for walk-ons, he did not find a welcome wagon rolled out to greet him. "The first thing my freshman football coach attacked was my talent," Brown recalled in an interview during the early 1990s.

"He said I couldn't run the ball and that I wasn't any good . . . if a coach addressed me at all, it was to needle."[23] The only African American on the 1953 freshman football team, he sat on the bench for the season. The basketball program didn't accord him that much; he didn't make the freshman team at all. But as was often the case throughout his life, Jim Brown accepted the card that was handed to him and found a way to turn an impossible situation around.

While it is hard to imagine anyone being better running with a football than Jim Brown, those knowledgeable in lacrosse consider that game to be his real forte. As Molloy had predicted, Brown flourished under Simmons's encouragement. A two-time All-American midfielder, Brown would become the first African American inducted into the National Lacrosse Hall of Fame (1984), and he remains the only athlete of any color who was *also* inducted into both the College Football Hall of Fame and the Pro Football Hall of Fame. Brown summarized his feelings about the relative merits of the two sports in a quotation that appears on his plaque in the lacrosse hall: "I'd rather play lacrosse six days a week and football on the seventh."[24] The Orange lacrosse team went undefeated, 10–0, in 1957, Brown's senior year. There being no championship tournament at the time, the national title was awarded each year by the U.S. Intercollegiate Lacrosse Association (USILA) in the form of the Wingate Trophy. Hopes were high in Syracuse, but the trophy went to Johns Hopkins University, which was also undefeated—with a record of 5–0. Jim Brown and goalie Oren Lyons Jr. were the only nonwhites on either team, and it was widely believed that Syracuse's "diversity" was a factor in the USILA decision. "For most of you, this is the first time you have felt the sting of racism," Coach Simmons told disappointed members of the team. "That lesson has far greater value than the Wingate or any other trophy."[25] The 1958 NCAA *Lacrosse Guide* called Jim Brown "the greatest lacrosse player in the history of the sport,"[26] a partial fulfillment of the vision that had motivated Molloy to campaign for Brown's admission to his alma mater.

Basketball, the sport most tightly controlled by Andreas, remained a sore point for Brown throughout his career at Syracuse, but that did not prevent him from shining when he was permitted on the court. The addition of Brown would increase the number of African American players on the varsity basketball team to three, the greatest number of black players that had ever been on the team. But three was also one more than Andreas allegedly allowed. Brown would have to compete for floor time with Vince Cohen, the team's leading scorer, and Manny Breland, the playmaking guard. Forced to play as a second-stringer, Brown somehow managed to average more than 13 points per game for the basketball team while continuing to set new records in football and lacrosse. According to Breland, Brown brought a startling combination of assets to the hardwood. "He was able to break a game wide open on sheer strength. He could drive the length of the court and nobody could stop him," Breland says. "He was quick . . . he had a good shot . . . and he was a tremendous leaper. At 6 feet 2 inches, he could dunk the ball at will. You didn't want to fight him under the boards."[27] But Coach Guley kept Brown on the bench for the greater part of every game, even when it meant ensuring a Syracuse loss. Fed up after two seasons, Brown did not return to the basketball team as a senior. His roommate, Vincent Cohen, who became a successful trial lawyer and U.S. attorney in Washington, DC, often expressed admiration and empathy for Brown. "It's frustrating playing every day and demonstrating that you're better than three-fourths of the team, and still not getting the opportunity. That can damage your pride," says Cohen, who was named an All-American forward as a senior in 1957.[28] Cohen and Breland say they believe Syracuse would have been a good bet for a national championship had Brown stayed with the squad and been given appropriate floor time as a starter.

In track and field, Brown's event was the decathlon, arguably the most demanding of all traditional athletic competitions. A test of versatility and endurance, the decathlon is composed of ten events, each of which is a competitive specialty in its own right: long jump, shot put, high jump, discus, pole vault, javelin, 110-meter hurdles, and 100-, 400-, and 1500-meter races. Competitors score points based on their performances in each event, with the winner determined by the highest point total. Brown finished fifth in the 1954 Amateur Athletic Union national championship meet in St. Louis, competing against elite track-and-field athletes, most of whom were specialists in several decathlon events. Combined with his team obligations in football, lacrosse, and basketball, Brown successfully competed at a national level in thirteen sports that year.

As for football, Jim Brown ran right through the internal opposition that had kept him on the bench as a freshman—and then through the defenses of every team that Syracuse played against for the next three years. At first, Schwartzwalder reportedly found Brown moody and unable to take criticism. A former military officer, the coach seemed to despise the cavalier way in which Brown would withdraw from team calisthenics to do his own exercise program, on some occasions, to catch a nap in plain view of his teammates. On more than one occasion, Schwartzwalder read Brown the riot act, but he never sent him packing, claiming that his hands were tied by alumni pressure. "I was told by people that I *had* to take him back. They didn't care what concessions I had to make," the coach said. "Must have been a thousand people come to see me."[29] It is possible that Brown's record-breaking productivity on the field may have played some role in tempering Schwartzwalder's impatience with insubordination. After all, Schwartzwalder was a leading exponent of the old-school running game and, pain-in-the-neck troublemaker or not, the kid from Long Island averaged 6 yards per carry as a sophomore. Whether it was due to alumni pressure or his own judgment as a coach, or both, Schwartzwalder found reason to let Brown stay in the program. As a senior, he averaged 123 yards rushing per game.

With the aid of television, which was conducting a successful transcontinental yardage campaign of its own during the 1950s, Brown's achievements were transforming him into a legendary figure at a speed unprecedented in amateur athletics. Brown's success and fame reflected brightly on the program that was seen as having mentored or "produced" him. Ben Schwartzwalder was Jim Brown's coach, and it therefore stood to reason that Schwartzwalder was the best coach in the nation for a promising black student athlete who had hopes of becoming a star. Syracuse emerged in the late 1950s as *a*, if not *the*, school of choice for black athletes.

Instead of the golden age of lacrosse that Ken Molloy had dreamed of, Jim Brown launched a golden age of Syracuse football that brought benefits to the team and the entire university for years to come. The football program was energized for more than a decade by a succession of extraordinary African American students whose choice to play football for Syracuse can be attributed, at least in some part, to Brown's influence. Ron Womack, a 1967 high school senior from Charleston, West Virginia, turned down offers from a half dozen other schools to come to Syracuse. "They sold the same pitch to each of us," he recalls. "'Come here, and you can be like Jim Brown.'"[30] David Johnson, a top academic student on a nationally ranked high school football team in Montclair, New Jersey, turned down an offer from Harvard to accept a Syracuse football scholarship. The reasons behind his decision were complex; they included being told by a high school teammate that his father, a Harvard graduate, "didn't allow blacks in the house." But Johnson described his choice of Syracuse this way: "Jim Brown called me on the phone. What more do I need to say?"[31] Moreover, scholarship athletes weren't the only students drawn to Syracuse by Brown's star quality. Jim Brown restored Syracuse University to a place in the consciousness of the African American intelligentsia that it had not occupied since the abolitionist founders established a policy of admitting all races in the 1870s. In 1961, for example, singer-songwriter Garland Jeffreys, a Brooklyn native, chose Syracuse, knowing little about the university or the city. "My father wanted me to go Boston College," Jeffreys says, "but Jim Brown was my hero and it just came to me that I had to go to school where he went to school."[32] John Kellogg, an attorney, entertainment agent, and faculty member of the Berklee College of Music in Boston, tells a similar story about his decision in 1965: "I grew up in Cleveland watching Jim Brown play, and when it came time for me to choose a college, all I could think of was 'I have to go to the school that Jim Brown went to.'"[33] To varying degrees and in different ways, a generation and more of African American college students were influenced by the heroic images projected by Jim Brown in Syracuse, Cleveland, and Hollywood.

But the golden age of Syracuse football that Brown launched would come crashing to an end in 1970 when the protest of the Eight exposed the truth: Brown had transcended the normal expectations of a college athlete in four sports despite the obstacles in his path. How a teenager, even one with Brown's talents, managed to endure and thrive after being told by authority figures that he wasn't good enough to play for the freshman football team or have a starting position on the basketball team no matter how many points he scored is a mystery best explained by Brown's lacrosse coach, Roy Simmons Sr., and other believers in the power of the human spirit.

The arrival of Ernie Davis in 1958 was the first and most direct benefit to Syracuse of the Jim Brown legacy. Born in Western Pennsylvania, about 120 miles southeast of Penn State University, Davis attended high school in Elmira, New York, about ninety miles southwest of Syracuse. Both schools pursued him, as did UCLA. There was sentiment in the family for Penn State. There was also some sentiment for UCLA, the school that Jackie Robinson had attended, but Davis wanted to stay closer to home. He idolized Jim Brown, and the deal was closed when the man himself came knocking at the door.

Inheriting Brown's Number 44 jersey, Davis emerged as a pivotal player during his sophomore year, helping Syracuse to its undefeated national championship season in 1959. As a junior, he averaged 7.8 yards a carry; as a senior, he eclipsed Brown in career yards rushing with 2,386, breaking a school record that many Syracuse fans thought would outlive their children. And then came the *pièce de resistance*. At the end of the 1961 football season, New York City's Downtown Athletic Club awarded Davis the Heisman Trophy, the singular annual honor signifying "*the* best player in college football." It was the first time the Heisman had gone to an African American or to a Syracuse student. The school that had introduced Bernie Custis, the groundbreaking varsity quarterback, and the coach that had "produced" Jim Brown, the greatest running back in the NFL, had done it again. The Downtown Athletic Club had come in for increasing criticism, including from some its own members, for failing to award the Heisman without regard to race. The club had no written rule on racial restrictions, and as early as 1944, Buddy Young, a black University of Illinois running back, had been among the top vote getters. Jim Brown had made news in 1956 for finishing fifth in the balloting, but the trophy had gone instead that year to Paul Hornung, "the golden boy" from Notre Dame. Five years later, with the civil rights movement gaining attention in the national media, Davis's triumph placed Schwartzwalder at a major milestone in the ongoing struggle for racial equality in the sports world—and beyond. Drafted by the Cleveland Browns, Davis was preparing to join Jim Brown in a "dream" backfield when he was diagnosed with leukemia.

The triumphs and tragedy of Ernie Davis's life are chronicled in print and portrayed on the screen in *The Express*, a 2008 biopic. But there is a rarely mentioned aspect of Davis's brief life that helps illustrate how the shameful treatment suffered by Jim Brown during the mid-1950s continued into the next decade for Ernie Davis and others, including the Syracuse Eight.

Davis was a high school All-American in two sports at Elmira Free Academy; his other game was basketball. Elmira racked up a record of 82–10 while he wore the uniform and went 66–1, including a fifty-two-game winning streak that began during Davis's sophomore year. According to the Elmira *Star-Gazette*, "Many people who saw him play thought Davis was better in basketball than football."[34] College basketball coaches around the country took notice. A 6-foot 4-inch guard, Davis was recruited for basketball by schools that didn't play intercollegiate football, and other athletic departments offered him scholarships in both sports or in the one of his choice. But the Syracuse basketball program, still under the control of athletic director Lew Andreas and head coach Marc Guley, showed no interest in recruiting the most celebrated high school basketball star in New York State, despite the fact that Syracuse basketball had particular need of Davis's talents at the time. In 1957–58, the Orange had just one reserve guard: Bill Stearns, a transfer student from nearby Cortland State. It had been five years since he played his first intercollegiate basketball game for Cortland, making him ineligible under NCAA regulations. When this was discovered, Syracuse was forced to forfeit all seven games in which Stearns had played, including wins over Georgetown, Army, and Canisius. Neither Andreas nor Guley admitted guilt, error, or even failure of due diligence in the fiasco. Instead, Andreas solicited letters from the athletic directors of the seven opponents, in which they declined to accept the Syracuse forfeits. These letters had no standing; the rules had been broken and the forfeits were not reversible. But Andreas recorded a winning season of 11–10 rather than the 8–13 season calculated by NCAA regulations.[35] Despite the team's troubles, Andreas and Guley saw no need for the services of a high school All-American guard who happened to be enrolled on campus.

Ernie Davis was in the middle of his junior year at Syracuse before he played basketball for the Orange. Midway through the 1960–61 basketball season, Davis and his football teammate, John Mackey, joined the SU basketball team. The two African American players were joined by a white teammate, Don L. King, as well. Like Davis, Mackey had been a top-level prep player. During Mackey's three varsity seasons at Hempstead High School on Long Island, the school chalked up a record of 63–2. King, who hailed from Buffalo, had been an all-city guard. Their addition to the team should have been great news for Syracuse basketball fans; the Orange were suffering the worst basketball season in school history.

Given their demonstrated reluctance to embrace black players, it seems unlikely, even under such desperate circumstances, that Andreas and Guley would have asked for the help of Davis and Mackey. Schwartzwalder, who had played football and wrestled as a student at the University of West Virginia, may or may not have suggested the idea, but if he had opposed it, it is certainly unlikely that Andreas and Guley would have proceeded without his support. Schwartzwalder had always encouraged his football players to go out for a second varsity sport as a way of staying in shape year round. But whatever convinced Andreas and Guley to accept the black students, their arrival should have, at the very least, improved morale.

With the football team still basking in the glow of its 1959 national championship, the basketball team had gotten off to a 1–9 start.

Davis, Mackey, and King made their first appearances in Syracuse basketball uniforms on the road at Alfred University on January 20, 1961. Earlier that week, the Orange had given up 103 points in a 25-point loss to Canisius and dropped a home game to Niagara by 22. Although the only publicity for the addition of the three footballers was word of mouth, Davis's return to the basketball court packed the Alfred gym with relatives, friends, and fans who made the seventy-five-mile trip from Elmira on a snowy January night, just to see him play. Cheered on by what sounded like a hometown crowd, Syracuse won its second game of the season, beating the Alfred Saxons 79–66.

Handed a miraculous opportunity to salvage the remainder of a disastrous season, Guley kept Davis and Mackey on the bench, using them strictly as scrubs for a roster that had dropped nine out of ten without them. In a sad replay of Jim Brown's experience, Ernie Davis got minimal playing time, while starter Terry Quigley, described in the yearbook as "a defensive standout," averaged 2.9 points per game and grabbed not a single rebound for the Orange in twenty games. When Quigley sustained a serious foot injury in late February, Guley relented and put Davis in the starting lineup for the last three dates on the schedule.

When spring mercifully arrived, the Orange found themselves at 4–19. Davis had appeared in a total of nine games, averaging 10.2 points per appearance (second highest on the team) and 9.6 rebounds (highest on the team). Mackey, a forward, averaged 4.7 points in six appearances. Like Jim Brown before them, Davis and Mackey had endured their fill of Coach Guley's basketball team; neither returned as seniors. Yet King returned to the basketball team as a senior the following year. He may have been sorry he did. The Orange went without a victory until March, managing to avert a winless season with a pair of victories on the road in the last two games of the 1961–62 season, finishing at 2–22.

Alumni—at least those more interested in winning than maintaining racial quotas—were furious. Andreas anticipated the situation by having Guley's letter of resignation on his desk well in advance of the end of the season. Having been hired as "interim" coach twelve years earlier, Guley went out as a lame duck. After retiring, he spent the next eighteen years as a physical education teacher at an elementary school in Cazenovia, New York.

Fred Lewis, hired by Andreas to replace Guley, had achieved an impressive win-loss record of 89–38 at Southern Mississippi College (now University) in Hattiesburg. There is no record of the job search in Andreas's papers. (When he bequeathed papers to the university, Andreas included no documents dated after 1952.) Lewis, a two-time All-American at Eastern Kentucky, was a native New Yorker who had played for multiracial Long Island University teams before transferring to Eastern Kentucky. He had begun his coaching career with multiracial teams at Amityville High School on Long Island. His plans for resurrecting Syracuse basketball were not about excluding anyone. The biggest problem he faced after taking the reins from Guley was how to convince talented kids with multiple offers to come play for a college team that had compiled a record of 6–43 over the previous two seasons.

A decade after the campaign to prevent Jim Brown from being admitted to Syracuse, Fred Lewis succeeded in pulling off one of the great recruitment feats of all time by bringing Dave Bing, the most sought-after high school basketball player in the country, to Syracuse. How did Lewis convince the nation's top prospect to choose the school with the worst recent record in Division I college basketball? Ironically, he lured Bing by enlisting the help of a graduating senior whose experience in the basketball program had been both professionally unproductive and personally insulting: Ernie Davis.

On the eve of a conference held in New York to commemorate the fiftieth anniversary of Davis's Heisman Trophy, Bing described his first meeting with Davis, which took place on the Syracuse campus in December 1962:

He was honest and frank. He told me about the good experiences
and the bad experiences he had at SU. I walked away thinking,
"What an impressive human being." And I thought that if SU could
help develop a human being like Ernie Davis, then I wanted to go
there and try to follow in his footsteps. The way he handled himself
on and off the field with such dignity set a standard, I believe for
everyone at Syracuse to follow. I remember when I was getting ready
to leave campus that weekend, he told me I had an opportunity to
be the "Ernie Davis of basketball." That was the clincher for me.[36]

Jim Brown brought Ernie Davis to Syracuse, and Davis provided
similar help to Syracuse in the recruiting department. Not only did
he help the university snag Dave Bing, the player most responsible for
the turnaround of Syracuse basketball in the mid-1960s, but Davis
also helped to recruit a suitable replacement for himself: Floyd Little, the next great Number 44 running back. These were the last of
Davis's gifts to the university; Bing and Little were both Syracuse
freshmen when Davis died in December 1963.

Floyd Little had grown up in New Haven, Connecticut, attending public schools until his grades and athletic abilities won him a
scholarship to prep at Bordentown Military Institute in New Jersey.
He was the first African American student to attend the school. As a
senior at Bordentown, Little was vigorously recruited by the service
academies, especially West Point, which assigned General Douglas
MacArthur the task. Summoning Little to dinner at his Waldorf-
Astoria suite, MacArthur pitched the virtues of Army, going so far
as to suggest to the eighteen-year-old that if he enrolled for college
at West Point, he might one day become the first black general in
U.S. history. Little was leaning in that direction until Schwartzwalder, a retired Army colonel, pulled out a big gun of his own. He
brought Ernie Davis with him on a visit to the Little family. Floyd
Little recalled the experience in a 2008 interview: "[Davis] was well-
dressed, he was very articulate, and he was sharp. He sat on the
couch between my mom and my sister, said, 'What's up?' and put
his arms around them. He had just won the Heisman, just signed the

contract with Cleveland, and just signed a contract with Pepsi. And there he was, at my house in the ghetto of New Haven, Connecticut, talking to me about going to Syracuse and what it did for him. All my mom and my sisters could say is that if they could *produce* someone like that, then you have no alternative as to where you ought to go."[37]

After enrolling in Syracuse, Little picked up right where Davis had left off, showing little evidence of feeling any pressure from the Number 44 legacy as he broke records set by his distinguished predecessors. Three times an All-American, Little rushed for 1,065 yards in 1965, eclipsing the single-season bests of both Brown and Davis. In the 1966 Gator Bowl, Little ran for 216 yards against Tennessee, surpassing Brown's standing record of 197. The number one draft pick of the Denver Broncos, Little still holds most of the team rushing records he established over the course of a nine-season, Hall-of-Fame career. As far as the sports world could see in the mid-1960s, Schwartzwalder, a coach who seemed to have a knack for guiding the talents of black students on the football field, had done it again.

Of all the African American student athletes who played for Syracuse during the Schwartzwalder regime, from Bernie Custis (1947) to the Syracuse Eight (1970), Little appears to have been the most comfortable in his relationships with Schwartzwalder and with the university. A history major, he confirmed his positive feelings for the school on the plaque bearing his name in the College Football Hall of Fame, thanking Syracuse for making him "a student first, an athlete second."

Schwartzwalder's reputation as the most successful white coach of African American football players extended beyond the three superstar running backs who wore Number 44. Art Baker (1958–60) and Jim Nance (1963–66), a pair of fullbacks from Pennsylvania, added to his standing in that regard and in other ways as well. Baker and Nance both demonstrated a degree of individual athletic prowess that transcends what is possible in football or any team sport by competing as college wrestlers and winning national championships in their weight divisions during what most football players prefer to think of as the off-season. Schwartzwalder had wrestled and played football as a college student at the University of West Virginia; he fully understood the level of personal commitment and self-control required for success in collegiate wrestling. After watching both Baker and Nance accomplish the almost impossible feat of winning the highest national titles in the toughest of all collegiate sports, while also excelling on the football field under the rough conditions he imposed, Schwartzwalder did not likely agree with Andreas's often-expressed belief that black athletes "didn't have any guts when the chips were down."[38]

In 1959, Baker went undefeated in the 191-pound wrestling division, winning the Eastern title and then the NCAA national championship tournament in his weight class. Both were firsts for Syracuse students and for African Americans. While Baker's wrestling season would have sufficed to make 1959 a very good year for any athlete, there were pleasures yet to come. That autumn, Baker enjoyed the foliage as a member of Syracuse's undefeated national championship football team. Schwartzwalder, in an off-handed reference to the growing fame of sophomore Ernie Davis, called Art Baker "the most underrated player on our team."[39] Baker, who ran 100 yards in 10.1 seconds at a (football season) weight of 220 pounds, was drafted by both Philadelphia (NFL) and Buffalo (AFL) in 1961. He chose the latter, a short drive from his family's home in Erie, Pennsylvania, and became the workhorse of the Bills' backfield in his rookie year, running with as many as 31 carries in a single game. During the off-season, Bills owner Ralph Wilson signed Cookie Gilchrist of the Toronto Argonauts, the leading rusher in the Canadian Football League, by guaranteeing Gilchrist the starting fullback position in Buffalo— Baker's job—as part of the deal.[40] It was a tough break for Baker; he played in just three games for the Bills in 1962. Technically, he could have tried to jump to Philadelphia, but at this point NFL teams were loath to take players who had signed with the upstart league, hoping to discourage others from doing the same. Baker crossed the border and signed with the Tiger-Cats in Hamilton, about seventy miles from Buffalo. His best season for the Cats was 1964, when he rushed for 726 yards, averaging 4.8 yard per carry.

If the feat of winning a national collegiate wrestling title while playing big-time college football seems impossible, consider this: Jim Nance did it twice. As a sophomore in 1963, he was the first African American to win the NCAA heavyweight wrestling championship; he repeated as champ as a senior in 1965. According to collegiate wrestling historian Jay Hammond, Nance achieved more than an impressive win-loss record in the sport; he was a transformative figure who "brought a level of speed, strength and athleticism to the heavy-weight class that had rarely been seen before," Hammond wrote in *Amateur Wrestling News*. "He created the mold for the many great big men that were to come."[41] Nance was just as impressive on the gridiron. While sharing backfield duties with Floyd Little in 1964, Nance led the Orange in rushing with 951 yards on 190 carries, a 5.0 average. Choosing the (then) Boston Patriots of the AFL over the Chicago Bears, he got off to a roaring start in 1965 as the league's rookie of the year. Nance was at his peak the following season, leading the AFL in rushing with 1,458 yards (on a 14-game schedule), scoring 11 touchdowns, and winning Most Valuable Player honors.

Schwartzwalder's association with so many remarkable African American athletes—Brown, Davis, Little, Nance, Baker, and others—occurred during the period when the Jim Crow era of college sports was ending once and for all. Although there is no evidence that it was Schwartzwalder's intention to foster that kind of a social breakthrough, the coach's admirers often attribute the success of his players, black and white, to his ability to build character in young men. This interpretation of his coaching style takes on added dimension when considered in light of the fact that two of the pioneering labor leaders in the history of professional sports, John Mackey and Billy Hunter, were African American student athletes who played football for Schwartzwalder at Syracuse.

Mackey (1961–63) turned down a commission in the U.S. Naval Academy at Annapolis to play for Schwartzwalder. A tight end for the Orange, he set a team record for yards gained by a pass receiver during his junior year and helped Syracuse to a 15–14 victory over the University of Miami in the Liberty Bowl. After earning a bachelor's degree in economics, he joined the Baltimore Colts, playing in five Pro Bowls on his way to the Pro Football Hall of Fame. Statistics don't adequately tell the story of Mackey's impact on football, either on or off the field. As a player, he redefined the function of the tight end position in football offense. Bringing explosive speed to a position that was usually limited to blocking assignments, pitch-outs, and short passes, Mackey was the first tight end to become a long-ball receiving threat. The son of a minister, he possessed a strong sense of community responsibility, and he expressed this through his activism on behalf of the NFL Players Association. Following the consolidation of the AFL into the NFL, he was elected as first president of the newly united players association, serving from 1970 to 1973. Under Mackey's leadership, the organization began to function in the manner of a labor union, engaging in collective bargaining and employing strikes and other labor tactics. In that regard, Mackey played a role in defining the economics of contemporary professional football.

In the last years of his life, Mackey shared the fate of many of his colleagues on the football field when he gradually succumbed to the dozens of unremarked concussions and other head injuries he had suffered during thirty years of playing the game, from childhood to retirement from the pros. At the beginning of his dementia, when he still enjoyed periods of clarity, Mackey resolved to his wife, Sylvia, to do something that would help those heading for the same fate.

Sylvia Mackey became a crusader for the cause and was instrumental in the NFL's adoption of the 88 Plan for retired players. Established in 2007 through a joint agreement between the league and the NFL Players Association, the plan provides financial support for inpatient care, or home custodial care and outpatient treatment, for former players with dementia, Parkinson's disease, Alzheimer's disease, or amyotrophic lateral sclerosis (ALS, also known as Lou Gehrig's disease). The plan was named in honor of Mackey, who wore jersey Number 88. When John Mackey died in 2011, Sylvia donated his brain to the Center for the Study of Traumatic Encephalopathy at the Boston University School of Medicine. The center conducts research on chronic traumatic encephalopathy, as well as how this cause of dementia can be prevented and treated.[42]

Billy Hunter, who played wide receiver for Schwartzwalder from 1962 to 1964 while majoring in political science, made a lasting impact on labor relations in pro sports as well. A highly regarded NFL prospect, Hunter was dogged by injuries during a brief pro career, spending a season each with Miami and Washington before giving up football to earn law degrees at Howard and UC Berkeley. Appointed as U.S. Attorney for Northern California by President Jimmy Carter, Hunter was one of the youngest federal prosecutors in history. He gained the national spotlight pursuing such high-profile cases as the Patty Hearst–Symbionese Liberation Army affair and the Rev. Jim Jones "People's Temple" mass murder. Entering private practice, he turned his attention to representing professional athletes. In 1996, Hunter became executive director of the National Basketball Players Association. During almost two decades, he led the players in major labor actions, resulting in abbreviated NBA schedules in 1998–99 and 2011–12.

Hunter's spectacular career is foreshadowed in a college incident that links him to the Syracuse Eight story. The Civil Rights Act, forbidding discrimination in public accommodations, became federal law during the summer of 1964, ending the legal protections that had enabled Jim Crow laws to operate in southern states. But, as with school desegregation, the change did not come overnight. The process would be long and drawn out as "segregation forever" diehards forced court case after court case. Ever since enrolling in Syracuse, Hunter had been appalled that Syracuse continued to schedule intercollegiate football and basketball games at stadiums and arenas that maintained segregated seating policies, and he certainly saw no reason for the university to remain complicit with the "holdouts" now that segregated seating was a violation of federal law. Beginning in the summer of 1964—following Lew Andreas's retirement as athletic director—Hunter circulated a petition demanding that the university articulate a clear policy of refusing to schedule games in any such venues, and threatening an athlete boycott of any Syracuse athletic event at a segregated venue. Every black student athlete on the Syracuse campus signed the petition, including John Mackey (Hunter's roommate) and Dave Bing, who was about to transform Syracuse basketball in the post-Andreas era. "Oh yeah, it worked," Hunter recalled with some relish in a 2011 interview. "There was no question about it. It definitely worked. [Athletic department administrators] were *scrambling*, man. They didn't know what to do."[43] The action that Hunter initiated brought an end, once and for all, to the policy of passive complicity with racial segregation that Andreas had instituted in the 1930s. The long-forgotten humiliations suffered by Wilmeth Sidat-Singh at the 1937 Maryland football game and the 1938 Navy basketball game were acknowledged.

The university's new policy was put to the test at the end of the 1964 football season when Syracuse received an invitation to play Louisiana State in the Sugar Bowl at Tulane Stadium in New Orleans on New Year's Day 1965. Syracuse accepted the invitation but made nondiscriminatory seating at the stadium a contingency for participation. City officials were in a pickle. The Sugar Bowl had never allowed "mixed seating" since the game's founding in 1935. But several weeks earlier, New Orleans had lost a major event because of the city's segregated seating policy. The AFL had scheduled its annual All-Star game for Tulane Stadium, but yanked the event after a group of players from both the East and West teams, led by Cookie Gilchrist, had threatened to boycott the game. To compound the embarrassment for New Orleans, the AFL had not moved the game to the North, but to Jeppesen Stadium in Houston, which had reversed its segregated seating policy in order to host the All-Star event. Rather than threaten the future of the city's signature college football game as well, Sugar Bowl representatives agreed to end Jim Crow seating. As Hunter relates the story, Coach Schwartzwalder did not criticize him for getting involved in a political action; in fact, he praised Hunter for showing "leadership" and rewarded him by naming him a team captain.[44]

The racial integration of seating at Tulane Stadium for the 1965 Sugar Bowl took on wider meaning for New Orleans and for other Southern cities that were considering resistance to the Civil Rights

Act of 1964. The NFL was planning to expand in the South with three new franchises at this time. Miami and Atlanta were both approved on a fast track, and the Dolphins and Falcons began league play in 1966. But NFL owners (as well as network television executives) were hesitant to grant a franchise to New Orleans for a number of reasons, and the city's failure to accommodate the AFL All-Star game over race issues posed a serious threat to the city getting its first major league professional sports franchise. With Tulane Stadium set to become the home field of the proposed NFL franchise, the accommodation of Syracuse's policy on seating for the Sugar Bowl game emerged as a litmus test of New Orleans's readiness to host major sports events. The Syracuse–LSU game went off without a hitch, and the New Orleans Saints were approved as a league franchise months later. Once again, without any apparent intention to do so, Ben Schwartzwalder found himself associated with a historic civil rights breakthrough in the sports world.

What happened over the course of the next five years that made Schwartzwalder react so harshly and uncompromisingly to the Syracuse Eight in the chain of events that took place in 1969 and 1970?

An easy answer is that the complaints made by the Eight were not about the policies and politics of higher learning institutions or government, but rather about the way Schwartzwalder was running *his* football program. Perhaps, as a former military man, he would not tolerate what he perceived as insubordination. There is, no doubt, some truth in this as a partial explanation for Schwartzwalder's actions, but it would have been naïve for either the coach or the students to think they could separate themselves from the currents of American history that surrounded them during the late 1960s. One hundred years after the outlawing of slavery, the legal battle against Jim Crow had finally been won in the courts and in the Congress. But it was clear that the longer saga of American race relations would continue, moving into uncharted territory as new African American voices asked new questions.

It could reasonably be argued that the undoing of Ben Schwartzwalder's image as a facilitator of racial progress in college athletics would begin with his inconsistent responses to demands that he hire a black assistant coach. On some occasions, he publicly agreed to make such a hire. On other occasions, he denied agreeing to any such thing or made a joke of it. At one juncture, he even claimed he had already taken care of the issue by having Floyd Little visit spring practice sessions, during which time he had designated Little as an "interim coach." In the end, Schwartzwalder would make the hire, but his behavior in the intervening fourteen months would destroy his credibility with the black players on his team, setting the conditions for the Syracuse Eight walk off.

There were many reasons why the black students on the football team believed they would benefit from having at least one black assistant on the coaching staff, but perhaps the most pressing was a need to alleviate the sense of isolation and alienation they experienced at the hands of the very same authority figures who had recruited them with promises to act in their best interests if they would sign on the dotted line. Ron Womack's story is a case in point. An offensive guard at Stonewall Jackson High School in Charleston, West Virginia, he was the first African American in state history to receive the Thomas Hornor Award as Best All-Around Academic Athlete (1967). Among the offers that Womack turned down when he chose Syracuse was a full *academic* scholarship (requiring no football) to Brown University. "My high school advisor told me that I'd never be able to keep up with the courses at Brown," Womack says.[45]

Womack received a much friendlier impression of Syracuse. He recalls Schwartzwalder telling him that, as a fellow West Virginian, he would understand his problems and give him special attention. "The coach was a personal friend of Mrs. Janie Johnson, my high school social studies teacher," Womack explained. "Mrs. Johnson, who was white, would invite me into her home for a steak dinner and, well, that was socially very unusual. And while I was there, Coach Schwartzwalder could call me on the telephone to talk about all the great opportunities Syracuse had to offer me." Mrs. Johnson also supplied Schwartzwalder with the extraordinary details of

Womack's personal life: he was the sixth of ten children; his father, a coal miner, had died of lung cancer when Womack was eight, and his mother had suffered a fatal heart attack two years later. "Schwartzwalder told me, and this is an exact quote, 'If you come to Syracuse, *I will be like a father to you.*'"[46]

As a sophomore member of the varsity in 1968, Womack was sharing a position on the line with a white player. He felt his performance justified more playing time, so he went to see Schwartzwalder about it. Womack says that the coach told him not to worry and that his time was coming. Several weeks later, Womack was told to see Dr. Pelow, the team physician, for reexamination concerning a condition he had developed before coming to college. "It was puzzling because they knew about it while they were recruiting me, and it wasn't bothering me." Based on the examination, Pelow declared Womack unfit to play football. "I believe that excluding me from playing was a blatant racist act to punish me," says Womack. "In retrospect, the head coach may also have been attempting to send a message to the remainder of the black players."[47]

Another incident pointing to the need for a black coach involved Dana "D.J." Harrell. An outstanding athlete, Harrell had lettered in football, basketball and track at Brebeuf Jesuit, a Catholic high school in Indianapolis. "The school had just opened a year before I enrolled, and despite the fact that we didn't have a track and we didn't have a real football field of our own, we had some of the best teams in the state," says Harrell, who quarterbacked the team to a 10–0 record in his senior year. Like the other Syracuse Eight players, Harrell had multiple scholarship offers to choose from, but Syracuse held several powerful attractions. For one thing, it was Jim Brown's school, and Harrell had grown up watching Brown play for Cleveland; for another, he says, he had been told by Syracuse recruiters—presumably speaking on behalf of the program—that he would be given a fair chance to try out for quarterback. "I knew that black high school quarterbacks were often converted to other positions when they played for predominantly white colleges," he explains.

"But while the other schools who recruited me told me right up front to forget about playing quarterback, Syracuse was the only one that told me I'd have a shot."[48]

At his first freshman practice, Harrell took a few snaps from scrimmage, and that was the sum total of his fair shot. He was converted to a strong safety as a freshman in 1967. Remaining on campus the following summer as he prepared to join the varsity pass defense, Harrell was one of several members of the team who took a job on the grounds crew of Archbold Stadium, the crumbling turn-of-the-century horseshoe that was the team's home field before the opening of the Carrier Dome in 1980. One day, as Harrell sat by himself eating lunch, some white football players on the crew were fooling around, spraying each other with a garden house. They decided to train the hose on Harrell, and he asked them to stop. The incident turned into something much worse when one of the white players walked up to Harrell and sprayed him in the face. "The nozzle was maybe two inches from my face," he recalls. "It escalated into a fight and I whipped his ass. Then two or three of them came at me, so I picked up an axe handle, put my back to the wall, and said, 'Okay, come get some.'" They did, and Harrell got the best of the tussle.[49]

According to Harrell, when Schwartzwalder was apprised of the incident, he showed no interest in learning the sequence of events or in disciplining the instigators. Instead, he lectured Harrell about not fighting with his teammates. Schwartzwalder's one-sided response caused a racial fracture on the team. "The split—whether *I* was right or wrong or *they* were right or wrong—played out along racial lines," Harrell says. Having attended a Jesuit school where all involved would have been called to account for their behavior, Harrell was emotionally distraught by the experience. But he felt there was no one on the coaching staff for him to talk to; Schwartzwalder's word was law to his assistants. Instead, Harrell made a complaint to the Human Rights Commission of Syracuse and Onondaga County.

In his account of the "Football Discrimination Crisis," John Robert Greene documents the fact that Schwartzwalder did make a promise to hire a black coach. According to Greene, "In mid-1968, in the presence of a number of reputable witnesses, Schwartzwalder told a Human Rights Commission investigator [responding to Harrell's complaint] that he 'would get a black coach right away,' and his statement was accepted by those present as a commitment; but when asked about his promise some months later, Schwartzwalder said he had meant the comment sarcastically."[50] Over the next eighteen months, Schwartzwalder would repeat this pattern of behavior.

During the football off-season in the winter of 1968–69, there was no easing of tension on this issue. Black members of the football team participated in a demonstration held at a home basketball game, Syracuse vs. Niagara, at Manley Field House on February 20, 1969. Organized by the Student African American Society, the Black Students Association, and other campus groups, about one hundred protesters remained seated during the playing of the national anthem before tip-off, with fists clenched in the "Black Power" salute. When the music ended, some stood up, fists still in the air, and walked through the aisles and out of the building; others stayed for the game. The student organizers released the following statement: "This demonstration is in protest of the racist attitudes existing in Syracuse University, as well as in the community, that affect blacks of Syracuse, as

4. *Daily Orange* article, February 28, 1969, explains the silent student protest at Manley Field House during the Syracuse vs. Niagara game.

recently exemplified by the treatment of black students and athletes. If this reflects any disrespect to the national anthem or the country, it is minor when compared to the blatant disrespect shown to the blacks in this country. We stand united as black students."

Chancellor William Tolley, who had recently announced he would retire in September 1969 (after twenty-seven years in office), met with Schwartzwalder and suggested the coach hold a special team meeting to talk about racial issues, pointing out that it would allow students to air their grievances in a private setting rather than in places where they were bound to cause public embarrassment for the university. Schwartzwalder, who had been given free reign over the football program since his brief tussle with Tolley in the early 1950s over increasing the number of football scholarships, agreed to do it but lived to regret it. "Before the talk, the team was a unit," Schwartzwalder said. "After that, it was two groups, one black, one white. If I had known what was going to happen, I would have refused to hold the stupid meeting."[51] When shown the coach's statement years later, John Lobon said, "We were divided, black and white, long before the meeting, but he refused to see that."[52]

Kevin McLoughlin, a sophomore in the spring of 1969, was among those who attended the football team's special meeting on the subject of race relations. A white student walk-on, he had impressed the coaching staff during winter workouts and was invited to the upcoming spring practice to take his best shot at a place on the defensive line. This was his first team meeting for the upcoming spring football practice, and he was excited to be there. "I remember it very vividly. Ben asked all the walk-ons to raise our hands, telling us he just wanted to make sure there were no reporters in the house," McLoughlin says. "Then he came down the aisle and stood right over me, asking me what year I was in, and when I said I was a sophomore he inquired as to why I hadn't gone out for the freshman team. I told him I was a forestry student. The academics were very demanding and I wanted first to establish myself as a student. Then he asked how I was doing in school and I told him I was on the Dean's List both semesters. Well, he looked all around the room and in a voice loud enough for everyone to hear, he said, 'Well, I'm a betting man,' and then, looking down at me over his glasses, he said, 'I'll bet you a quarter you're not around this spring when we put the pads on.' I mumbled something and nodded, feeling completely embarrassed that the head coach would take this much interest and time in a nobody walk-on at the beginning of a very important closed-door team meeting attended by the entire football team, the athletic director, and all the coaches and PR people. Even the team chaplain, Father Charles, was there. After Ben walked away, one of the guys whispered to me, 'The coach likes you.' I didn't know if he was kidding or what."[53]

Things escalated from exciting to bizarre when the meeting began.

"Coach Schwartzwalder spoke as if the black players had betrayed him, and he looked like he just could not believe they acted that way toward *him*," McLoughlin recalls. "He mentioned how Jim Brown had some problems, 'but we worked them out.' He began saying something like, 'After all I've done . . .' but he couldn't finish his sentence. It was all very awkward. He did try to bring these race issues into a broader perspective by mentioning that he couldn't change how things are done on the outside world and that he knew that some of these things just aren't fair. But he pounded his fist into his open palm to emphasize that 'on this football team everybody is treated the same.' The black players were there, right in front of him, but it was as if he was talking *about this team problem*, like they weren't really there. Then he continued again. 'You know, some people used to call me a. . . .' He stopped himself, but you knew what he meant to say. You could even hear the beginning of the 'n' sound. There was a long silence after that. It lasted a few seconds or maybe longer. I don't know. Then he finally said, 'You know, some people used to call me a lover of Negroes.' He went on to mention that Syracuse had black players long before a lot of college football teams and he was proud of that fact. The meeting ended. No one had talked but Ben, and nothing was really resolved. I recall trying to start a conversation with John Godbolt, who was sitting close to me, but he just shook his head sadly and walked away."[54]

McLoughlin decided to stay at the gym and work out after the meeting. The place was empty. He later learned that everyone automatically got a day off from workouts whenever there was a team meeting. Alone in the gym, he says, he had a feeling that things had gone very badly at the meeting. McLoughlin was personally acquainted with three of the African American players. As a freshman, he had lived down the hall from Bucky McGill and John Godbolt, who were roommates, and all three had taken a math class together. "My mother had a graduate degree in math, and when we'd get stumped on a tough homework problem in math, we'd call her on the phone for the answer," McLoughlin says. "Those guys introduced me to Ron Womack, and he became a friend, too. So I knew those guys pretty well, and I just couldn't see how any of them or any of the other black student athletes would be able to respond to Coach Schwartzwalder after that meeting."[55]

John Lobon, who had participated in the demonstration at the basketball game, was also at the team meeting. He remembers the anger Schwartzwalder directed toward him and the other black students in the room. The message Lobon took away from the meeting was a threat. "It was about ownership . . . and control," Lobon says. "If you don't do right, I can take your scholarship."[56]

The team meeting did not change Schwartzwalder's behavior regarding the hiring of a black staff member. According to Greg Allen, Schwartzwalder continued to flip-flop on the issue, making assurances one day, retracting them the next. In a memo written a few weeks after the team meeting, Dean James Carlton affirmed to Edward Piskor, Vice Chancellor for Academic Affairs, that the coach had met with "a black faculty member, a black graduate student, and a black community leader" and told them "he would seek a black assistant coach." Yet some weeks after that, Schwartzwalder told Carleton, "Just so you don't get any wrong ideas, I told those people I'd *look* for one and I looked all the way home and all the way back to school this morning and didn't find any!"[57] The black football players continued to reiterate their demand, but spring and summer passed and the 1969 football season opened with their demands unanswered. When Schwartzwalder was challenged on the subject, he claimed that Floyd Little's visits to spring practice in 1969 were what he meant when he said he would bring in a black coach, and now that he'd done that, he didn't see any reason to further discuss it. "That was a real turning point," according to Alif Muhammad, who at the time was called Al Newton. "We realized beyond any doubt that they had no problem lying to us about anything."[58]

Meanwhile, back on the football field, the 1969 season—the tenth anniversary of the national championship season—was not a happy one for the Orange. After a 3–1 start, the team finished with a 5–5 record; it was the first time in twenty years that Schwartzwalder had come up with anything less than a winning record.

Events trended downward for the team's African American players over the course of the 1969 season: Fullback Alif Muhammad led the team in rushing for the second year in a row, averaging 4.5 yards on 154 carries. (By contrast, Larry Csonka had averaged 4.3 yards on 261 carries as the team's fullback and leading rusher in 1967.) As the season wore on, Schwartzwalder called an increasing

Table 2
Syracuse Football 1969—Season Rushing Statistics

	Player	Att	Yds	Avg	TD
FB	Al Newton	154	689	4.5	4
QB	Randy Zur	112	195	1.7	4
RB	Greg Allen	81	362	4.5	1
RB	Ron Trask	48	166	3.5	0
QB	Rich Panczyszyn	42	97	2.3	1
RB	John Godbolt	35	106	3.0	2
RB	Mike Chlebeck	27	142	5.3	0
RB	Rich Phillips	17	53	3.1	0
FB	Marty Januszkiewicz	16	59	3.7	2
RB	Robin Griffin	9	62	6.9	0
RB	Larry Giewont	4	15	3.8	0
QB	Frank Ruggiero	3	-6	-2.0	1

number of quarterback keepers, with the effect of keeping the ball in white hands as much as possible. The team's three white quarterbacks, Randy Zur, Rich Panczyszyn , and Frank Ruggiero, combined for 156 carries—that's two more than the starting fullback. Halfback Greg Allen, the team's second leading rusher, was averaging 4.5 yards a carry, but had only 81 carries, while Zur, averaging just 1.7 yards per carry, ran with the ball 112 times. John Godbolt had averaged 4.7 yards per carry in 1968, a higher average than anyone on the 1969 team, yet he was all but benched for the season, with only 35 plays from scrimmage. On defense, John Lobon, Bucky McGill and Duane Walker, all starters in September 1969, and all black, were spending more time on the bench with each passing week. John Lobon summarized the situation this way: "The issue was this: were the best being played? We said no."

4

End of an Era

During his twenty-five seasons as head coach, Ben Schwartzwalder created and presided over Syracuse University football's most impressive and extensive period of success. A former high school coach, Schwartzwalder had just three years of collegiate experience at much smaller Muhlenberg College when he took over a Syracuse team that was reeling from the longest string of losing seasons in its history. After stabilizing a program in free fall, he did not merely restore the team to its prewar regional prominence, but built it into a formidable national power. Having never previously played in the postseason, the Orange appeared in seven major bowl games under Schwartzwalder and won the Lambert Trophy (awarded annually to the "best independent college team in the East") four times. At his retirement, Schwartzwalder's record of 178–96–3 (153–91–3 at Syracuse; 25–5 at Muhlenberg) placed him sixteenth in career wins on the all-time list of college football coaches, ahead of such iconic figures as Knute Rockne of Notre Dame and Bud Wilkinson of Oklahoma.

By the time the Syracuse Eight enrolled at the university in the late 1960s, the glory days of the Schwartzwalder era had passed. From 1949 to 1967, the coach had compiled a stunning record of 124–58–2 at Syracuse—a winning percentage of .681. By contrast, during his last six years at Syracuse, the team played .400 ball at 29–43–1. Almost one half of the losses recorded during Schwartzwalder's twenty-five-year reign at Syracuse occurred during those last six seasons. There are many plausible explanations for the decline; purists boil it down to a case of Schwartzwalder's old-school grunt-and-run ground game having finally outlived its effectiveness in the

5. Syracuse University head football coach Floyd "Ben" Schwartzwalder. Portrait Collection, University Archives, Syracuse University Libraries.

age of the college passing game. But "Old Ben," as the coach took to calling himself during the fourth quarter of his career, showed little interest in updating his playbook. As the Syracuse Eight controversy swirled around him during the 1970 season, Schwartzwalder seemed to equate changes on the football field with changes in the political arena: "I realize college football is under scrutiny," he said in an Associated Press interview. "A lot of folks want to do away with it. Sure, there's a chance. A lot of people want to do away with our form of government, and they're pretty much the same type of people."[1] For more than twenty years, the coach's comments to the press had typically been terse and tightly focused on issues pertinent to recent or upcoming games. But by the end of the 1960s, times had changed. "Nobody wants to talk about football anymore. All they want to talk about is *that*," he complained in *Sports Illustrated*, pointing at a newspaper on his desk with an eight-column banner splashed across the front page: "Schwartzwalder Quizzed on Black Issue."[2] The coach had an odd tendency to refer to himself in the third person. "Old Ben's not thinking about retiring," he assured fans across the nation. "Old Ben's thinking about coaching."[3]

But a comeback wasn't in the cards. There were no more postseason invitations for Schwartzwalder after Syracuse's trip to the Gator Bowl in 1966. After compiling an 8–2 record in 1967, six wins were as good as it got for him. Following the shock of a losing record (5–6) in 1972—his first losing season since 1949—Schwartzwalder announced his intention to retire after just one more campaign. But a hoped-for last hurrah was instead a definitive disaster. The team went 2–9 in 1973, including embarrassing blowout losses at home to Bowling Green State (41–14) and archrival Penn State (49–6). "I knew that the team had some great years under Schwartzwalder, but by the time I was old enough to start attending games, they were just a kind of mediocre team," recalls Betty Tily, who grew up in the Syracuse area and has worked for the university most of her life. "We just kept thinking, 'Maybe if they get another coach, they'll start winning.'"

Schwartzwalder's long and awkward final act did not matter much in terms of his legacy; his place in the College Football Hall of Fame was already secured by his career stats, his longevity, and his national championship. His ascent into the football pantheon was fast-tracked by another factor. The privately endowed colleges of the Northeast had invented American football in the late nineteenth century and dominated its early development. But decades had passed since one of them had taken the national title when Schwartzwalder pulled off that feat with the 1959 Syracuse team. It wasn't exactly Princeton, Yale, or Cornell, but Syracuse was close enough to make the coach a sentimental choice for every honor the game's gatekeepers could bestow. In 1977, Schwartzwalder received college football's equivalent of the Oscar for lifetime achievement: the Amos Alonzo Stagg Award,[4] bestowed each year by American Football Coaches Association on the "individual, group or institution whose services have been outstanding in the advancement of the best interests of football."[5]

The Schwartzwalder name—the Schwartzwalder-Syracuse "brand" he had forged during the most successful years of his career—was thoroughly identified in the sporting public's mind with the racial integration of college football. Just as any discussion of professional baseball and the civil rights movement must include mention of Jackie Robinson, Branch Rickey, and the Brooklyn Dodgers, any discussion of college football and the civil rights movement must touch upon Jim Brown, Ernie Davis, Ben Schwartzwalder, and the Syracuse Orange. Whether one believes that Schwartzwalder gained this distinction by conscious effort or that it fell upon him by circumstance, this aspect of the Schwartzwalder legacy was put in doubt by the Syracuse Eight protest. The sports commentators, historians, and documentary filmmakers who praised Schwartzwalder as foresighted for making Bernie Custis his starting quarterback way back in 1949, and who gave him credit for mentoring Ernie Davis past the color barrier to the Heisman back in 1962, might not have had kind words for an aging coach whose response to the grievances of his black players in 1970 was to suspend them from the team, effectively ending any chance of them becoming professional football players. Schwartzwalder's collected letters reveal that the coach's treatment of the Syracuse Eight in 1970 had made him a national lightning rod for racial anxieties and resentments.[6]

The key ingredient to Schwartzwalder's success—the signature strategy underpinning his Hall-of-Fame career, the thing Ben Schwartzwalder is remembered for to this day—was a tough and relentless running game that could wear down a defense both psychologically and physically. It is difficult to imagine how his strategy could have worked so well for so long if it had not been for Jim Brown (1955–57), Art Baker (1958–60), Ernie Davis (1959–61), Jim

Nance (1963–65), and Floyd Little (1964–66). Despite having bene-
fited so greatly and for so long from the talent, dedication, heart, and
performance of young black men, Schwartzwalder seemed unable to
connect these athletes with the struggle for racial equality that was
on the front page of the newspaper just about every day he served as
their coach.

In 1970, Orange football player Joe Ehrmann was often identified by Schwartzwalder to the press as a spokesman for the white
players who opposed allowing the Syracuse Eight to rejoin the team.
Ehrmann, who lived under the authority of football coaches from
grade school in a working-class Buffalo neighborhood until his retirement from pro football, says that he was manipulated by Schwartzwalder into opposing his black teammates, and has come to regret
the role he played in their exclusion. A pastor now with an inner-city
ministry in Baltimore, Ehrmann is cofounder, with his wife, Paula,
of Coach for America, an organization dedicated to transforming the
lives of young people through sports mentorship. In his 2011 book
on the impact of coaching, Ehrmann identifies Schwartzwalder as
an extreme example of what he terms a "transactional" coach—an
authoritarian who is willing and able to use players to further his
aims without taking responsibility for the effects that his methods
of control may have on their psychological or emotional well-being.
Ehrmann writes of Schwartzwalder, "He knew what he wanted out
of me and he knew how to get it. He loved my anger, leveraged my
needs, and used my 'mean streak' to service his mission perfectly."[7]

When Jim Brown came to Syracuse in August 1970 to attempt
to negotiate terms for reinstating the suspended black players,
Schwartzwalder told Brown that "white bigoted players would not
permit their return."[8] In a series of conversations with individual
white players, Brown learned that while some resented what they
saw as "special treatment" for players who had broken the rules,
others wanted to see their black teammates reinstated, if for no other
reason than to improve the team's chances for the coming season.

When the Syracuse Eight story began to break nationally in the
spring of 1970, sportswriters and football fans across the country

were astonished to see Ben Schwartzwalder in conflict with black students in the Syracuse football program. John Crittendon, sports editor of the *Miami News*, had covered many race-based sports stories in the South and elsewhere for years, but he found something special about the Syracuse case. "The curious thing is that this would happen to Ben Schwartzwalder. Schwartzwalder was recruiting Negroes back when the NFL still had a quota system," he wrote. The writer continues, "Schwartzwalder and Penn State's Rip Engle broke most of the color lines in the South, bringing blacks to play on grass where no Negro in a football uniform had ever walked before. In his twenty-one years at Syracuse, Schwartzwalder has produced more big name football players than any coach north of the Mason-Dixon line . . . [and] . . . so many of them were black. The five top names on the Syracuse rushing record list read like a college hall of fame for ball carriers—Larry Csonka, Floyd Little, Ernie Davis, Jim Brown, and Jim Nance. Except for Csonka, all of them are black."[9]

With African American enrollment in higher education rising across the country in the late 1960s, the African American students who joined the Syracuse football team during this period were surprised and disappointed to find "the school of Jim Brown and Ernie Davis" to be something less than they had imagined. "They [the recruiters] created the impression that Syracuse was not only a fair place, but that there were a lot of African American students," says Ron Womack. "We didn't realize they were just talking about one black superstar every four years. Being a young high school student, I didn't do the math." Womack remembers meeting the other black recruits during freshman orientation in August 1967. "We walked across campus to Booth Hall and got on an elevator together. In that small confined space, with no one else around, we all looked at each other and said, 'Where are the rest of 'em?' Later that day we met Dave Johnson, a black athlete who was an upperclassman. We said to him, 'There's got to be more.' And he said, 'No, this is it, and it's very unusual that they brought in six at one time.'"[10] But the students who would become the Syracuse Eight didn't necessarily view themselves as worse off than other black students who were playing ball for predominantly white universities. "There were double standards for white and black players everywhere, no question about it," says Bucky McGill, a starting defensive end in 1969 who chose to walk off the field during spring practice 1970. "This was the system that developed at many or most schools, not just at Syracuse."[11]

McGill and his teammates were an impressive group of young men. They weren't merely high school football stars, but also bright students with academic records ranging from good to exceptional. Since the 1920s, African American students in their position— including notable activists like Paul Robeson and Brud Holland— had chosen to patiently endure racial indignities at predominantly white college campuses to get their diplomas and/or their shots at playing pro ball. So what led the Syracuse Eight to act so decisively that they would put their promising futures at risk?

"I recently told the story of the Syracuse Eight to a group of students at Western Kentucky University," Greg Allen said in 2011. "They were athletes, mostly black, some white. When I told them what we did in 1970—that we had scholarships and we were on the team but that we refused to play until something was done about the way we were being treated—these kids just looked at me like they thought I was crazy. The story just turned them upside down. You should have heard them. 'You *had* a scholarship, and you did *what*? *Why* did you do that, man? *How* could you do that?'"[12] Duane "Spoon" Walker got a similar reaction when he told the Syracuse Eight story to students at Saginaw Valley State University. "The whole mindset of student athletes today is *me* as opposed to *we*," he said. "They have pretty much lost the focus of what they represent to the community."[13]

A straightforward response to the questions of these bewildered twenty-first-century college students might be, "My dignity was more important to me than the material advantages I might be sacrificing." Bucky McGill offers a different explanation of why he and his teammates were willing to risk what they been told was their one best chance to make it in America. According to McGill, "there was something in the air" that made accepting the status quo unacceptable at that time, in that place. It is tempting to dismiss this as overly simplistic or romantic. But many who lived that moment in American history—and particularly those who lived it on college campuses—know there is more to it than that.

It was 1970, and that was not a time for serious young black men in America to suck it up and take it, but rather a time to do something about it—and do it now. Pride, self-respect, and self-reliance had crystallized as the measures of dignity during the 1960s, and the Syracuse Eight decided they would not back down from those principles. Without a theorist or mentor to organize them or urge them on, they followed their hearts and the examples of the civil rights leaders they had grown up respecting. They had been invited by recruiters to follow in the footsteps of Jim Brown and, ironically, that is exactly what they chose to do. They excelled at what they did and they were not willing to accept the toleration of their presence as a substitute for respect. So they spoke truth to power. They took action to relieve themselves of specific humiliations they were suffering and needless dangers they were facing. They made no threat of violence. The only leverage they could bring to bear in support of their demands was the choice to withhold their labor, no small thing to descendants of slaves. "I think the most important influence on our decision was Dr. Martin Luther King's practice of nonviolent protest," Greg Allen says. "The system was wrong and we didn't want to take it anymore," adds McGill.

A decade of assassinations, riots, and war appeared to be spiraling into some kind of unfathomable apocalypse. President Richard M. Nixon, who had won office in 1968 on a "peace with honor" platform, had instead expanded the Vietnam War into Cambodia, sacrificing that country as collateral damage in a wider war against a communist menace that posed a threat which, to many, would appear to have been exaggerated. As American soldiers were dying in the heat of what the media was still calling the Cold War, members of the Ohio National Guard turned their guns on unarmed students at Kent State University, killing four at an anti-war demonstration. From an expanding seat in the middle of the American couch, those leaning left saw fascist shock troops devouring the young, while those leaning right saw "us," at long last, striking back at "them," the domestic enemy. The line between patriotism and foolhardiness blurred beyond reasonable distinction. Growing numbers of students feared graduation from college because of the unwanted choice of international destinations it seemed to present: Vietnam vs. Canada. In a stalemated war producing tens of thousands of casualties and little else that anyone could put a finger on, the definition of "peace with honor" was revealed as "war and more war, with no end in sight." Educators and administrators began to see themselves as babysitters for a generation of lambs awaiting slaughter, and this was not the kind of job that had drawn them into their relatively poorly paid profession. Unable to function under these conditions, many campuses suspended classes. Syracuse was one of them.

Given all that was going on that spring, the complaints of scholarship athletes enjoying free rides at a private university may seem trivial at first glance. But time has only proved the courage of those who have something worth risking and choose to risk it. Like Rosa Parks going about her business on a city bus in Montgomery, the Syracuse Eight entered a larger struggle at the point where their own lives intersected it. The issues they raised in Syracuse in 1970 got them thrown off the football team and effectively blacklisted from pro football. But their local complaints gradually exposed problems that were national in character. The things that got the Eight kicked off the football team have since been addressed so thoroughly at Syracuse and elsewhere that a student athlete of any race at almost any school in the United States today would be astonished to think of what the Syracuse Eight were asking for as anything but "givens."

So what exactly did the Eight do that caused the man who was personally responsible for bringing each of them to Syracuse to banish them from football?

Spring practice commenced on Wednesday, April 8, 1970, and the black coach that had been promised thirteen months earlier was nowhere to be seen. On the following Monday, ten of the eleven African Americans in the Syracuse football program signed their names to a document containing four complaints about how they were being treated: bias against black players in academic advisement; quotas limiting black participation on the team; the failure to hire a black assistant coach as promised; and poor medical care, especially in sports-related injuries. The document was delivered to the office mailbox of Coach Schwartzwalder.[14]

Bias in Academic Support

Believing they could succeed as college students, they demanded the same level of academic support routinely offered to other students at the university, including white members of the football team. The most pressing particular in this regard was an end to the practice of assigning them assistant football coaches as academic advisors rather than faculty members from their chosen fields of study. "The courses they had us take, such as 'Techniques of Football' and 'Theories of Basketball,' were good for one thing only: they kept you eligible to play for the team. But they were worthless when it came to graduating," says Alif Muhammad.[15] A National Merit Scholarship finalist in high school, Muhammad's attraction to a Syracuse engineering program had persuaded him to forego offers from such schools as Harvard, Princeton, and the U.S. Naval Academy. In effect, the Syracuse Eight were rejecting two stereotypical assumptions about them that underpinned the practice of placing them in so-called "basket-weaving courses": (1) the students refused to see themselves as a bunch of dumb jocks who could succeed at nothing other than playing football; and (2) they refused to believe that their race made them any less capable than any other students admitted to the university.

Bias in the Depth Chart

Frustrated by artificial limitations on the number of nonwhites who were permitted to play in the backfield, they demanded an end to quotas, believing they and the entire team would benefit if the assignment of positions were determined solely by merit. Quotas in athletics (as well as in admissions) were once common at majority-white schools that accepted students of color. At Syracuse, athletic quotas were most closely identified with basketball, where Lew Andreas's "rule of two" limited the number of nonwhites who could appear on the court at one time. But the rule of two was already a thing of the past in Orange basketball in 1970.

"When Fred Lewis came here as head basketball coach in 1962, he didn't care what color you were, as long as you could play," said Jim Boeheim, who was a Syracuse freshman that year. "Whatever had gone down in the past, after Fred brought in his first two groups of recruits, we had some of the best college prospects in the country: Dave Bing, Vaughn Harper, Sam Penceal and Val Reed. The rest of us were Upstate kids, like George Hicker and myself."[16]

Boeheim had grown up in Lyons, New York, about fifty miles west of Syracuse. He says that before coming to the university, the only black people he knew were a family in town who had two sons with whom he sometimes played ball. Joining the varsity in his sophomore year, Boeheim learned that his roommate would be Dave Bing. "I remember walking into the dorm room and seeing Dave's stuff there. Given my background and the fact that I wasn't a scholarship player, I never thought I'd be assigned to room with Dave. It turned out to be one of the best days of my life, and I knew it even then. I already knew what a great player he was, and I soon found out what a great guy and great leader Dave is. He had a tremendous influence on me. I learned right away that what's important in sports is your talent, how you develop it and use it, and what kind of teammate you are. Those principles have served me throughout my career." Boeheim would remain a part of Syracuse basketball for the next half century, becoming the most successful head coach in Orange history, with more than nine hundred career victories to his credit.

But if diversity was bringing benefits to Syracuse basketball and basketball players, things seemed to be moving in the opposite direction in the football program. During Schwartzwalder's early years at Syracuse, when there were so few blacks playing football (or attending) predominantly white universities, the presence of a few black players on a team could be taken as evidence that the program was making positive efforts at racial inclusion. But after the federal civil rights legislation of 1964, increasing numbers of African American students won admission to institutions across the nation, so their impact on collegiate sports also increased. Quotas, where they existed, could no longer remain invisible.

The Syracuse basketball program, under Fred Lewis, adapted to the new conditions and thrived as never before. The football program under Schwartzwalder did not adapt and paid the price for the duration of his tenure and beyond.

During the first few years after the Civil Rights Act of 1964 ended laws requiring segregation, Schwartzwalder attempted to comply by recruiting an unprecedented number of black athletes, including all of the Syracuse Eight. That effort brought to Syracuse some tremendous talent, as well as a contingent of politically aware and academically accomplished African American students. In 1969, for example, Greg Allen joined a student group that was lobbying for the addition of an African American studies program to the Syracuse curriculum. Activists had sought Allen's participation in the hope that having a high-visibility athlete on their committee would attract student attention for their cause. Soon after the group presented a proposal to Chancellor John Corbally, Allen got a call to come to the field house and see the coach. He recounts the meeting:

> I'm sitting there thinking he wants to talk to me about the coming spring practice, but I didn't really know what this was about. Ben looks at me over his glasses and says, "What's this I hear about you and this black crap?"
>
> "Coach, if you're talking about the black studies program, yes, I attended the meeting, but it's nothing radical."
>
> "Well, you're going to have to make up your mind. Do you want to be black, or do you want to be a football player?"
>
> "Coach, I'm going to be a football player for a short time, but I'm going to be black for the rest of my life. This is a good cause and it won't interfere with me being a football player."
>
> "I guess you've got some real thinking to do, Allen."

And that's how our meeting ended. I left his office not knowing what to say. I wasn't all that familiar with black studies when the group first asked me to get involved. So they made their case, and it seemed like a good idea to me. What right did the football coach have to tell me not to get involved in something like this? How did he even know that I had been at the meeting?[17]

By spring practice in 1970, the competition for positions in the backfield was pretty crowded. There were five African American players (Allen, Bulls, Godbolt, Griffin, Muhammad) who were limited to competing for two starting spots, as well as several white players (Marty Januszkiewicz, Roger Praetorius, Larry Giewont, John Rosella), who could compete for all three running-back positions or for the quarterback spot. The decision to recruit so many promising running backs carried negative consequences for the team; with a limited number of scholarships available, some of the squad's other needs were bound to suffer. For example, Schwartzwalder attempted to compensate for the lack of defensive recruits by turning some of his "excess" black offensive backs into pass defenders. Of course, not all offensive backs can be expected to excel as pass defenders.[18]

The team's suffering was not as great as the individual suffering. Every scholarship student, white or black, competing for a spot in Schwartzwalder's backfield, had turned down excellent opportunities to try out for backfield positions at other schools. While all contenders for backfield positions faced this situation, the pain was not equally shared among those who lost. For students who came from middle-class or well-to-do families, going off to college on a football scholarship was a proud achievement, and ending up on the bench or with a different position or not making the team could be terribly disappointing. But for students who had been told since they were children that a pro sports career was their one real chance for success in life, a lack of opportunity to at least give it one's best shot could constitute a personal disaster of the first order.

Perhaps no one suffered more from the over-recruitment of offensive players and the extension of quotas at Syracuse into the late 1960s than John Willie Godbolt of the Syracuse Eight. Godbolt had grown up in Father Panik Village, a crime-ridden public housing project in Bridgeport, Connecticut. "It was one of the worst projects in the country," according to Bucky McGill, Godbolt's roommate. McGill, who grew up in a modest working-class neighborhood on the East Side of Binghamton, New York, still recalls his shock when he accompanied Godbolt on a visit home: "Everywhere you walked, you stepped on broken glass. I remember thinking the glass was as abundant as the blades of grass on a lawn."[19] While still in high school, Godbolt had fathered two baby daughters, and he was determined to make sure they got out of Father Panik Village as soon as possible.

A blazing fast runner capable of sudden, unexpected acceleration, Godbolt had lettered in football, basketball, baseball, and track at Bassick High School in Bridgeport. Intent on going to college and becoming a pro athlete, he considered himself (at 6 feet 1 inch, 205 pounds) too short for basketball, and chose to focus on football. Several schools expressed interest in Godbolt, but Frank Dorio, an assistant football coach at Bassick—and a 1937 Syracuse alum—secured an offer from Schwartzwalder and captured Godbolt's attention with tales of the exploits of Jim Brown and Ernie Davis. It's even possible that Dorio mentioned Wilmeth Sidat-Singh, who had been his teammate at Syracuse. Godbolt's decision to accept the Syracuse offer made the Bridgeport newspapers.[20]

At first, things seemed to be working out well for Godbolt. As a sophomore in 1968, he averaged 4.7 yards per carry in 68 rushing attempts for 389 yards. He also returned kicks on special teams, averaging 18.2 yards per runback. In his best performances that season, Godbolt ran for three touchdowns in a 31–0 shutout of William and Mary. But Schwartzwalder seemed to take a personal dislike to Godbolt, and with an overabundance of running backs on the bench and a quota to observe, the coach kept Godbolt on the bench much of the 1969 season. Godbolt did get one moment to shine. In an October game against Wisconsin in Madison, injuries to white players forced Schwartzwalder to play three blacks in the backfield—Godbolt,

Allen, and Muhammad. Godbolt scored two touchdowns in a 43–7 upset road victory. McGill recalls Schwartzwalder's response, which has stayed with him for more than forty years: "The brothers were so happy because we witnessed all three blacks in the same backfield most of the game, and we won," he says. "During our jubilant walk off the field, Ben comes over to John and says, 'Don't be too happy, it's a short walk from the parlor to the outhouse.' At that point John's body language just went limp and I was wondering why Ben would say these harsh words at this time. The next week at practice, John's name had fallen deep on the running back depth-chart list."[21]

Greg Allen, from Plainfield High School in northern New Jersey, joined the varsity in 1969. Instead of being paired with Godbolt in the backfield, as conventional analysis might dictate, Allen became Godbolt's replacement. Allen certainly deserved a first-string place in the backfield. Rushing for 4.5 yard per carry, he was also a spectacular asset on special teams. In the 1969 Penn State game, Allen racked up 172 yards in punt returns, setting a single-game Syracuse record that still stands. Godbolt lost his special team position to Allen. But for reasons having nothing to do with fair competition, Allen's addition as a primary player in the backfield resulted in the removal of Godbolt in favor of Ron Trask, a white player whom Godbolt had outperformed in every statistical category.

The squad's leading ground gainer in 1969 was fullback Alif Muhammad, who chalked up 689 yards that season. Schwartz-walder might have been confident he had two candidates for his next great running back in Allen and Muhammad. But Godbolt sat on the bench in 1969, as did Robin Griffin, a 6-foot, 193-pound half-back out of Easton, Pennsylvania. (Griffin, it should be noted, initially supported the Syracuse Eight protest, but would break with the group in August 1970, agreeing to Schwartzwalder's terms for rejoining the team. He was the only African American on the seventy-two-player roster during the 1970 season. Even so, Griffin was assigned to a defensive back position.) Two more black hopefuls for rushing positions were scheduled to join the team at spring practice in 1970: Dick Bulls, a sophomore who had been an all-city fullback

John Godbolt Falls Victim to Quotas

In 1968, Syracuse's three primary running backs were fullback Alif Muhammad and halfbacks John Godbolt and Ron Trask. When Greg Allen earned a placed on the 1969 team, either Godbolt or Trask would have to get less playing time. Comparing their performances in 1968, Godbolt comes out ahead of Trask in every significant statistical category: yards per carry, touchdowns, total yards, and even pass receptions. But Coach Schwartzwalder did not play more than two blacks in the backfield at the same time. So in 1969, Godbolt's plays from scrimmage were cut by more than half, while Trask got the same amount of playing time he had the year before. This was part of a larger pattern leading up to the Syracuse Eight protest. In 1969, Schwartzwalder cut the playing time of virtually every returning African American player on the Orange football team, regardless of personal performance.

Year	Pos	Rushing				Receiving				Plays from Scrimmage			
		Att	Yds	Avg	TD	Rec	Yds	Avg	TD	Plays	Yds	Avg	TD
1968													
John Godbolt	RB	68	321	4.7	6	7	68	9.7	0	75	389	5.2	6
Ron Trask	RB	46	160	3.5	1	1	39	7.8	1	51	199	3.9	2
1969	Pos	Att	Yds	Avg	TD	Rec	Yds	Avg	TD	Plays	Yds	Avg	TD
John Godbolt	RB	35	106	3.0	2	0	0	0.0	0	35	106	3.0	2
Ron Trask	RB	48	166	3.5	0	1	9	9.0	0	49	175	3.6	0

in Buffalo at Grover Cleveland High School, and freshman tailback Ron Page out of Mont Pleasant High in Schenectady. Presented with the opportunity of moving past three varsity upperclassmen—Allen, Godbolt, and Muhammad—in pursuit of an open "black" backfield position, Bulls chose instead to join them in the protest. Page, who was never part of the protest, was red-shirted in 1970.

"They tried to play each of us against the other," Allen says.[22] "It wasn't healthy competition; it was a form of control." McGill points out that Godbolt suffered a disadvantage in that crowded fight for a "black" position in the backfield. "Schwartzwalder seemed not to like John, and I was not sure why until I heard Ben tell John that he reminded him of Jim Brown."[23]

The All-White Coaching Staff

The Syracuse Eight reiterated the demand they had been making for more than a year that the athletic department make tangible efforts to add an African American to the all-white coaching staff. The need for mentors, role models, and advocates among students of all types is generally acknowledged in college sports today, and the Eight had plenty of good reasons for wanting a black coach in the program. For one thing, they said, they were weary of authority figures who saw them only in terms of stereotypes. They needed someone on the staff who might have more relevant advice for them than "don't be like Avatus Stone!" They wanted someone in a position of relative authority who they could depend on to say something to a player or coach who used the word "nigger," and who might help them get some relief from the hundred daily slights and humiliations that were acceptable in the institutional culture of the program. Schwartz-walder had publically agreed to hire a black coach, but had played the students for fools by telling them that Floyd Little's visit to spring practice constituted the hiring of a black coach. By showing such blatant disrespect for their concerns, the coach made it difficult for the players to respect him.

Medical Care

Alarmed by their experiences with team physician Dr. William E. Pelow, the students demanded better medical treatment for *all* team members, without regard to race.

A veteran who served in both world wars, and an accomplished golfer who had won several amateur tournaments, Pelow was a close personal friend of Schwartzwalder. Both were members of the Bellevue Country Club in Syracuse and they played together often, with Pelow offering much needed help to Schwartzwalder, a lefthander who had come to the game—and country clubs—relatively late in life. Dr. Pelow was a sixty-six-year-old retiree when Schwartzwalder hired him. Although ministering to the medical needs of dozens of young football players might be construed as a physically demanding job, he remained team doctor until he was seventy-four, retiring then only because Schwartzwalder's departure forced him to do so.

Dr. Pelow's medical specialty was gynecology, which is an unusual qualification for a doctor charged with the care of seventy or so male athletes in one of the roughest of contact sports.[24] Dr. Pelow spent more of his career as an administrator than as a practicing gynecologist, and while that is not a credential for treating men's sports injuries, it did provide him with useful skills in his job. He had served as chair of the Onondaga County Medical Society's Compensation Committee for two decades and for a term as chair of the Compensation Committee of the New York State Medical Society. This proved to be excellent preparation for filling out insurance forms, an increasingly important part of a team doctor's work during the 1960s.

In presenting an accurate picture of the medical care afforded to the football team, it should be pointed out that the athletic trainer was in charge of taking care of most of the day-to-day bumps and bruises requiring ice, heat, or taping, and Syracuse's trainer, Jules Reichel, was probably among the best in the business. In a career that began in Syracuse in 1931, Reichel is credited with inventing a mouth guard for Syracuse football players that became a model for such equipment and with developing several techniques for wrapping common injuries.[25] He was inducted into the National Athletic Trainers' Association in 1965. "Julie was the nicest man you will ever meet, and a great trainer," according to Bucky McGill, who didn't sustain any injuries while playing for Syracuse that were considered serious enough to require a doctor's attention. "I learned to tape ankles using Julie's 'Louisiana heel-lock' technique and as a youth football coach, I sometimes still use wraps that Julie taught me."[26]

But Reichel's authority was limited. Athletes with more serious injuries were treated by Dr. Pelow. "We used to call him 'The Butcher,'" says John Lobon. "One of the first things people told you was to stay away from him. I thought it was a joke, until I saw him, one day, draining fluid from a player's knee in the locker room. That's a pretty common procedure and it isn't all that painful. But the guy was in agony, screaming in pain, and the doctor just kept going about his business. He didn't seem to notice."[27]

Ron Womack had a different kind of experience involving Dr. Pelow. Shortly after Womack complained to Schwartzwalder about not getting the playing time he felt he deserved, he was called in to see Dr. Pelow. "Supposedly, he was going to check the status of a condition I had, which he was already treating," Womack says. "I couldn't understand why; I was feeling fine. But after examining me for a few minutes, the doctor declared me medically ineligible to play football at Syracuse. I have no doubt in my mind that Coach Schwartzwalder used the doctor to shut me up. I had complained about sharing my position with a white player who I didn't think was performing at the same level I was. I was black and I had spoken my mind. He perceived me to be a 'troublemaker.'"[28]

Any number of stories told by Orange football alumni who had come under Dr. Pelow's care might suffice to support the Syracuse Eight's claims about him. This one is provided by Kevin McLoughlin, whose football career ended as a result of the incident he describes:

I hurt my wrist in practice, and it seemed pretty bad, so I was directed by Coach Joe Zombathy to show it to Dr. Pelow. He looks at my wrist and puts two fingers around it and starts to shake it up and down. I was already in terrible pain and that only made it worse, but he just kept shaking my wrist and looking at it. Then he hurries me over to Coach Schwartzwalder and picks up my wrist again, dangling it in Schwartzwalder's face and he starts shaking it again. He says, "Coach, this looks pretty bad. Better send him over to the hospital." One of the other football assistants drove me over to Crouse Hospital and I walked into the emergency room by myself, with all my football equipment on. I had been told by some of the other guys that if you ever get injured, the best thing to do was to get away from Dr. Pelow as soon as possible, and try to see Dr. Murray or Dr. Sugarman. They were orthopedists over at Crouse, and really knew how to treat sports injuries. Luckily, I was able to get in to see Dr. Sugarman. After a series of x-rays, he says, "Your wrist is broken in two, maybe three places and all the other carpals are out of place. You haven't moved it since the injury, have you?" So I tell him what happened with Dr. Pelow, and as I'm describing it, everyone in the room—a few nurses and doctors and whoever else was there—everyone stops what they're doing and they all look in my direction and roll their eyes up at the ceiling. It never healed exactly right, and I still can't bend it back to this day.[29]

On April 14, 1970, the day after the protest document was sent to Schwartzwalder, the African American students who endorsed it all showed up at practice. Schwartzwalder made no mention of it, but his silence came through loud and clear. The players began their protest action the next day, staying away from scheduled drills that week and from an intra-squad scrimmage on Saturday. The following week, Floyd Little arrived on campus to assist in spring practice 1970, as he had in 1969. In an interview with the *Daily Orange*, the student newspaper, Little said that the type of treatment the Syracuse players were complaining about was "going on all over the country." Like the veteran athletes who had counseled young black athletes to steer clear of the planned boycott of the Mexico City Olympic games two years earlier, Little advised the Syracuse students to avoid becoming involved in a football team boycott and instead to keep focused on advancing their individual careers. "They've got to go out there and do it for themselves or they'll never have a chance," said Little, who was coming into his own at this time as a star running back for the Denver Broncos. He expressed particular concern for Alif Muhammad, who he believed had the makings of an NFL fullback: "He has all the ability to play pro ball but I don't know if he is willing to pay the price."[30]

New York then, as now, is a state all but bereft of nationally competitive college football powers. News of the player walk-off at Syracuse, perhaps the only school in the state capable of mixing it up in Division I, found its way to the New York City metro area, where many Syracuse alumni live. The *New York Times* reported the story, instantly turning it into a media event: "Negroes Boycott Syracuse Drills."[31] Coincidentally, it was one of the last times that the newspaper of record used the term "Negro" in a headline.[32] The article prioritized Little's response to the players' demands as the catalyst for the boycott and mentioned that the athletes went through a practice of their own after a meeting with Chancellor Corbally the previous day.

With no response to their demands forthcoming, the students continued to stay away for the balance of spring practice. Since no official action had been taken against them all spring, their status as members of the team remained uncertain into the summer. As far as they knew, no action had been taken to remove them from the team. Schwartzwalder addressed that important detail by filing carbon copies of eight identical letters, dated July 6, 1970, addressed to Allen, Godbolt, Lobon, Griffin, Harrell, McGill, Muhammad, and Walker at their homes (illus. 6). The letters notified them that by "voluntarily withdrawing" from spring practice, they had also withdrawn from the football team. But the coach added that if they had "any interest in returning," they needed to make appointments with him before August 1.

In March 2012, five of the surviving members of the Syracuse Eight were shown carbon copies of the letters addressed to them

July 6, 1970

Mr. John Lobon
49 Mahl Avenue
Hartford, Connecticut 06120

Dear John:

This spring you voluntarily withdrew from football practice.

The coaching staff now is busy making plans for fall practice. If you have any interest in returning to football, it is essential that you see me personally before August 1.

Your status will be discussed at this time. If I do not hear from you, it will be assumed that you have no interest in competing in football for Syracuse University.

Please call the football office (ext. 2517) to establish a time convenient to both of us for the interview.

Yours truly,

F. B. Schwartzwalder
Head Football Coach

FBS/flb

6. Form letter dated July 6, 1970, from Coach Schwartzwalder to boycotting players, addressing their "voluntary withdrawal." Although the letters were filed as "sent," the players never received them. Ben Schwartzwalder Papers, University Archives, Syracuse University Libraries.

(retrieved from university archives), but none of them remembers ever receiving any such letter. "We were waiting for some kind of word from the football program or from the university all summer long, and nothing ever came," said McGill. "These letters were not mailed. This is unbelievable!" Allen, Lobon, McGill, and Muhammad reacted in precisely the same way.[33]

Members of the Syracuse Eight said they believed that during the late 1960s Schwartzwalder started taking systematic measures to reduce black participation in the Syracuse football program. It began, they argue, in 1968 when Ron Womack was unexplainably declared "unfit to play football" and then placed on the injured list, never to be reexamined (and therefore never to be reinstated). All through the 1969 season, Schwartzwalder reduced the playing time of African Americans, including his most productive running backs.

Another measure the members of the Syracuse Eight believe the coach put in place is described here in a newspaper account of a complaint made against Schwartzwalder in 1970 to the Human Rights Commission: "The three athletes claimed the coaching staff shifted black players from their regular positions to ones with which they were not familiar the day before the team would travel to an away game. . . . [In accordance with NCAA rules] they could not be on the traveling squad, which consists of the first two men [on the depth chart] for each position. On Monday, after the road game, they would be shifted back to their original position."[34]

The recruitment of new black players fell from six in 1967 to three in 1968 and two in 1969. Members of the Syracuse Eight believe that, in reaction to their protest, Schwartzwalder allegedly planned to cut six of them (Godbolt, Harrell, Lobon, McGill, Muhammad, and Walker) as punishment for their disloyalty, leaving the seventy-two-man squad with only two African American athletes (his choices were Allen and Griffin). "Instead of dealing with the team problems, Coach Ben Schwartzwalder has eliminated us," Dana Harrell told a reporter in August 1970.[35]

Of the issues raised by the Syracuse Eight, only one—the hiring of a black coach—received a response from university administration during the summer of 1970, when the chancellor took an interest in it. John E. Corbally, who replaced William Tolley in September 1969, was approached by the Syracuse Eight, and he agreed to get involved. Greg Allen was encouraged by the development. He had met Corbally while serving on the student committee advocating the introduction of an African American studies program to the university curriculum, and Allen found the chancellor to be fair-minded and willing to listen. The youngest chancellor in the school's history, Corbally seemed eager to focus on the difficult task that had convinced the trustees to hire him: defining new academic roles and programs for Syracuse, a private university, in the face of the vigorous growth of the public State University of New York system, which had been little more than a collection of small teacher's colleges before World War II. In statements to the press, Corbally denied that there was any truth to the students' complaints of discrimination but added that he recognized "the existence of misunderstandings between certain student-athletes and the football coaching staff."[36]

Schwartzwalder promptly arranged a trip to Tallahassee to consult with Jake Gaither of Florida A&M University. Gaither had just retired after twenty-five years as head coach at A&M. He was among the most successful African American coaches in college football during the segregation era, compiling a record of 203–36–4 during a career roughly parallel to Schwartzwalder's, and he had guided his team to six Black College National Championships. Gaither had played by the rules of the segregated South, but he had also made important contributions leading to change. In the late 1940s, Gaither had founded an annual June coaching clinic on the Florida A&M campus, and over the years he persuaded Bear Bryant of Alabama, Woody Hayes of Ohio State, and other top white coaches from all-white schools to participate.[37] The clinic played a key role in the eventual integration of Southern college sports, helping to prepare the region for the transition it faced after the repeal of Jim Crow laws. In 1960, on the heels of the Syracuse national championship, Gaither had named Schwartzwalder chairman of the football clinic "faculty," putting him at the head of a table that included such coaching greats as Sid Gilman of the Los Angeles Rams and Rip Engle of Penn State. Gaither's recommendation was as good a credential as any candidate might hope to get for the position of assistant coach at Syracuse that Schwartzwalder was asked to fill. Carlmon Jones was a tackle on the Florida A&M team during Gaither's final season before retirement.[38] On July 25, 1970, the *Syracuse Post-Standard* trumpeted the result of the Florida head-hunting trip: "SU Names First Negro Grid Aide." The hiring of Carlmon Jones, Syracuse University's first African American athletic coach (in any sport), qualifies as the last civil rights milestone Schwartzwalder's name can be associated with at Syracuse.

Gaither's seal of approval notwithstanding, Jones was a curious choice for the job. An offensive lineman who had played nearly every offensive position as well as defensive end and tackle, Jones brought knowledge and experience to the table; however, he had just graduated from A&M that spring.[39] At twenty-three, he was not much older than some of the Syracuse seniors.[40] Although Jones possessed technical knowledge and in-game experience, Alif Muhammad believes that Schwartzwalder chose him more for what he wouldn't do than for any of his capabilities. "Carlmon Jones was a good guy and he'd been a football player, which was also good," Muhammad says, but given his age, he wasn't in a position to challenge authority. Muhammad recalls peeking in on a coaches' meeting in August 1970. "I'll never forget that. It was a very intense session. There were all these X's and 0's going on [at the blackboard] and all this intense discussion. And there's Carlmon, sitting by himself in the back of the room. I remember thinking, 'I *sacrificed*—and this is what I got?'"[41]

A look at the university's archival list of football coaching personnel for 1970 supports the impression of Jones as a marginal member of the staff:

Floyd (Ben) Schwartzwalder, Head Coach
Theodore Dailey, Defensive Line
Daniel Fogarty, Defensive Backs
Joseph Krivak, Receivers

Wally Mahle, Freshman Coach
Rocco Pirro, Offensive Line
John Seketa, Freshman Assistant
James Shreve, Offensive Backs
Joseph Szombathy, Defensive Ends/Linebackers
Carlmon Jones, Assistant[42]

While the other assistant coaches are listed alphabetically and are identified with their specialties, Jones is at the bottom of the list with no specific responsibilities. This cannot be attributed to his joining the staff so soon before the beginning of the 1970 season; he is listed exactly the same way (bottom of the list, no specialty) for each of the four years he spent at Syracuse.[43]

Although the hiring of Jones was something less than a triumph for African American student athletes, it is worth noting that no action at all was taken (nor was much even said) about any of the other issues raised by the Syracuse Eight. As almost any contemporary athletic director will readily confirm, racial quotas in team assignments, racial bias in academic support, and inadequate medical care for student athletes are not trivial matters in American collegiate sports. But with Jones on staff, at least it could be said that something on the black students' agenda had been acted on. Corbally told Schwartzwalder to resolve the situation by drawing up conditions that would allow the players who had protested to rejoin the team in time for the football season.[44]

At this point, just a month before the first game of the 1970 season, Schwartzwalder revealed *his* vision of a happy ending for the student protest. Winning, which had always been the coach's top priority, remained so. But his focus no longer seemed to be on winning football games. Duane Walker told a reporter, "He's more concerned with fighting us than the teams on the schedule."[45]

5

End of an Error

The students who had boycotted spring practice left for summer recess with no official response to their grievances and with no official change in their status as members of the Syracuse football team. They had been ignored, but they knew the situation could not continue this way indefinitely. Chancellor Corbally's success in finally getting Schwartzwalder to hire a black coach (Jones reported for work on August 1) was taken as a sign that things were moving in the right direction as the Syracuse Eight anxiously awaited word from the athletic department or the university to confirm the next step toward solving the problems they had articulated. What they and the chancellor did not know is that Schwartzwalder had secretly and unilaterally decided the players' futures with the football team.

Schwartzwalder filed with his other administrative papers carbon copies of the letters to each of the players who had participated in the boycott. All were dated July 6, 1970. He later donated the carbons to the Syracuse University Archives as part of his collected papers. These letters contain two key pieces of information for the players: (1) by missing spring practice, they had, as far as the coach was concerned, "voluntarily withdrawn" from the Syracuse football program; and (2) any who wished to discuss a change in that status could do so by making an appointment to meet one-on-one with the coach before a deadline of August 1, 1970. The players spent their summer at home waiting for some type of communication from the coaching staff or university administration. "We were watching the mailbox all summer long, and we were all in touch with each other," said Bucky McGill, forty-two years after the date on the letters. "If any of us had been sent that letter, every one of us would have known about it. It never happened."[1]

The first actual communication from the football program to any of the Syracuse Eight occurred in mid-August, when Greg Allen and Robin Griffin received telephone calls from members of the coaching staff inviting them to fall practice. The others were not officially contacted about their status, but instead were left to presume their exclusion after word spread that two of their colleagues had been invited to camp.

If all the boycotters had committed the same offense, why an amnesty for two, and the stiffest sentence possible for the others? Allen says the other boycotters pressed him for an answer about what he was going to do. He turned to his father for some advice, "I was nineteen, just turned twenty years old and I was still a kid. It was a big decision for me, and I wanted to seek his counsel," Allen explains. "And he told me, 'Greg, this is one of those moments when you have to become a man. I can't make a decision for you, you'll have to decide for yourself. But you'll have to live with the decisions.'" Allen ultimately refused the offer of reinstatement when he learned it was not extended to the others. "This was typical of Schwartzwalder," Allen says. "He wanted to show us he had the power to divide us. He wanted to trivialize us by trivializing everything we stood for. We all wanted to go back and play. It wasn't that I just wanted to boycott and end my whole college career. I wanted—we all wanted—to just get this behind us and go back out and play and go on maybe to careers in football."[2]

Like the Syracuse Eight, the chancellor had taken the hiring of Carlmon Jones as a sign that Schwartzwalder was now ready to address the grievances of the African American players, or, at the very least, as a proof that Schwartzwalder could be forced to take positive actions if the full authority of the university administration was invoked. Neither was the case. Hiring Jones and then marginalizing his duties amounted to little more than a tactical maneuver on the part of the coach. But adding Jones to the staff was not the first step on a path of reform. Jim Brown, who had both suffered and prospered from his relationship with Schwartzwalder, made the following observation about his former coach when he came to Syracuse in the summer of 1970. "Ben has always been a powerful, strong, stubborn man," Brown said. "And now he's old. He's inflexible. Ben is building a fortress around himself. He seems to be afraid of his job."[3]

With six prominent players, each with two years of varsity experience, being dropped from the squad, the press would expect an explanation. That job fell to athletic director James H. Decker, who had held the job since Andreas's retirement. In a *Syracuse Post-Standard* article headlined, "SU Snubs Six Black Varsity Grid Players," Decker explained the process by which these decisions were made: "Head Football Coach Ben Schwartzwalder held interviews with all of them and told [the dropped players] personally they would not be invited back for this season."[4] According to each of the surviving members of the Syracuse Eight, those "interviews" never took place.

Jim Brown's assessment that Schwartzwalder had become "afraid of his job" is a piercing insight that escaped the many experienced local and national sportswriters who covered the Syracuse Eight story. For some two decades, Schwartzwalder had defined his job as winning football games, and that meant putting the strongest team possible on the field. But in the summer of 1970, and for at least two years preceding that date, the athletes he kept on the bench had already proved themselves to be the best Syracuse had at their positions. It wasn't just about anything so mundane as chalking up a win on a Saturday afternoon anymore. If another national championship or even a bowl invitation was a priority on the coach's list of things to do in 1970, he showed little evidence of it.

Joe Ehrmann describes Schwartzwalder in terms suited to a deeply politicized culture warrior, circa 1970. "He used to count the guys on the opposing team who had mustaches and long hair, and tell us they were all 'pinko commies.' It was like an extra incentive to beat them," Ehrmann said in a 2006 interview.[5] Ehrmann recalls the campus visit of Dave Meggyesy, a Syracuse football alumnus who had just retired from a seven-year career as an NFL linebacker.

Students, and especially team members, were normally encouraged to turn out for events involving sports alums. This was not the case with Meggysesy. An activist in the anti–Vietnam War movement, Meggysesy had just written *Out of Their League*, a controversial exposé of life in the NFL, one of the first books to take on the wholesome image the league had been promoting since the 1950s. Further, Meggysesy's appearance on campus was sponsored by the Syracuse chapter of Students for a Democratic Society. "Schwartzwalder called me into his office and told me that he didn't want me or anyone else on the team to go hear Meggysesy speak," Ehrmann said.

Schwartzwalder had stalled and made sarcastic jokes about hiring a black coach, but in the end he had complied. Corbally's call for an act of conciliatory spirit toward the black players seemed to send him into rebellion. His invitation to Allen and Griffin to return included a precondition that they sign documents apologizing for disrupting spring practice, renouncing their ties to the other boycotting players, and pledging loyalty to him (illus. 7).

To create a rationale for banishing some players and readmitting others, Schwartzwalder wrote a memo asserting that Griffin and Allen "were reinstated because, in my judgment, and that of the staff, their spring action was based on duress."[6] No evidence or explanation of "duress" is offered. Greg Allen fervently denies that he was pressured by anyone to participate in the boycott of spring practice. "It's a total falsehood," he says. "Even if there was any truth in it, how would he have found out about it? He hadn't even talked to any of us since the whole thing began." Allen dismisses Schwartzwalder's claim to have had "meetings" with him and the others that summer. "I don't think any of us believed he could have blatantly fabricated the facts."[7]

Schwartzwalder's choice of Griffin and Allen makes sense in strategic terms. Griffin had agreed, before the boycott, to give up on competing for a backfield slot in exchange for a position in the defensive backfield.[8] This gained him favor with Schwartzwalder in two ways: he had shown himself willing to follow orders, even if it meant suppressing self-interest; and Griffin's return to the squad on defense would not put any pressure on the backfield quota, which Schwartz-walder apparently aimed to maintain indefinitely. Griffin signed the documents without comment. Schwartzwalder's offer of amnesty to Greg Allen was extended with other things in mind. Allen was the chosen one for "next great Syracuse running back."

In 1968, there had been talk in the newspapers of John Godbolt as "the next Number 44," and more recently, attention had been on Alif Muhammad as the likely chosen one. But Schwartzwalder had identified Godbolt as someone who "reminded him of Jim Brown." Cutting loose Alif Muhammad, the team's leading rusher for the preceding two seasons, would probably never have been an option for Schwartzwalder when he was at the top of his game as a coach; Muhammad was the kind of power fullback that he had made the foundation of his best teams. But cutting such a player was clearly an option for the Schwartzwalder of 1970.

Alif Muhammad, Dana Harrell, and Duane Walker filed a joint complaint against Schwartzwalder with the county's Human Rights Commission (this was Harrell's second civil rights complaint against Schwartzwalder). When their complaint to the county was found to have merit, Muhammad filed a complaint with the New York State Human Rights Commission.

During 1969, the team's offense had suffered from the benching of Godbolt and the diminished playing time of Muhammad. The only game in which Syracuse scored more than three touchdowns that season was a 43–7 victory over Wisconsin, when Schwartz-walder had been forced to play Allen, Godbolt, and Muhammad at the same time because of injuries to white players. But the defense had been a bright spot through it all, rated fifth in the nation during an otherwise mediocre (5–5) season, and it had at least kept Syracuse in the game during losses to two ranked teams: Penn State (15–14) and West Virginia (13–10). In 1970, by eliminating three of his best defensive players in one fell swoop—Lobon (linebacker), McGill (defensive end), and Walker (defensive back)—Schwartzwalder prob-ably did at least as much damage to the Syracuse defense as he had done to the offense. Minutes after the season's opening game kickoff,

CODE FOR SYRACUSE ATHLETES

An athlete at Syracuse University:

Is aware of the value of intercollegiate athletics to the institution and to himself, and will accept participation as an opportunity for self-development and for contribution to the institution. He also accepts the responsibility that accompanies the opportunity by regular attendance at practice, by an all-out effort, by loyalty to his team, and support of the University.

Conducts himself as a gentleman always, on and off the campus, and never, through misbehavior, embarrasses his University, coach, teammates, fellow students or family.

Considers it a privilege to represent Syracuse University and as an athlete realizes that he will be in the public eye and hence is careful in his associations.

•Meets all University appointments and obligations promptly and regularly, both in the classroom and on the athletic field.

Conforms absolutely to the training rules established by the coach of his sport.

Obeys the instructions and orders of departmental staff members that are normal and necessary operation of the sports program.

Reports immediately director of athletics, or his representative, any suspected attempt the contest or any unusual request from outside sources for information about his team. He neither bets himself, nor takes bets on any athletic event.

Retains his amateur standing as defined by the National Collegiate Athletic Association and the Eastern College Athletic Conference, and will not sign, or agree to sign, a professional contract during his period of collegiate eligibility, nor will he agree to be represented by an agent or organization for the marketing of his athletic ability during this period.

Knows that willful disregard of this code can result in suspension from his athletic squad and/or other disciplinary penalties, and possible gradation or cancellation of financial aid.

Understands that when he feels that he cannot live up to this code, he so indicates to the proper University official and withdraws from his sport.

_____, 1970

In requesting reinstatement as a member of the Syracuse University football squad, I concede that dismissal from the squad was a logical consequence of missing football practice for a protracted period during the Spring, 1970. I further recognize that this absence from practice for a protracted period affects my status with regard to the initial depth chart. In support of my request for reinstatement and as evidence of my desire to contribute meaningfully to the success of the football team, I make the following commitments to the coaching staff and to the tri-captains of the football team. I understand that these commitments are required of every member of the football squad.

I. I have reread and reaffirmed acceptance of the Code for Syracuse Athletes.

II. I promise a cooperative attitude and commit myself to 100% effort in all drills and other assignments.

III. I am willing to play any position designated by the football coaching staff.

IV. I will accept and follow all training rules established by the coaching staff and all rules and decisions related to such matters as training table, trip lists, trip schedules, ticket allocations, and housing. I understand that these rules and decisions will apply equally to all members of the squad.

V. I agree that it is a disservice to the team and to individuals concerned to air grievances in the public arena. The grievance procedure outlined in Item VI is the logical approach to the resolution of past and present complaints and dissatisfactions and I will follow the proposed procedure.

VI. I agree that all complaints or grievances will be taken up initially with Coach Schwartzwalder or with an assistant coach. If this discussion does not resolve the grievance, I shall discuss it with the Director of Athletics. If still dissatisfied with the result, I will discuss the problem with the Chairman of the Athletic Governing Board.

Signed: _____

7. Syracuse University Code for Athletes and Request for Reinstatement, which Coach Schwartzwalder asked returning players to sign. Ben Schwartzwalder Papers, University Archives, Syracuse University Libraries.

Sequence of Events in the Syracuse Eight Story
April–September, 1970

April: The Syracuse Eight send a written list of grievances to Head Coach Ben Schwartzwalder. When Schwartzwalder refuses to discuss the grievances or acknowledge receiving the document, the players stop attending spring practice sessions.

June: Chancellor John E. Corbally orders Schwartzwalder to hire an African American assistant coach, noting Schwartzwalder had agreed to do this more than a year earlier. It is the only Syracuse Eight grievance addressed by either Corbally or Schwartzwalder.

July: Schwartzwalder complies with the Chancellor's order by hiring Carlmon Jones, the first African American athletic coach in Syracuse University history. Schwartzwalder files copies of a July 6 form letter addressed to the eight players—but never received by any of them—requiring that they contact him by August 1 or be removed from the team.

August: Schwartzwalder offers reinstatement, via phone call, to only two players. Greg Allen refuses to rejoin the team unless all of the Eight are reinstated. Robin Griffin rejoins the squad. Corbally urges Schwartzwalder to reinstate the Syracuse Eight.

September: Responding to Corbally's late-August request, Schwartzwalder drafts a reinstatement document to be offered to each of the removed players, requiring them to disavow the protest they had staged in April. The players refuse to sign. Meanwhile, some members of the Eight file complaints with the county and state Human Rights Commissions. After the state commission intervenes on September 21, the university announces that all eight players will report for practice on September 23, with language of the reinstatement document to be negotiated. Upon arriving at practice, four of the players are declared academically ineligible, and four others are scheduled for physicals, making them ineligible to play in the game against Kansas on September 26. After failed attempts to change the language of the documents, Corbally agrees to the suspension of the Syracuse Eight for the 1970 season.

Houston connected for a 99-yard touchdown on the way to a 42–15 shellacking of the Orange.

Bucky McGill and D.J. Harrell were in the Astrodome for the Houston–Syracuse game—as spectators. They hoped, by being there, to make a statement to the public and the team about what Schwartz-walder was doing to Syracuse football, and sympathetic members of the black community in the city of Syracuse provided them with airplane tickets. Had McGill, Lobon, and Spoon Walker been permitted to play that day, Syracuse would have been in a much better position to cover Houston's passing game, which featured two All Americans: wide receiver Elmo Wright and tight end Riley Odoms. "I always wondered if Wright could have made that 99-yard score with Spoon on him," says McGill. When the game ended, the Syracuse players exited the field through a portal just under where McGill and Harrell were seated. "The entire team, including the coaching staff, looked up and glared at us, as they walked into the tunnel," McGill recalls. "We just stared back." Schwartzwalder avoided their stare, but took note.

Although Schwartzwalder would have to struggle through two more lopsided losses before he could put together an effective pass defense, he was much quicker in getting ahead of the competition in the media war against his former black players. By announcing the return of Griffin and Allen, Schwartzwalder effectively seized control of the narrative where it most counted: on the sports pages.

But not everything went according to script. In an extraordinary show of personal courage, self-sacrifice, and loyalty to comrades, Greg Allen declined Schwartzwalder's offer unless or until the other banished students were afforded the same opportunity. The coach's assertion that Allen had been pressured into casting his lot with the other boycotting players was at risk of appearing to be self-serving fiction. Allen was clear and sharp in his response to the press: He had acted just as each of his colleagues had acted—on his own volition. He considered the offer an attempt by the coach to dilute the substance of the serious issues raised by the players by pitting them against each other, just as he pitted them against each other in "unhealthy competitions" for top positions on offense.

"We had been told that we would have a black assistant coach at spring practice, but we didn't have one," Allen told *Sports Illustrated*, explaining what had happened back in April. "Now that there is a black coach, I feel the whole problem can end if the others are permitted to play this fall."[9] This was precisely the conciliatory endgame Corbally had suggested.

Allen's rejection of Schwartzwalder's invitation left the coach without his preferred candidate for running back. But if he was worried about the 1970 football season, he hadn't shown it yet. The boycott and its aftermath had brought the number of black students on the roster from an all-time high of eleven down to one—Robin Griffin. That was two black students fewer than were on the roster the day Schwartzwalder took over a 1949 Syracuse team that included Bernie Custis, Bill Haskins, and Horace Morris.

During the last week of August, more than three weeks in advance of the Houston game, the chancellor had asked the coach to reinstate all the players who had been involved in the boycott. After the invitations to Griffin and Allen only, little had been said about the documents that the two suspended players would have to sign to rejoin the team. Griffin had accepted the offer whole and without comment; Allen never got to that point, refusing reinstatement out of hand because of the unfair exclusion of his teammates.

When Corbally asked that all the players be allowed to rejoin the team, the coach complied by holding a meeting at which he offered the reinstatement document to each of the removed players. Given the terms of reinstatement, Schwartzwalder may have suspected that they would either refuse to sign the document or, if they did sign, that they would in doing so undermine the basis of their protest.

The grievances presented by the boycotting players in spring 1970 were not accounted for or even mentioned in the conditions for reinstatement. Each player wishing to rejoin the team would have to pronounce himself guilty of missing spring practice and agree that Schwartzwalder's decision to remove the player permanently from the team had been a reasonable response to the protest. The document begins:

I concede that dismissal from the squad was a logical consequence of missing football practice for a protracted period during the Spring, 1970. I further recognize that this absence from practice for a protracted period affects my status with regards to the initial depth chart.

Schwartzwalder had benched or reduced the playing time of black players in the past without giving a reason. Now he had a reason he could give: they had protested against him doing it.

Each point in the document was an abstraction that seemed designed to obfuscate and bury the substance of the issues the Eight had raised. As part of the agreement, each player would have to agree never to mention any grievances against the program to anyone but the coaching staff. The document continues:

> In support of my request for reinstatement and as evidence of my desire to contribute meaningfully to the success of the football team, I make the following commitments to the coaching staff and to the tri-captains of the football team. I understand that these commitments are required of every member of the football squad.
>
> I. I have reread and reaffirmed acceptance of the Code for Syracuse Athletes.
>
> II. I promise a cooperative attitude and commit myself to 100% effort in all drills and other assignments.
>
> III. I am willing to play any position designated by the football coaching staff.
>
> IV. I will accept and follow all training rules established by the coaching staff and all rules and decisions related to such matters as training table, trip lists, trip schedules, ticket allocations, and housing. I understand these rules and decisions will apply equally to all members of the squad.
>
> V. I agree that it is a disservice to the team and to individuals concerned to air grievances in the public arena. The grievance procedure outlined in Item VI is the logical approach to the resolution of past and present complaints and dissatisfactions and I will follow the proposed procedure.

VI. I agree that all complaints or grievances will be taken up initially with Coach Schwartzwalder or with an assistant coach. If this discussion does not resolve the grievance, I shall discuss it with the Director of Athletics. If still dissatisfied with the result, I will discuss the problem with the Chairman of the Athletic Governing Board.

In essence, the document was an overwhelming endorsement of the status quo that had led the Syracuse Eight to stage their protest in April, and not one of the players was willing to sign it. The season opened in Houston on September 19, with no new reinstatements; Robin Griffin remained the only African American on the team.

The chancellor had publically agreed to allow Schwartzwalder to set conditions for the return of the suspended players, and now he had little choice but to berate the Syracuse Eight for their refusal to meet those conditions. But on September 21, the Monday following the Houston game, that course of action became impossible. The university received word from the New York State Human Rights Commission that it was prepared to take legal action to force the reinstatement of the suspended black players. If the chancellor abandoned the Syracuse Eight now, he would appear to be opposing the state's Human Rights Commission, an awkward position for an academic administrator. Corbally informed Schwartzwalder of this, and the two worked out what appeared to be an agreement to reinstate all the players who had participated in the boycott. The chancellor announced that the suspended players would report for practice on Wednesday, September 23. The returning players would still be expected to sign documents, but the wording of those documents would be subject to negotiations.

For a day or two, it was widely assumed that the Syracuse Eight would rejoin the team for the home opener against Kansas on Saturday, September 26. The press loved this happy ending, declaring the whole mess over and praising Schwartzwalder as the hero of the story—a strict disciplinarian who had made strategic compromises for the good of the team and the university.

But when the Syracuse Eight showed up for practice on Wednesday, Schwartzwalder would not allow them to take the field.[10] John Godbolt, John Lobon, Dana Harrell, and Duane Walker were declared academically ineligible and turned away. No further explanation was given. Greg Allen, Richard Bulls, Bucky McGill and Alif Muhammad were told that, in accordance with NCAA rules, they would each need to have a physical exam, followed by a three-day waiting period, before they would be eligible for full contact workouts. Allen and Muhammad were sent to Dr. Pelow's office that day; Bulls and McGill had appointments scheduled for Thursday. Technically, none of them was eligible for Saturday's game.

That was the closest the suspended players ever came to rejoining the team. Negotiations for "rewording" the documents that Schwartzwalder insisted upon proved fruitless.

By keeping the boycotters off the practice field on their day of "reinstatement," Schwartzwalder clearly marked them out as separate from the team. "It was very divided," Joe Ehrmann says. "I don't remember having conversations with any of the black athletes. The white players got all their information from the coaching staff. [That was how] it ended up becoming 'us' versus 'them.'"[11]

To the surprise of the members of the Syracuse Eight, four of the students learned they were ineligible because of "academic difficulties." Harrell, Lobon, and Walker had all been in good standing academically for two years or more at this point. (Some think it possible that Godbolt, who was depressed over his unwarranted demotion to the bench in 1969, may have fallen behind in his studies, but those records are not available.) "We were told we would *all* be allowed to return to the team," says John Lobon. "But when we reported the next day we were told that four of us would not be allowed to return for academic reasons. It was the first I heard of it. That evening we had a meeting to discuss what had happened. We agreed that they were once again trying to divide us, and that if we let them do it, we would be defeated as a group. It only made us stronger as a group."[12]

Finally, the medical exams given to the four "academically eligible" players provided Schwartzwalder with yet another option for keeping them off the field, if all else failed. With confidential medical reports on file, the coach had the option of placing any or all of them on the injured list for the Kansas game, for the entire season, or, if need be, forever, as he had done in the case of Ron Womack. That option was exercised immediately on Dick Bulls, who had undergone leg surgery as a freshman. In less time than it took for an x-ray to be developed in 1970, Dr. Pelow reversed his own previous decision on the surgery and declared Bulls out for the season.

Meanwhile, Corbally was coming under tremendous pressure from alumni. No matter what the chancellor said or did, even after he agreed to the suspension of the Syracuse Eight, Schwartzwalder boosters considered Corbally the enemy for daring to get involved in a football matter. They found eager allies among those who were unhappy with the new chancellor for other reasons, especially his suspension of classes amid the spring 1970 anti-war protests, and his subsequent decision to permit seniors to graduate without taking final exams. In May, at Syracuse University's One Hundredth Commencement (Corbally's first as chancellor), the keynote speaker was Julian Bond, a civil rights activist who helped to found the Student Nonviolent Coordinating Committee and led protests against Jim Crow segregation in the South. Although the choice of Bond as speaker was not Corbally's decision alone, it brought him a new wave of negative mail. The student valedictory address also drew the ire of some alumni, as the speaker called for the impeachment of President Richard Nixon (it would be several more years until that idea became mainstream sentiment).

Corbally's critics mercilessly derided him as soft on student radicals, while lauding Schwartzwalder's no-nonsense, play-by-the-rules stand against the boycotting players. The chancellor attempted to justify his stance by advising alumni of information that was not carried in the press. In a response to criticism from two longtime alumni donors, Corbally wrote, "Let me explain to you in confidence a few of the errors . . . which have led to our current situation. Two and one-half years ago in the presence of a number of reputable witnesses, Ben told an investigator from an earlier Human Right Commission that he 'would get a black coach right away.' This statement was accepted by those present as a commitment. Ben now reports that it was 'sarcasm.' A number of reputable witnesses have told me that Ben has told them that a coach in today's world should not recruit blacks."[13] But many Orange football fans, convinced that the team's chance for future glory was tied to the coach of the 1959 national champions, were simply not interested in facts, details, differing perspectives, or anything that did not express unmitigated support for Schwartzwalder.

More progressively inclined alumni were only slightly friendlier to Corbally. They freely expressed their dismay at what they saw as a lack of leadership from a chancellor who allowed himself to be suckered and bullied by a "redneck" football coach. Alumni donations from all sides nosedived through the summer. "I remember the chancellor showing me two stacks of letters on his desk, one very tall, the other very short," says Alif Muhammad. "He pointed at the big pile and said, 'That's the mail running in favor of Schwartzwalder.'"[14] Corbally, a Navy veteran who had been awarded the Purple Heart in the Pacific, now found himself in a new kind of battle.

John Brown Jr., an offensive tackle for Syracuse's 1959 national championship team and a member of the Pittsburgh Steelers in 1970, was the only football alumnus who came forward, on his own volition, to volunteer his services as a mediator in the conflict. An African American who had no history of conflict with Coach Schwartzwalder, Brown seemed an ideal candidate for the job. Having gotten no response to his offer from Schwartzwalder, Brown wrote a letter to Chancellor Corbally (illus. 8), in which he articulated the problems leading up to the impasse. There is no record of Corbally responding to Brown.

On August 27, the *New York Times* reported that "68 members of the football team walked off the practice field . . . in an apparent symbolic counter-boycott to one staged earlier in the year by suspended black players."[15] Quarterbacks Paul Paolisso and Randy Zur told the *Times* that the squad fully supported Coach Schwartzwalder and his staff in the controversy involving the suspended black

                                        John Brown, Jr.
                                        3397 Colwyn Road
                                        Shaker Heights, Ohio

Dr. John E. Corbally
Administration Building
Syracuse University
Syracuse, New York 13210

Dear Dr. Corbally:

          Recently I was made aware of a very serious situation in the
Syracuse University Athletic Department. Being an alumnus of Syracuse
University and a member of the Syracuse University football team from
1957 to 1962, I feel it is my obligation to become involved.

          I have talked to Coach Swartzwalder and a representative group
of black athletes who are, and who have been confronting each other for
some time.

          It is a deplorable situation that I feel should never have taken
place. In retrospect, it was fore-seeable and could have been prevented
years ago.

          Speaking from experience, the black athlete is recruited, in
most cases, from black oriented environment and thrust into a hypocritical
non-black society. In most cases he is not accepted as just another student
who happens to have a skill. He is expected to be a super humanoid, devoid
of all feelings and ability to think.

          I am not one to judge who is right or wrong in this situation but
I feel as though a solution can be found amiable to both sides. A man has
the right of peaceable dissention without repercussions. He has the right
to try to change a situation or system that is detrimental to his performance, his peace of mind and the total system.

          Syracuse University in 1957, in spite of its progress in the field
of education was an alien place for a black student. From what I have been
able to find out, changes have been made toward helping blacks become fully
qualified students. The same changes should be made in the Athletic Department in making black men athletes as well as students.

I have offered my services to Coach Swartzwalder to act as a mediator in this dispute.

I am still available and will do all I can to preserve the tradition of Syracuse University football.

Yours truly,

John Brown - 1962

CC: Coach Ben Swartzwalder
     Mr. Alan Newton

8. Letter from John Brown Jr. (class of 1962) to Chancellor Corbally, August 19, 1970, addressing the circumstances surrounding the boycott and offering to act as a mediator. Ben Schwartzwalder Papers, University Archives, Syracuse University Libraries.

players, and they planned to continue their demonstration for at least two more days. Schwartzwalder had made it clear in the letters he wrote but never sent to the Syracuse Eight that missing a practice was equivalent to quitting the team, but there was no word on whether the coach planned to enforce that rule on the students involved in this second boycott of practice in 1970.

This three-day counter-boycott culminated with the release of a document called "the players' petition" (illus. 9), which was signed by most members of the 1970 team. Despite its name and its look,

---

The signatures above represent sixty-eight members of the 1970 football team at Syracuse University.

The fact that nobody has asked for our opinions on pertinent questions concerning the team, we have decided to set forth our opinions in writing for the benefit of whomever are interested.

1. As far as we are concerned, there are no racial questions involved.

2. It would appear that ten members of the squad and their advisors are attempting to dictate the football policy of Syracuse University. This we will not permit.

3. We have implicit faith in our head coach and believe and insist that it should be his sole opinion as to whether a coach should be added to the present staff or whether a coach should be deleted from said staff. We feel that he has well earned that right by his record over a period of many years.

4. We will not accept anything concerning this problem which in our opinion is being forced upon our group.

5. That we the above are one hundred per cent behind our coach's opinions on football matters and will abide by said opinions regardless of the attempts being made by others to dictate otherwise.

6. That our recent practice sessions have been the best that we have had in years and in our opinion cannot be improved upon.

7. Never has the spirit been as great as it exists on our practice field this year.

8. We have many great football players on our team and they have indicated that they expect this team to be the best team that has represented Syracuse University in years.

9. It is to be understood that the above represents the concerted opinions of sixty-eight players and is not to be construed as being the opinions of a committee representing this group.

---

9. A petition signed by sixty-eight white members of the Syracuse football team in support of Coach Schwartzwalder, alleging that racial inequality did not exist on the team. Ben Schwartzwalder Papers, University Archives, Syracuse University Libraries.

the document did not ask for anything in particular. Of its nine numbered statements, the third is easiest to connect to an actual event. In apparent reference to the hiring of Carlmon Jones, it asserts, "We have implicit faith in our head coach and believe and insist that it should be his sole opinion as to whether a coach should be added to the present staff or deleted from the said staff." The racial context of the hiring is completely ignored, and indeed the very first point made in the document is that "there are no racial questions involved" in any of the football team's recent problems. However, the document's list of signatures contradicts that claim: the petition presented the typed names of all of the white players in the football program (including freshmen and redshirts) next to a blank line reserved for each signature, whether a player signed or not. Some white players did not sign,[16] but Robin Griffin (varsity) and Ron Page (redshirt) evidently were not even given the opportunity to sign: their names appear nowhere on the list. A white-players-only petition suggests that "racial questions" were very much involved.

There were certainly white players who saw the spring walk-off by their black teammates strictly in terms of a violation of training rules, and they adamantly opposed reinstatement of the Syracuse Eight, especially if it was granted without appropriate punishment. Bill Coghill, a tackle who had done a two-year hitch in Vietnam, was perhaps the most outspoken among them. At one point, Coghill called for a boycott of the Kansas game if any of the suspended players were taken back, but he dropped that plan when a majority of the seventy-two players voted against the action. "I think we lost some pride," he said of what initially appeared to be Schwartzwalder's decision to reinstate Allen, Bulls, Muhammad, and McGill for the Kansas game. "But I will go along with what the team decides."[17] Gary Bletsch, a senior defensive back, spoke for many of his teammates when he told the *Syracuse Post-Standard*, "I didn't understand how they could be taken back and I'm not sure I understand how they would want to be taken back." In that interview, Bletsch advanced a proposal by Robin Griffin to resolve the situation by guaranteeing all the suspended players a chance to return to the team after sitting out 1970.[18]

However one may feel about their opposition to reinstatement for the Syracuse Eight, it is hard to imagine Coghill, Bletsch, or any of the white players who spoke publically on the subject as bigots or thugs whose threats of violence were restraining Schwartzwalder from doing the right thing. Nonetheless, during the three days between the announcement of "reinstatement" of September 23 and the home opener versus Kansas, Schwartzwalder increasingly referred to white player resentment as a formidable obstacle to allowing members of the Syracuse Eight back on the team. As game day drew closer, the coach ratcheted it up a notch, informing the mayor, the chief of police, and other concerned parties that he feared a violent attack on the black players should they take the field on Saturday.[19] Schwartzwalder placed himself as a moderating force between allegedly dangerous white students and dangerous black militants on the Orange football team.

Schwartzwalder had introduced the possibility of racial violence into the narrative in late August, telling Jim Brown that he hesitated to reinstate the suspended black players because he feared the threats of angry white players. Brown saw through the ruse and called the coach's bluff, forcing Schwartzwalder to admit that the real reason he wouldn't take back the black players was because he didn't want to. A month later, Brown was gone.[20] With no one, least of all city officials, giving any credence to Brown's assessment of the situation, Schwartzwalder gave his "white bigoted students" ploy another try, escalating it into an urgent public safety issue by telling Syracuse Mayor Lee Alexander that if the black students showed up to play, there was no telling what the whites might do.[21] In addition to filling the city with fear, the prospect of a race riot had the effect of marshaling public sentiment against reinstatement. Although Schwartzwalder said that white students had threatened violence, black students were generally perceived as the source of possible violence by vocal members of the city's white community. On the day before the game, members of the Syracuse black community held a demonstration at City Hall, urging Mayor Alexander to cancel the game in order to protect black students and the entire community from violence.

Any beliefs the Syracuse Eight held that their talents on the football field might move Schwartzwalder to reconcile had come to naught. "We were convinced the coach was getting rid of us, no matter what it did to the team," says Duane Walker. "It wasn't like Ben would get fired if he had a bad season. He could just blame it on us." Any faith the Eight had that being on the right side of the issues might count for something was proving to be misplaced, as well. No one at the university, not even the chancellor, seemed capable of standing up to Schwartzwalder.

Nor could the government offer effective help. Although the complaint filed with the county's Human Rights Commission (illus. 10) was found to have merit, the commission's authority appeared to be limited to recommending, but not enforcing, a remedy. When Muhammad filed a seven-point complaint with the New York State Human Rights Commission, the state's commissioner, Robert Mangum, sent a telegram to Schwartzwalder specifically requesting that he "restore 8 black players to the Syracuse football squad" (illus. 11).

Although Schwartzwalder proclaimed all the players "reinstated," he simultaneously took actions that would prevent them from actually playing. But anyone who cared to read the newspapers carefully knew well before game time that there was no chance any of the Syracuse Eight would be playing football that Saturday. For example, an Associated Press story that appeared the day before kickoff stated: "Ironically, of the eight reinstated, four were ineligible for active status for academic reasons and the remaining four cannot play against Kansas because NCAA regulations require three days of physical preparation before full workouts."[22]

Even forty years after the fact, what remains most galling for the Syracuse Eight players was how little public attention was given to the issues they risked their careers to raise. It was as if all their demands had been met with the hiring of Carlmon Jones. Not even something as universally and undeniably important as the team's medical care ever came up for public discussion. Why was the basic story all about whether the coach should show mercy to malcontent rule breakers? What about racial discrimination? On the day Syracuse University

STATE OF NEW YORK .: EXECUTIVE DEPARTMENT

DIVISION OF HUMAN RIGHTS   :

   on the complaint of   :

. AL NEWTON, JR.   Complainant, :

      against   :   COMPLAINT NO. *V-CE- 688-70*

SYRACUSE UNIVERSITY, ATHLETIC DEPARTMENT AND   :
COACH, BEN SWARTZWALDER
                      Respondent. :

I,____Al Newton_____

residing at __611 Walnut Ave, Syracuse_____Tel No.__478-4680_____

charge _Syracuse University, Athletic Department and Coach, Ben Swartzwalder____

_____Tel No._____

whose address is__Syracuse_____

with an unlawful discriminatory practice relating to education on or about _____

__July, 1970 and continuing_____

because of my RACE (XX), COLOR (XXX, RELIGION ( ).

The particulars are:

1. I have been playing football at Syracuse University since Fall, 1967. Initially
I put forth maximum effort to play my best and to retain a good attitude towards
my fellow players and coaches.

2. During my Sophmore year I became aware of a double standard in choosing players
for team positions.

Preferential Treatment for Players:

A. Upon information and belief, the procedure is for an upper classman with the
most experience to be given priority for an open position. Black players are placed
in accordance with this policy. White freshman players, however, have moved into
varsity slots without any experience as a varsity player.

B. The lack of disciplinary procedures caused the coaching staff, which we believe
to be discriminatory and racist, to act arbitrarily on disciplinary issues. Black
players have been given more severe penalties for less severe acts than whites.

C. Furthermore, when the traveling squad list was posted, black players would be
shifted from their regular position to one with which they were unfamiliar on
Thursday, the day the list was posted. Thus, they could not be on the traveling
squad, which consists of the first two men for each position. On Monday after a
road game, they would be shifted back to their original position. On information
and belief, this did not happen to white players.

3. On different occasions black players have been subjected to derrogatory comm
by players and coaches. This has been brought to the attention of the head coac
and administration without anything being done.

Complainant: Al Newton, Jr.   Complaint No._____

Respondent: Syracuse University, Athletic Department and Coach Ben Swartzwalder

4. On different occasions the hiring of a black coach was promosed by the Athletic Department. We do not feel that these promises were made in good faith as the University did not actively seek out applicants and at least in one instance, did not follow through on one applicant. Finally after bringing the matter to higher administrative personnel and a boycott, a black coach was hired. We feel that had white players requested a change or addition to the staff, the matter would have been given prompt and serious attention.

5. Ben Swartzwalder said to several black players "Be a football player first and Negro, Black or whatever, you want to be second". I do not feel that as blacks we should be expected to ignore violations of our civil rights. Nor do I feel that we should be subjected to what we believe to be discriminatory practices that demean our pride and dignity.

6. As a result of our efforts to protect our human and civil rights, as well as our dignity, we have been told that we "cannot re-join the team under any circumstances". We feel that had white players attempted to protect their rights, they would be permitted to return to the team.

7. I therefore charge the respondent with an unlawful discriminatory practice in violation of the Human Rights Law of the State of New York by denying me the use of its facilities because of my race and color. I am Black.

I have not commenced any civil, criminal or administrative action or proceeding in any court or administrative agency based upon the same grievance.

STATE OF NEW YORK   ) ss:
COUNTY OF ONONDAGA   )

_____
(Signature of Complainant)

____Al Newton____, being duly sworn, deposes and says: that he is the Complainant herein; that he has read the foregoing complaint and knows the contents thereof; that the same is true of his own knowledge except as to the matters therein stated on information and belief; and that as to those matters he believes the same to be true.

Subscribed and sworn to before me
this 3 day of September , 1970

_____
(Signature of Complainant)

10. Complaint filed with the Syracuse-Onondaga Commission on Human Rights, September 3, 1970, by Al Newton, Dana Harrell, and Duane Walker against Syracuse University, the Athletic Department, and Coach Schwartzwalder for racial discrimination. Ben Schwartzwalder Papers, University Archives, Syracuse University Libraries.

Telegram

F SY LDA 004 PDF SXRX TDSY OSSINING NY 18 1026P

COACH BEN SCHWARTZWALDER

ATHLETIC DEPT SYRACUSE UNIVERSITY

SYRACUSE NY

URGENTLY REQUEST YOU RESTORE BK 8 BLACK FOOTBALL PLAYERS TO THE
SYRACUSE FOOTBALL SQUAD AND MAKE THEM ELIGIBLE FOR PARTICIPATION IN
SATURDAY'S OPENING GAME PENDING A RESOLUTION OF THE CONTROVERSY. THIS
MATTER HAS BEEN PLACED BEFORE THE NEW YORK STATE DIVISION FOR HUMAN
RIGHTS AND I FIRMLY BELIEVE FROM THE FACTS AVAILABLE TO ME THAT IT
CAN'T BE CONCILIATED TO THE SATISFACTION OF ALL PARTIES CONCERNED XØ
TOWARD THAT END I WILL BE HAPPY TO FLY TO SYRACUSE TO MEET WITH YOU
AND YOUR CHANCELLOR AND THE BLACK PLAYERS TUESDAY SEPT 21 AT ANYTIME

WU 1201 (R 5-69)

Telegram

YOU DESIGNATE AS A FIRST STEP TOWARD RESOLVING THE PROBLEM AT A
TIME WHEN OUR NATION IS HEROICALLY STRUGGLING WITH THE PROBLEMS
OF THE WAR IN VIETNAM AND THE MIDEAST CRISIS I REFUSE TO BELIEVE
THAT WE CAN'T SIT DOWN AND SETTLE THE RACIAL DIFFERENCES OF THE MEN
ON THE FOOTBALL SQUAD OF ONE OF OUR GREAT UNIVERSITIES I APPEAL
AGAIN TO YOU TO MAKE THE BLACK PLAYERS ELEIGIBLE FOR YOUR OPENING
GAME SATURDAY AND URGE YOU TO SIT DOWN WITH ME ON TUESDAY TO
RESOLVE THE ENTIRE MATTER.

                    ROBERT J MANGUM

                    COMMISSIONER OF HUMAN RIGHTS

                    STATE OF NY 270 BROADWAY NEW YORK NY

WU 1201 (R 5-69)

11. Telegram from New York State Commissioner of Human Rights
Robert J. Mangum to Coach Schwartzwalder, asking that the boycotting
players be reinstated. Ben Schwartzwalder Papers, University Archives,
Syracuse University Libraries.

opened in 1870, Rev. Dr. Jesse T. Peck, the founding board chair, told the faculty, "The laws under which you will do your work say . . . there shall be no invidious discriminations here against women or persons of any nation or color."

During the last week of August 1970, before the hope of reasonable compromise had completely slipped away, the Eight had reached out to Jim Brown. Since retiring from pro football five years earlier, Brown had made his way in Hollywood from supporting roles to stardom in some eight feature films. He had not been back to campus much in recent years, but he responded dutifully to the appeal of these undergraduates, flying into Syracuse and offering himself to all involved as an honest broker.

Brown expressed to the boycotters that his primary goal was to negotiate their reinstatement on the team so they would be able to maximize their chances for careers in the NFL. When Schwartzwalder greeted him with the premise that opposition from white players was preventing him from reinstating the black players, Brown drove straight up the middle to see for himself.

He met with team co-captains Paul Paolisso, Randy Zur, and Ray White. "They agreed to discuss the status of the Black players," Brown says, recalling how he shuttled among the interested parties. "The Black players [then] agreed unanimously to return to the squad, with the hope that some kind of impartial monitoring system could be enacted to prevent a continuation of past injustices and to prevent retributions. With that commitment, I then went back to Ben and he informed me 'that under no circumstances could he accept the Black players back on the squad.'"[23]

Although Brown had gotten Schwartzwalder to stop hiding behind "bigoted white students" and speak the truth, Brown could not budge him on allowing the suspended players to rejoin the team. Brown conducted his own inquiries over the next few days, and called a press conference to announce his findings. He verified the Syracuse Eight's charges of poor medical treatment and of racial discrimination in the assignment of positions. He did not comment on the charge of biased academic support, lacking proper access and time to investigate the issue. But Brown added some charges that had not appeared in the April list of grievances, including casual, unchallenged use of the word "nigger" by the coaching staff and legally questionable payoffs to white players (and white players only) by team boosters. By bringing up the "n-word," Jim Brown, the de facto poster child for Syracuse's recruitment of African American athletes and students of all types for more than a decade, was making a statement.

Brown's press release was written in the first person for distribution to reporters at his press conference (illus. 12). Engaging the press, Brown held nothing back in analyzing the situation. He placed the blame squarely on Schwartzwalder. The crime here was not football players missing spring practice; it was a man past his prime recklessly threatening the futures of talented young men who dared to stand up for what they knew to be right. Every sports reporter in the area covered the event, but in the available accounts, only Arnie Burdick, sports editor of the *Syracuse Herald-Journal*, wrote of what had happened to Ben Schwartzwalder since his glory days, and of the consequences for the Syracuse football program. Burdick quoted Brown at the press conference as stating: "The problem here at Syracuse centers around Ben Schwartzwalder and the Athletic Department. Ben has always been a powerful, strong, stubborn man. And now he's old. He's inflexible. . . . Ben is building a fortress around himself. He seems to be afraid of his job. He's got his mind made up, but keeps blaming the white players for the decision. . . . Ben even said that he has some bigoted players—those are his words—that would not permit the suspended black players to return to the squad."[24]

Throughout the crisis, Schwartzwalder had ignored serious complaints made by his African American students, not even bothering to attempt to refute them. He had given all of his energy to assigning blame: the black players were guilty of breaking the rules; the white players were guilty of bigotry against the blacks; the chancellor was guilty of sticking his nose in the coach's business. Given an opportunity by Burdick to respond to Brown's criticisms, this was the best Schwartzwalder could muster: "I don't have any desire to even attempt to dignify the various statements. However, I would like to say that the word 'bigoted' is not in my vocabulary."[25]

Despite what Brown said about Schwartzwalder at the press conference, Schwartzwalder's image as the maker and mentor of great black student athletes was so strong in the sports world that it survived the criticisms by Brown, the person most qualified to offer judgment on it. Three weeks later, the day before the Syracuse–Kansas game, former New York Yankees shortstop Phil Rizzuto had this to say on his daily CBS radio network sports program:

> I don't know of another school that has turned out as many outstanding black football athletes as Syracuse. The list sounds like a "Who's Who": Jim Brown, Ernie Davis, John Mackey, Floyd Little, Jim Nance. These are but a few of the men who had brilliant college careers at Syracuse—and most went on to pro ball and big money. And the man who coached them, who brought out that latent talent in all of them, is in his 22nd year at Syracuse, an old paratroop hero named Ben Schwartzwalder. Ben was hit this year with a series of charges by most of the black athletes on the team . . . charges of discrimination . . . of inferior medical treatment . . . of under the table money to the whites and not to the blacks . . . of a double standard in choosing players for the team . . . of ignoring derogatory remarks by whites against blacks . . . of refusing to hire a black assistant coach. Most of these allegations—if not all of them—don't ring true. Ben isn't that kind of a guy. Even Jim Brown wouldn't call Schwartzwalder a biased person the last time I talked with him.[26]

The September 26 home game against Kansas appeared to be the last chance for the suspended players to return for the 1970 season, and events built to a crescendo as Saturday approached. Newspaper accounts differ on what occurred leading up to the game, and on what happened off the field in Syracuse that Saturday.

William Morrissey, covering the Syracuse Eight story for the Associated Press since it began in April, published an article dated September 25 in which he reported that, after three days of meetings

Jim Brown
Press Release
September 3, 1970
SYRACUSE UNIVERSITY

Acting as a concerned alumnus, I undertook an investigation of the football
impasse that was brought to my attention at Syracuse University.

I regret to report my findings, after numerous meetings with the Chancellor,
John Corbally, Jr., the coaches, Ben Schwartzwalder and his staff, and the
Black and White players, four cases of discrimination, as follows:

1. Cases of name calling, "Nigger", "Dumb", etc.
2. Poor medical treatment to Black players.
3. Illegal money given to White players.
4. A double standard in choosing players for positions.

Not even after these findings I had hopes of some kind of compromise bringing
all parties together.

I then contacted Chancellor Corbally and he stated that, "the matter was out of
my hands, and in the hands of the head football coach." I then contacted Ben
Schwartzwalder, the head coach.

Upon talking with Ben, he stated, "even if I would be willing to take back the
Black players, there were bigoted players on the team who would not permit the
suspended Black players to return to the squad." "Bigoted players", gentlemen,
was his statement, not mine. I was then referred by the coach to the tri-captains.

After much deliberation concerning the possible reinstatement to the squad of the
Black players, the tri-captains agreed to discuss the team's position concerning
the status of the Blacks.

I then met with the Black players to determine their willingness to return to the squad. After a brief discussion, they agreed unanimously to return to the squad with the hope that some kind of impartial monitoring system be enacted.

With this commitment I then went back to Coach Schwartzwalder, who subsequently informed me, "under no circumstances could he accept the Black players on the squad." I then requested to meet with the entire squad.

I met with the tri-captains and about twenty-five other White football players. I asked them if it were possible to return the Black players to the squad and if there would be any penalties. Joe Ehrmann, acting as the spokesman for the group stated emphatically, "that under no circumstances would they accept them back on the squad."

I emphasized that this would mean the end of the careers of these players, limiting their chances of making a professional football living. I once again asked them to reconsider their decision. I was then told by a number of the White players that the coaches had gotten them to sign a petition saying that they would not play with the Black players.

Now, gentlemen, I refuse to believe that the Syracuse community, the large alumni of this great institution knowing that Blacks have fought so diligently for Syracuse's recognition in all endeavors will tolerate the persistent demonstrated acts of discrimination which are so evident as I now address you. Ladies and gentlemen I'm convinced that these acts will not go unchallenged.

12. Press release written by Jim Brown following his inquiries into the boycotting SU football players' allegations of racial discrimination, and distributed at a press conference, September 3, 1970. Ben Schwartzwalder Papers, University Archives, Syracuse University Libraries.

involving Schwartzwalder Corbally, Mangum, and Syracuse Mayor Lee Alexander, "reinstatement had been recommended by Schwartzwalder, upon a vote of the team members."[27] The article further states that there were "declarations by some white athletes that they would not play in the Kansas game because of the way in which eight suspended black players were reinstated on the team."

None of the "white athletes" who made these declarations are named. The odd anonymity of the white athletes is made more odd by another claim in the same article: "A statement issued by *the team* said only that they would accept the suspended players in order to play the Kansas game. Later, some white members said they would not play the game themselves, declaring that they had been forced to accept the reinstatement by threat of a court order banning the game"[28] (emphasis added). In pro football, a "statement issued by the team" usually means a statement issued by owners or front office executives. But who is "the team" in college football and how does it issue a statement? Was this another spontaneous act by sixty-eight football players, like the "players' petition" and the "counter-boycott" of the previous month?

The Morrissey article reports a demonstration by "about 100 Negro residents and students" in front of City Hall in downtown Syracuse. Concerned by the threats of violence made against the Syracuse Eight, the demonstrators met with Mayor Alexander and urged him to cancel Saturday's game as a way of assuring the safety of the black players. "The statements by the white players on Wednesday polarized the community," Alexander said. "Some of the white players more or less presented themselves as white men wronged."[29]

The mayor declined to cancel the game, choosing instead to deploy police to the University Hill area including the full contingent of the Syracuse Police Department's mounted division. Their very presence may have been enough to instill fear in many citizens that a race riot was imminent.

On Saturday, September 26, 1970, supporters of the Syracuse Eight, mostly students and local black residents, formed a picket line in front of the box office at Archbold Stadium about an hour before the game. Picket signs included, "Ben's the foe—he's got to go!" and "Why let the Eight become racist bait?" More than one hundred uniformed officers on foot and on horseback blanketed the area between the stadium and the Marshall Street commercial district as a county sheriff's department helicopter hovered overhead. Not one of the reinstated players was listed in the game program, nor were they in uniform.

The *Syracuse Post-Standard* reported on page 6 of Monday's paper: "Police say they moved in to control a crowd of about 300—mostly blacks—although there were some whites who appeared to be of high school age. They say persons were throwing rocks, swinging clubs and looting stores." With people throwing rocks, swinging clubs and looting stores, some readers might have expected a front-page story or more extensive coverage. But in what seems to be a description of an entirely different event, the article goes on to say that there were a total of three arrests in the area that day, two for disorderly conduct and one for obstructing traffic, and that all three suspects were white men, ages twenty to twenty-two. Perhaps the most telling line in the article was this rare admission: "What actually happened remains to be reported."[30]

On that same Monday, the *New York Times* ran an article concerning the future status of the Syracuse Eight, but included this two-sentence capsule on the riot: "Saturday's game here against Kansas ended with a melee between the police and youthful spectators. Syracuse lost, 31–14, and there were reports of looting, the use of tear gas and rock-throwing. Six white youths were arrested." The "reporting of reports," while popular in twenty-first-century online rumor mongering, was considered little more than anemic journalism in 1970. The *Times* might have done better by referencing two stories on the riot it had carried in its Sunday edition.

A piece that appeared on the front page of the sports section gave the riot short shrift:

Syracuse University preserved order around Archbold Stadium today with maximum security measures, but Kansas ran wild on the football field en route to a 31–14 victory over the Orange-men. . . . The demonstrators distributed literature to spectators entering the stadium, but did not block their paths or pursue a con-frontation with police officers, who mingled around the gates and probably outnumbered them. Shortly after the kickoff, the protest-ers left the stadium. About an hour later, 14 police cars were dis-patched to the area following reports of windows being smashed in several stores.[31]

Another story, with no byline, appeared in the news section of the *Times*, painting quite a different picture of events, beginning with its headline: "Police Disperse Brick-Throwing Mob at Syracuse University." In this version, the mob of three hundred rioters consists of mostly white students rather than blacks, and a Syracuse police-man and an Onondaga County Sheriff's Deputy "were hurt by flying

13. Police officers positioned outside Archbold Stadium to control picket-ers at the September 26, 1970, game against Kansas. Student Publications Reference Collection, University Archives, Syracuse University Libraries.

14. Police discharged tear gas and pepper fog spray when protesters in support of the Syracuse Eight marched from Archbold Stadium to Marshall Street on September 26, 1970. Several arrests were made. Student Publications Reference Collection, University Archives, Syracuse University Libraries.

rocks." The article presents mostly unconfirmed reports, but it does describe two specific acts of vandalism: "small group of youths . . . broke windows at the administration building and the adjacent Hall of Languages"; and "some youths smashed the windows of [Syracuse] Police Chief Sardino's car, flattened its tires, and ripped off its antenna and radio microphone." In this article, the arrest total is put at six rather than three.[32]

One source of information barely mentioned in any of the available articles was the Syracuse Police Department. Having discharged

15. Police on horseback were dispatched to control protesters picketing in support of the Syracuse Eight, September 26, 1970. Student Publications Reference Collection, University Archives, Syracuse University Libraries.

tear gas and pepper fog spray on the streets that day, the department may have been in need of a riot to justify its use of force, its budget, or both. But if a store had a window broken or its inventory looted that day, the papers never said which one. The *Syracuse Post-Standard* offered a description of only one of the three arrests it reported: "Policeman Maurice P. Richer, who made the arrest, said [Edward] Coleman was holding a large tree limb in his hand and 'appeared ready to throw it at other policemen across the street.' Richer said he used 'necessary force' in apprehending Coleman and, in the process, the youth was injured. Coleman was taken to Crouse-Irving Memorial Hospital where he received five stitches for a wound on the top of his head."[33]

Riotous behavior was certainly displayed in the *Post-Standard*'s letters to the editor during the week that followed. In the Wednesday

the **daily orange**

Vol. 69, No. 7   Daily Orange, Syracuse, N. Y., Tuesday, Sept. 29, 1970   10 Cents

"I don't want to hear anything about police brutality."
— Police Chief Thomas J. Sardino

Photo By Steve Schmitt

Stadium protest becomes M Street confrontation

By TOM BRYAN

What began as a peaceful picketing of Saturday's SU-Kansas football game reached near-riot proportions in the late afternoon when police, nearly one hundred strong, confronted a crowd of more than 400 students on Marshall Street. For more than two hours police suffered a barrage of flying rocks, bottles and wood but quickly retaliated with repeated gusts of pepper gas and frequent attacks with their nightsticks.

City and university officials had feared all week long that violence might occur at Saturday's game. They combatted the possibility with security precautions described by one police officer as the most severe since Richard Nixon's visit to the city in 1968. Three hours before game time carloads of city police began arriving at Archbold Stadium. By kickoff nearly one hundred police were inside the gates, numerous others, many with cameras, were atop campus buildings, and the south side of the stadium was jammed with paddy wagons, police buses (including the campus shuttle bus) and Onondaga County Sheriff Department personnel. Dozens of police guarded the stadium's entrance gates while additional police cars and motorcycles patrolled the campus. Their watch was aided by two police helicopters which hovered above the campus all day.

Entrance gates picketed

For more than one hour before the game two hundred black students, joined by more than one hundred whites, picketed outside the three main entrances to the stadium. While many walked in the picket lines, others handed out leaflets to those attending the game and attempted to convince them not to enter the gates.

Ticketholders were welcomed to "rinso-white stadium" by hecklers, most of whom were white, and were asked why they were "supporting a racist institution." Calls to "whistle Dixie on the way to the game" and "bring your white sheet next time" greeted many of the spectators. Fathers were often asked to explain racism to their children, a point hecklers thought would carry the issue home to many dinner tables.

Although few would-be football fans were seen heading for home, attendance for the game (25,000) fell far short of the expected 32,000.

At the sound of the national anthem from within the stadium, pickets quietly left the stadium. Most of the black students congregated at the BSU, while more than one hundred whites moved to the M Street beach. More than two dozen police watched as the students walked down South Crouse Avenue. At one point a student stepped into the street, snapped to Nazi attention and roared "sig heil" to a passing motorcycle cop. He skidded to a stop and threatened to arrest the student. After a brief staring match, they both went their ways.

All was quiet for the moment on M Street. No police were in sight. But soon a group of high school youths walked into Douglas Stone's Ltd and "liberated" several articles of clothing. They moved from there to Discount Records and left with stacks of records and a record player. Uncle Bruce estimated the loss at $2,000.

As news of the looting spread, employees of Manny's lowered the infamous iron gate that protects the store. They did not have time to lock it, however, and it was raised by several of the youths. Before

anything could occur at Manny's four police cars sped the wrong way down M Street and blocked the street in front of Manny's. The looters left and hundreds of students lined the sidewalks and spilled into the street.

More police support was called in. City police formed a line in front of Manny's and sheriff's deputies formed a similar line by the Pizza King. The second line was backed by two shotgun-wielding deputies. The two lines moved toward each other and successfully cleared the street.

Syracuse Police Chief Thomas J. Sardino then arrived, amidst cheers and heckling from the crowd, and ordered that everyone keep off the streets. He was met with chants of "get out of our street, get out of our street." Simultaneously twenty people from both sides of the street sauntered across M Street and traded places. More people stepped onto the street and Sardino himself pushed them back to the sidewalk. One student ordered Sardino to "say please." The Chief countered, "You get back up on that curb. If I have to tell you again you'll be under arrest." Everyone backed up onto the curb and for a minute M Street was clear. Then one demonstrator walked in front of Carroll's, threw his picket sign on the ground and sat in the middle of the street. He screamed at Sardino and dared the chief to arrest him. A black youth, about 12, sat with the man. Sardino, on hearing the man's dare, wheeled around and headed for the demonstrator and ordered his arrest. As the man was dragged away he shouted, "I'm a Quaker and I believe in civil disobedience."

Sardino began to walk back toward his line of police. A beer bottle arched out of the crowd and landed just to his right. Another policeman whirled toward the crowd, hand on gun, as they ran back several steps. An armoured car pulled up and two gas-masked policemen jumped out with a pepper-fog machine. They promptly started it and for nearly fifteen minutes paraded up and down the street with Chief Sardino. Syracuse Mayor Lee Alexander arrived Kennedy style, and conferred briefly with Sardino. The order was never given to use gas at this time. The pepper fogger was put back in the armoured truck and tensions quickly lifted.

Rocks and horses

About one half hour later two mounted policemen rode down M Street. They, like Sardino, were met with cheers. And they were met with flying rocks. Both turned their horses to the crowd and charged up the beach, clubs swinging. Everyone ran for cover. More police were called in and a police line was set up on South Crouse Ave.

The crowd, now about three hundred, moved toward the line, singing "Power to the people," and blocked off both Marshall and South Crouse. Occasional bottles were lofted into the police ranks and soon police began moving the demonstrators back up M Street. The crowd roared, "No more pigs in our community." The pepper fogger was again brought out and police charged into the crowd. About one hundred students ran up South Crouse and University and were forced to stay on South Crouse for about 30 minutes. Several of the demonstrators, however, broke away and moved on the campus smashing windows in the Hall of Languages and the Administration Building.

In the meantime, the other 200 demonstrators were chased up M Street by police. The pepper fogger was turned on and a huge white

(Continued on page 5)

Photo By Bruno Joachim

Photo By Mike Silverman

16. An article in the *Daily Orange*, September 29, 1970, reports on the peaceful protest at Archbold Stadium, which escalated into a confrontation with police on Marshall Street on September 26. Student Publications Reference Collection, University Archives, Syracuse University Libraries.

edition alone, a variety of angry readers blamed the disturbance on "red activists," "the anarchist faction," "eight bruising black football players," and, quoting a recent remark by Vice President Spiro T. Agnew, "a bunch of sick, tormented, frustrated, ill-mannered, lazy bums who have nothing but destruction and violence on their minds."[34]

Not much more was said about the riot until some twenty-eight years later, when it was described in an unofficial history of the university: "Shortly after kickoff, the protesters moved down South Crouse Avenue, paused at the Afro American Student Union, and proceeded to the Marshall Street area where they immediately blockaded the street. About ten minutes before the end of the game, some 300 protestors began to throw stones and rocks at sheriff's deputies. Although no windows were broken on Marshall Street, there was some looting, [Police Chief] Sardino's car was destroyed and six youths—all white—were arrested."[35] No eyewitness source is cited.

The "riot" came up again, this time some forty years after the fact, when 2011 Republican gubernatorial candidate Carl Paladino, a law student at Syracuse University in 1970, revealed in a Syracuse stump speech that he had personally helped Syracuse police put down the disturbance.[36] (Paladino is otherwise remembered for his promise, baseball bat in hand, to "clean up Albany," which he made in a television ad during his unsuccessful bid for office.)

Theoretical questions of what constitutes a riot aside, the Kansas game, like the Houston game, came and went, with none of the Syracuse Eight wearing the uniform or setting foot on the field. Unwilling to sign statements reducing their act of protest to the commission of a rules infraction, the Syracuse Eight gave up on the idea of playing football that season.

Having triumphed off the field, Ben Schwartzwalder began to turn his attention back to winning football games. After a third straight blowout loss, a 27–0 shutout at the hands of Illinois, Old Ben regained his coaching groove. The Orange rebounded from 0–3

Table 3
1970 Syracuse Football Schedule with Outcomes

Game	Date	Opponent	Venue	Score (Syr–Opponent)
1	Sep. 19	(15) Houston	Houston, TX	15–42
2	Sep. 26	Kansas	Syracuse, NY	14–31
3	Oct. 3	Illinois	Champaign, IL	0–27
4	Oct. 10	Maryland	Syracuse, NY	23–7
5	Oct. 17	Penn State	University Park, PA	24–7
6	Oct. 24	Navy	Syracuse, NY	23–8
7	Oct. 31	(15) Pittsburgh	Syracuse, NY	43–13
8	Nov. 7	Army	West Point, NY	31–29
9	Nov. 14	West Virginia U.	Morgantown, WV	19–28
10	Nov. 21	Miami (FL)	Syracuse, NY	56–16

with a five-game winning streak at the expense of Syracuse's most intense traditional rivals: Maryland, Penn State, Army, Navy, and Pittsburgh. A win over Miami in the season finale gave Syracuse a 6–4 record.

Schwartzwalder, who was lauded in one newspaper as having "molded a winner from the seeds of racial discontent," was named Eastern College Football Coach of the Year by United Press International.[37] "The charges of racism and turmoil that threatened his coaching existence are behind him and Ben Schwartzwalder tries hard not to talk about it," wrote one admiring reporter. Asked the hardball question of why he had not quit when lesser men surely would have, Schwartzwalder responded, "Because I made up my mind if the Germans ever stopped shooting at me I'd never complain about anything."[38] College football pundits across the country took notice of the miracle 6–4 season, and some predicted Schwartzwalder would lead Syracuse back into the Top Ten in 1971; even *Playboy* magazine, known for its left-leaning politics, forecast a Number Six ranking for the Orange.

Syracuse University Football—1970 Season Statistics

Date	Day	School		Opponent	Pts	Opp	W	L	T	Notes
Sep. 19	Sat	Syracuse	@	Houston	L	15	42	0	1	0	Houston ranked 15
Sep. 26	Sat	Syracuse		Kansas	L	14	31	0	2	0	
Oct. 3	Sat	Syracuse	@	Illinois	L	0	27	0	3	0	
Oct. 10	Sat	Syracuse		Maryland	W	23	7	1	3	0	
Oct. 17	Sat	Syracuse	@	Penn State	W	24	7	2	3	0	
Oct. 24	Sat	Syracuse		Navy	W	23	8	3	3	0	
Oct. 31	Sat	Syracuse		Pittsburgh	W	43	13	4	3	0	Pittsburgh ranked 15
Nov. 7	Sat	Syracuse	@	Army	W	31	29	5	3	0	Syracuse ranked 20
Nov. 14	Sat	Syracuse	@	West Virginia	L	19	28	5	4	0	
Nov. 21	Sat	Syracuse		Miami (Florida)	W	56	16	6	4	0	

Season Record: 6-4

Points: Syracuse 248, Opponents 208

Running backs:

Marry Januszkiewicz (FB)—769 yards on 199 attempts, averaging 3.9 per carry, scoring 8 TDs.

Roger Praetorius (HB)—474 yards on 114 attempts, averaging 4.2 per carry, scoring 3 TDs.

Larry Giewont, Ray White, John Rosella, Greg Wysocki, Mike Clebek, Drew Marciano, and Dennis Finnegin were all used as running backs; none had more than 20 rushing attempts.

It never happened. The year of the boycott, 1970, was Schwartzwalder's last winning season. The one week during the 1970 season that the team had spent at Number Twenty was the last national ranking of a Schwartzwalder team. After three more seasons, the coach retired at the age of sixty-one.

6

Aftermath

On December 9, a few weeks after the end of the 1970 football season, "The Report of the Trustee, Faculty and Student Committee on Allegations of Racial Discrimination in the Football Program" was delivered to Chancellor Corbally. In ten weeks of deliberations, the committee had met in twenty-eight four-hour sessions, interviewing about forty witnesses, including athletic director James Decker, Coach Schwartzwalder, members of the football coaching staff, current and alumni football players (white and black, including members of the Syracuse Eight), university administrators and faculty members. Although many of the problems described in the report were the result of standing policies instituted by former athletic director Lew Andreas, who was living in retirement in Syracuse, Andreas was not interviewed, nor does his name appear anywhere in the report. The committee noted that the university's Administrative Board on Athletics, which was technically charged with overseeing Syracuse intercollegiate athletic programs, had "abdicated" its responsibilities by not becoming involved in the eight-month football crisis. The withering of that administrative board into an honorific body was cited as a reason for "the long-standing authoritarian role of the head coach." But that is as close as the report came to saying a bad word about Schwartzwalder or other individuals. The committee concluded that racism in the football program was "real, chronic, largely unintentional, and sustained and complicated unwittingly by many modes of behavior common in American athletics."[1]

Ironically, the hiring of Syracuse's first black athletic coach, the one grievance of the Syracuse Eight that had been addressed by

Schwartzwalder, became a springboard for some of the report's most tangible criticism. The report rejected the Athletic Department's contention that the hiring of Carlmon Jones was evidence of its willingness to cooperate with African American students, focusing instead on the protracted period of unnecessary foot-dragging that had played such a pivotal role in poisoning the atmosphere between the white coaches and the black players:

> The Committee finds that the legitimate request [to hire a black coach], made as early as the spring of 1969 . . . was ignored; that the Athletic Department was grossly insensitive to the legitimacy and meaning of this request; that the signs of increasing estrangement between the Black football players and the White coaching staff were ignored; and that an effective corrective measure—the hiring of a Black assistant football coach—was not taken until *after* the Black athletes boycotted spring practice in 1970. The definition of the spring boycott of the black athletes merely as an issue of violating coaching authority, and the penalizing of these athletes without taking into consideration the broader context of their protest, was an act of institutional racism unworthy of a great university.[2]

The implications of the committee's interpretation of events were clear: The black members of the team had raised serious issues to the coaches in a reasonable manner, but the coaching staff ignored the players and the substance of what they said. With no functional channel available for registering complaints, the students were forced to go outside the system to be heard. They had violated a rule by walking away from spring practice, but their only alternative was to remain silent and continue to suffer what they believed was unfair treatment.

The report also took note of a disturbing trend for a program that had become so thoroughly identified with the development of exceptional black student athletes. The number of black recruits had been steadily declining since 1967, and not a single black freshman was anticipated to join the program in fall 1971.[3] With record numbers of

talented black athletes entering collegiate football programs at predominantly white universities in every region of the country during
the late 1960s, Syracuse was well-positioned to attract the best and
the brightest among them. Instead, the Orange was moving in the
direction of becoming an "all-white" team.

A closer look at the thirty-nine-page document shows that after
the report's critical analysis of events leading to the hiring of Carlmon Jones, it rejects all three of the other original contentions of the
Syracuse Eight.

The subject of "medical treatment" is disposed of in a few para-
graphs, ending with this conclusion: "The issue appears to be that a
system which seems geared to winning football games has become
associated in the minds of some of the players with one uninterested
in them as people." Dr. Pelow, the former gynecologist and hospital
administrator, is not mentioned by name. His qualifications were not
examined, nor was his practice investigated, either systematically or
anecdotally. He remained team doctor until his retirement at age
seventy-four, stepping down in conjunction with Schwartzwalder's
departure.

In the area of "academic advisement and assistance," the committee could find "no intent to treat Black and White athletes
different[ly]," noting that it was up to individual students to take
responsibility for choosing their majors, finding appropriate advisors, and seeking tutorial help.

Perhaps the most surprising finding was in the area of "team
positions" (i.e., quotas). Although the committee made no attempt at
statistically correlating the performances of African American players with their diminishing playing times, it concluded that "no pattern of racial discrimination" could be established.

Although the report was criticized as displaying a "pro-black"
bias, it was written with a practical strategy in mind. The committee's goal was to address long-term issues of institutional racism in
order to make the football team, the athletic department, and the
university a more welcoming place for African American students.

the daily orange

Vol. 69, No. 39   Daily Orange, Syracuse, N. Y., Thursday, Dec. 10, 1970   10 Cents

Racism report hits Decker, coaches, and Athletic Dept.

Blacks' grievances and actions are vindicated

After nearly three months of work behind closed doors, the Chancellor's Committee to investigate the allegations of racial discrimination in the football program returned a thirty nine page report supplemented by twenty one pages of appendices.

Composed of three basic sections, the report considers the specific allegations of racism by the black football players and the Committee findings after investigating the charges, the history of the controversy surrounding the suspension of the 8 black players (Al Newton, Dana Harrell, Duane Walker, Bucky McGill, John Godbolt, Rich Bulls, Greg Allen, and John Lobon), and finally a body of recommendations arrived at by the Chancellor's Committee.

In the General Summary of the report, the Committee, in "general agreement on all sections of the report," writes, "The Committee concludes that racism in the Syracuse University Athletic Department is real, chronic, largely unintential, and sustained and complicated unwittingly by many modes of behavior.

'Polack,' 'dirty kraut,') were never meant to be derogatory, but were simply a common feature of the special and intense relationships inherent in athletic life."

The other complaint that the committee substantiated was the harrassment of players who refused to conform to the political, social, and personal attitudes and activities viewed by the coaches as proper for a "student athlete."

The report reads: "The Committee concludes that the players increasingly did not conform to the coaches' conception of the student-athlete. Insensitive to changing student concerns, the coaches regarded as troublemakers those students whose personal values and political beliefs seem to conflict with their own."

Interestingly, the report indicates that the Committee could not substantiate the other specific complaints, over medical treatment, academic advising, discipline, etc. on racial grounds because the complaints seemed to apply equally well to both black and white players.

Coach Schwartzwalder
found to be so disfunctional that the Chancellor's committee

NEWS ANALYSIS
By BILL LEOGRANDE

Echoing the words of Dave Meggyesy and Jack Scott, the report of the Chancellor's Committee on racism begins with the sentence, "Athletics has long been an integral and prominent part of American life, expressive of many of our social values, attitudes, and behavior." The report goes on to characterize athletics at Syracuse as racist, authoritarian, lacking in sensitivity, unresponsive to changing ideas, poorly administered, and no longer under the control of the representative structures designed to formulate policy.

Though it never acknowledges the fact, the report is nearly a total vindication of the eight black players who were suspended. The Committee affirms their position that their just calls for a black coach were ignored by the Athletic Department; it agreed with their argument that their suspension was unjustified; it agreed that the central administration's handling of the affair was not appropriate, and it agreed that at least some of their specific allegations were true.

The report directly criticizes the coaches, the Athletic Director, and the members of the Athletic Governing Board; indirectly, it criticizes the Chancellor who directed the "inept and ineffective" conciliation measures attempted by the University during the fall crisis.

Where the Committee could not find evidence of racial discrimination, it generally concluded that all the players, both Black and White, were being mistreated. There was neither criticism of the Black players' actions nor of their position in the report, and there was little criticism of the White players. The fault was laid squarely upon the shoulders of the University administration.

Despite the seeming thoroughness of the Committee's investigation, there are a few glaring questions that remain unanswered by their report. In September, Norman Pinkard, Executive Director of the City/County Human Rights Commission suggested a five point program for conciliation of the dispute over the suspension of the players; 1) that coach Schwartzwalder identify what sort of committment he would expect from the eight before he would allow their re-instatement, 2) that he set up procedures to

17. Front page of the *Daily Orange*, December 10, 1970, addresses a report released by the Chancellor's Committee charged with investigating the allegations of racism against the SU Athletic Department and the football program. Student Publications Reference Collection, University Archives, Syracuse University Libraries.

Change had already come elsewhere in the athletic department—notably to the basketball program—and change would come to football, as well, although not right away. For the next three years, Orange football would dwell in the twilight of Schwartzwalder's career. During that time, the team tumbled from the mediocre plateau it had landed on in the late 1960s to a humbled level of performance Syracuse fans had not suffered since before Schwartzwalder's arrival. The Orange went 2–9 in the 1973 season, Old Ben's last, and then 2–9 again in 1974 with the team he left to his successor, Frank Maloney.

Along with other Orange football fans, Schwartzwalder would have to wait until 1979 for anything as glorious as a 7–4 record and an invitation to play McNeese State in the Independence Bowl in Shreveport, Louisiana. It was the team's first postseason game in 13 years. Syracuse won 31–7, led by two African American stars, Art Monk and Joe Morris. Enrolling in 1977, Morris proved to be the long-awaited "next great Syracuse running back," rushing for more than 1,000 yards in each of his varsity seasons. His 1,376 yards in 1979 still stands as the single-season record at Syracuse.

In one of Schwartzwalder's rare post-retirement comments on Syracuse football to the national press, he told *Sports Illustrated* in 1981 that he thought Morris was on a par with all the great Syracuse running backs he had coached. "He's in their class, yes sir," said Schwartzwalder. "He's like something out of a cannon."[4] Morris went on to become an NFL star, helping the New York Giants win the Super Bowl in 1987. Monk played for the Washington Redskins in four Super Bowls, collecting three championship rings.

Monk and Morris were the first Syracuse offensive players to make the All-America team since Schwartzwalder curtailed the recruiting of black students in 1968. A booster of Syracuse University and its football program throughout his professional career, Monk was elected to the Board of Trustees in 2005. "I had a very different experience at Syracuse, and it's clear to me that the willingness of the Syracuse Eight to take a stand on behalf of African American student athletes in 1970 was a necessary step toward positive changes in the program," said Monk, who was founding chair of the committee that created the Syracuse Eight Scholarship.[5]

John Corbally resigned in March 1971, after only eighteen months on the job. Although Corbally seemed to vacillate during the crisis, there is little doubt that he was convinced of the validity of the Syracuse Eight's grievances. In an October 1970 speech to the American Association of Universities in Bloomington, Indiana, Corbally enumerated and confirmed all four of the original points made by the black student protesters. Yet his judgment of those responsible for these conditions was not harsh. "This is not discrimination or racism," he concluded. "It is insensitivity."[6]

Before leaving office, Corbally took steps to assure that the terms of the athletic scholarships granted to the Syracuse Eight would be honored in good faith, without interference from anyone. That meant that they would continue to receive their full athletic scholarships as long as they maintained grade point averages of 2.0 or better. The outgoing chancellor also oversaw creation of a new governing body for Syracuse athletics. Composed of faculty members, administrators, alumni, and undergraduates, it was empowered to hear appeals of student-athlete grievances that were ignored or otherwise handled unsatisfactorily by athletic coaches and staff. Less than a year later, the NCAA, noting that coaches should not have the power to summarily absolve themselves of wrongdoing, adopted a rule that a majority of the members of an athletic governing body should consist of faculty and staff from outside the athletic program. Corbally had put Syracuse ahead of the curve before his departure. Having lost the war, he had done what he could to secure the benefits of an equitable peace.

The talents that had attracted the Syracuse trustees to hire him two years earlier were well known in the academic world, and his career quickly advanced with an offer to assume the presidency of the University of Illinois system. During eight years in office, Corbally was credited with revitalizing the flagship Urbana-Champaign campus and with turning the Chicago Circle campus into a modern urban university. His most well-known achievement was still ahead of him. As president of the John D. and Catherine T. MacArthur Foundation during the 1980s, Corbally convinced his board to make large no-strings cash awards to creative individuals, now called the "MacArthur genius grants."

Schwartzwalder died in 1993 at the age of eighty-three. His obituary in the *New York Times* mentioned his military service, the success of his unorthodox running defenses, and his restoration of the Syracuse team, which was flagging when he first took on the job. It

18. Coach Floyd "Ben" Schwartzwalder, 1965. Portrait Collection, University Archives, Syracuse University Libraries.

also makes mention of some of the running backs Schwartzwalder is credited with recruiting, including Floyd Little, Ernie Davis, and Jim Brown.[7]

As for the Syracuse Eight, they were left to reimagine their lives—without football.

7

Legacies

In a society where choosing which side to root for often takes priority over other forms of authentic discovery and engagement, it may be tempting to sum up the story of the Syracuse Eight as a conflict between a "racist white" football coach and a group of "militant black" student athletes. The temptation is worth resisting. What little truth there is in that characterization only tends to obscure the complexity of a more compelling human drama that touches not only on race and sports, but on generational conflict, American cultural history, the ability of institutions to cope with change, and the struggle of individuals for personal dignity.

On that last matter, personal dignity, the coach was as much consumed by that struggle as any member of the Syracuse Eight. If Floyd Burdette "Ben" Schwartzwalder seemed to be suffering an excess of pride as he reached his sixtieth birthday in 1969, it is not hard to understand what led him down that path. The son of lower middle-class parents in Point Pleasant, West Virginia, he was, at 5 feet 9 inches, 155 pounds, an unlikely candidate for a college football scholarship. He nevertheless earned one from the University of West Virginia, the most competitive football program in the state. Making up in moxie what he lacked in size, Schwartzwalder distinguished himself on the offensive line as the Mountaineers' starting center. Aiming for a career as a high school teacher, he completed bachelor's and master's degrees in physical education and entered the job market during the worst years of the Great Depression. In 1941, when Pearl Harbor was bombed, Schwartzwalder was a thirty-two-year-old high school gym teacher and football coach, working his fourth job in seven years. Answering the call for volunteers, he joined the U.S. Army's 507th Parachute Infantry, Second Airborne Division. As he had done as a college football player, he showed himself capable of uncommon physical fortitude and courage, parachuting onto the beach at Normandy on D-Day, recovering from wounds to fight in the Battle of the Bulge, and earning a chest full of medals, including the Bronze and Silver Stars. Impressed by his leadership qualities, General Dwight Eisenhower appointed Schwartzwalder military governor of Essen during the Allied occupation of Germany. He left the service six months later at the rank of major.

Spurred to extraordinary deeds and elevated to high position during wartime, Schwartzwalder did not return to the life he had been leading as a small-town high school gym teacher. With the help of Dr. Carl Schott, his college mentor, he stepped up to a job as head football coach at Muhlenberg College, and stepped up from there to national prominence as head coach at Syracuse University.

Having risen from obscurity and economic uncertainty on the strength of consistently dynamic performances over a period of twenty-five years, Ben Schwartzwalder could not have been pleased by parallel trends in his career and country that he discovered during the 1960s. After three Top Ten finishes in the AP Poll during the late 1950s (including Number One in 1959), Syracuse did not finish in the Top Ten during the 1960s and was not rated at all by the AP for most of the decade.[1] Schwartzwalder continued to log winning seasons, but the buzz had gone elsewhere in college football. In 1967, for example, Syracuse went 8–2, including victories over Berkeley and UCLA, but did not receive a single bowl invitation.[2] Something had gone wrong. The country was at war and traitors were out in the streets calling for surrender. Men—including his own football players—were not ashamed to wear their hair like women. Then there was this group of defiant black players who challenged his authority, wanting to play whatever positions they liked and demanding say-so on whom he could hire for his coaching staff. In Schwartzwalder's world, this was no way to run a football team, especially the one coached by him.

Like their coach, the Syracuse Eight were experiencing their own collisions of the life cycle and social change. All of the them were either solid or top students in high school, and in a period of expanding opportunities for African Americans, each had multiple offers of athletic scholarships, and in some cases academic scholarships. They had chosen Syracuse for a variety of reasons, ranging from attractive academic programs to the relative convenience of the school's location, but all agreed that the university's reputation as a place of opportunity for African American athletes was a factor in the decision. What better place to go than to the school that had opened its doors, without need of a court order, to the likes of Jim Brown and Ernie Davis?

High expectations made the subsequent disappointment all the more painful. Blocked from playing the positions they excelled at and/or benched for reasons not related to performance, they found their dreams of playing pro football under threat. Steered away from courses they needed to fulfill the requirements of their desired fields of study, they found their career aspirations threatened as well. A doctor unqualified to cope with their injuries posed a threat to their physical health. Seeing white players go unpunished for attacks against them, they could not be confident of their physical safety. Spied on in their private lives, their personal freedoms were at risk. When they complained about any of this to their coaches, they were ignored, ridiculed, or punished. When they felt they had no choice but to walk away from practice in protest, they were summarily pronounced guilty of a crime whose sentence, they came to realize, was exile.

The Syracuse Eight, all a year on either side of twenty, were desperate to realize the potential they had shown in adolescence. Schwartzwalder, at sixty, was desperate to maintain the position and reputation he had enjoyed in middle age. There is nothing unusual about either of these situations. Shakespeare covered them both in *King Lear* and *Hamlet*. But the familiar life passages of all involved were further complicated by the pitiless trajectory of history. Schwartzwalder, a consummate product of America's heroic moment

abroad and the egalitarian era it ushered in at home, failed to understand that what history had given him, it was now taking away.

During the age of scarce black athletes at predominantly white
colleges, Schwartzwalder had accommodated two or three per season and prospered. But the civil rights law ended that environment.
With black students enrolling in "white" schools in unprecedented
numbers, he no longer had the pick of black talent for his running
game. When black players began arriving in numbers on his team,
they presented a painful contrast to the coach. In his view, they had
wild frizzy hairdos and freakish clothes and had come from the
urban slums of the Northeast. The white players were a more familiar bunch to him. Most were good old boys from hardworking families in the steel mills around Buffalo or the rural towns of Western
New York and Pennsylvania. They took ROTC courses, and some of
them had even served in Vietnam. If they grew their hair too long, all
you had to do was tell them to cut it. They were grateful to be in college and they knew that they owed it to football and to the football
team and the football coach. They never complained about anything
and the worst thing they did was drink too much beer on Saturday
night and maybe get in a fight.

At a time when black players were showing up in numbers on
opposing teams and in the NFL draft, Schwartzwalder believed that
maintaining the old quotas was the best thing for his football team
because it was the best thing for football, and football was the best
thing for the country. It was a fatally flawed formula for success.
During his four final years as head coach, including the boycott
season of 1970, no Syracuse football team had more than two African Americans on the roster, and the team's season record declined
each year. In 1973, Schwartzwalder's last year at the helm, Syracuse
avoided a winless season with two November victories and finished
at 2–9. Having failed to bring back 1959, he had almost conjured
its opposite.

The actions of the Syracuse Eight were no less affected by the
particulars of history. Although some of them thought about transferring to other schools or contemplated accepting Schwartzwalder's

conditions for return to the squad, they felt the need to stand their ground and fight the injustices they had encountered so that others could avoid the suffering. In that regard, they were following the example of the heroes of the civil rights movement. After all, Rosa Parks had left Montgomery for Detroit *after*, not instead of, desegregating the public transit system in Alabama's state capital.

Jim Brown knew what was likely to happen to their pro football career hopes if the Eight went ahead with the boycott. He advised them to find a way to return to the team or face the prospect of being blackballed from the NFL. Although McCarthyism was just about dead and gone from the entertainment industry by 1970, the situation for football players who were seen as political radicals was getting worse, not better, at this time. Pro football made its real money from television, a federally regulated medium (much more so then than now), and the owners were committed to demonstrating the kind of patriotism the Nixon Administration liked to see. With anti–Vietnam War sentiment growing and government harassment of dissenters increasing, NFL owners were more eager than ever to show Washington which side they were on.

Moreover, with the AFL-NFL merger now a done deal, there would be no competitive alternative for blacklisted players. Even the Canadian league could no longer be depended upon as a refuge for outcasts. With the growth of the CFL during the 1960s, more than one-half of the positions on the league's coaching staffs were held by Americans. Most of these Americans (and, for that matter, most of their Canadian colleagues) were hesitant to do anything that might disturb their chances of one day snagging a lucrative NFL job south of the border. Each member of the Syracuse Eight who attempted to play pro football learned the truth of these matters the hard way.

The Syracuse football program suffered for years because of Ben Schwartzwalder's handling of the boycott, first with the losing teams of his lame-duck period, and then from lingering recruitment problems. The university that had once automatically attracted the consideration of so many elite African American football prospects now repelled them.

Frank Maloney was brought in from the University of Michigan staff to replace Schwartzwalder as head coach in 1974. One of his first moves was to hire away assistant coach Bill Spencer from Cornell. Spencer, an African American who specialized in working with pass receivers, helped Maloney to restore Syracuse's reputation among black student athletes and their families, and to rid the program of any remaining vestiges of the culture of tokenism. Spencer was instrumental in recruiting Syracuse's next great African American star, Art Monk.

Monk, who attended White Plains High School in the New York City suburbs, had started out as a lineman, playing both offense and defense. Hoping to transform himself into a pass receiver, he joined the White Plains track team as a hurdler and decathlete to improve his speed and agility. He showed his coaches what he had accomplished, and they moved him to tight end during his junior year. But his stats were unimpressive. By the end of his high school career, Monk had a total of only twelve completions.

Spencer, however, was impressed by everything about Monk: his grades, his work ethic, and his athleticism. Seeing Monk as a potential marquee athlete—just the kind they were looking for to restore confidence in the program—he convinced Maloney to offer Monk a full scholarship.

> Nobody made any promises or guarantees to me about making the team as a pass receiver, or anything like that. But they did tell me, "You will have a great chance to play early. You won't have to wait a couple of years before you get on the field. We need good players as soon as we can get them." That was important to me. Another factor was Bill Spencer himself. My Mom really liked him. One evening she caught me talking to someone from the University of Maryland on the phone, and she let me know just how much she wanted me to go to Syracuse and that Coach Spencer was a big part of it.[3]

The gamble on Art Monk was something unimaginable during the glory days of the Schwartzwalder era, when no "gambles" were taken in recruiting African American athletes. Eye-popping stats were a minimum requirement for consideration. Monk's arrival marked a turning point for the Syracuse program. A strong student and diligent about his training, he was, as one biographer put it, "determined to prove he was worth the scholarship he had been given. By the time he graduated from Syracuse in 1980, Monk had set school records . . . in receptions . . . yards gained in receptions . . . and kick return yardage."[4] A first-round draft pick by the Washington Redskins, Monk went on to a fifteen-year career in the NFL and induction into both the college and pro football halls of fame.

Monk's memories of his school days at Syracuse paint a picture that bears little resemblance to the experience of the Syracuse Eight. "We all got along pretty well together on the team, although the football players tended to congregate in black and white groups sometimes," he recalls. "Some people were more friendly than others, but

19. Syracuse University Chancellor's Award Medal, awarded to members of the Syracuse Eight in 2006 at a public ceremony in which they received a formal apology from the university. Photo courtesy Stephen Sartori, Syracuse University.

20. Jim Brown with the Syracuse Eight at the Chancellor's Award Ceremony. The group was recognized by Chancellor Nancy Cantor for an act of courage in standing up for their beliefs. From left to right: John Lobon, Clarence McGill (back row), Greg Allen, Dana Harrell (back row), Duane Walker, Jim Brown, Alif Muhammad (back row), Ron Womack, Richard Bulls. Photo courtesy Stephen Sartori, Syracuse University.

we did things socially with the white ballplayers. There was never any name-calling or anything like that. I've been asked about this before, and I can tell you that there wasn't even any kind of subtle hint of racism that I could pick up." Asked if he was surprised by that, enrolling just five years after the boycott and two years after Schwartzwalder's retirement, Monk replies,

> I never knew anything about the Syracuse Eight during my entire time as a student at Syracuse. The first time I ever even heard of them was at a reunion in 2005—that's twenty-five years after I graduated. I had never even heard anything about the Report of the Chancellor's Commission on Racism or any of the changes that were made because of it. I suppose in one way that's good because it shows how different a place Syracuse had become in

21. Halftime at the Dome: Nancy Cantor with the Syracuse Eight. In October 2006, at halftime of the Orange's 28–13 loss to sixth-ranked Louisville, the surviving members of the Syracuse Eight received their letterman jackets. Photo courtesy Stephen Sartori, Syracuse University.

such a short time. But in another way, it's kind of a shame. I had no idea for all those years of how much I owe those guys, and how much everyone owes them, for the sacrifices they made. Doing the right thing can have rough consequences and it can leave people feeling very lonely. When you see someone who has done something beneficial, you have to reach out to them and say, "I know what you did. Thanks."[5]

PART TWO

Interviews

Following are transcribed interviews with each of the surviving members of the Syracuse Eight. In answering a series of questions, the interviewees were able to offer—in their own words—their personal perspectives on events described in this book and on the forces that shaped their lives before and after football at Syracuse University.

8

Gregory Allen

Greg Allen had two years of football eligibility left after sitting out the 1970 season, and he announced his intention to play Orange football in 1971. Ben Schwartzwalder was remarkably amenable, welcoming Allen to practice without qualification. There were several plausible explanations for the coach's shift in attitude. Perhaps he realized just how close he had come to a bowl invitation or even a nationally ranked team in 1970, despite having discarded some of the best players on his squad. During 1969, Allen's only season playing for Syracuse, he had exploded for gains of 20 yards or more fourteen times, and the coach was ready for some of that. Perhaps he had rationalized that he had already agreed to let Allen back on the team a year ago, and now Allen had finally come to his senses and returned. Perhaps he thought that adding a third black student to his 72-man squad might serve as a rebuttal to the committee's report on racism, which had documented the declining number of blacks in the program.

In any case, on Wednesday, August 26, 1971, Greg Allen reported to fall practice. He saw Dr. Pelow for his annual mandatory physical, which he passed with flying colors. Five days later, he collapsed while walking on campus and was rushed to Crouse-Irving Hospital where he was diagnosed with infectious hepatitis. Allen would have to sit out his second season in a row.

"Sure, we've got some more tailbacks, but not like Greg," said Schwartzwalder. "He came here in shape this year and he wanted to play football. None of our other guys has the experience he has. I just hope we can get him back next year. I want him to play for me."[1]

22. Greg Allen, no. 17, in SU uniform, 1969.

The coach's wish came true. Allen reported healthy in 1972, and it looked as if he was set to have the banner year that was due him. Following an opening day 17–10 win against Temple, Schwartzwalder praised Allen to the press, placing him with Marty Januskiewicz and Roger Praetorius, the team rushing leaders for the past two seasons. The following week, Allen scored an early first-period touchdown on a 12-yard run, a bright spot in a 43–20 loss at North Carolina State. And then, as abruptly as it began, the rapprochement ended.

"I gave an interview to a paper down in North Carolina, and the reporter asked me if I had any regrets about the boycott," Allen says. "I told him that I thought the things we stood up for two years ago were still worthwhile, and that the report of the chancellor's committee had pretty much backed up what we had said." Allen remained with the team for the rest of the season, but after that interview, he became persona non grata. "Schwartzwalder didn't want to have anything to do with me anymore," he says. After twenty-one carries during the first two games, he was used sparingly, to say the least, running with the ball just twenty-seven times during the next nine games.

Statistically, Allen was the most reliable runner on the offense, averaging a whopping 5.5 yards per carry. But Bob Barlette, averaging 4.0, got more playing time. Even though Allen held (and still holds) the Orange record for most yards gained on punt returns in a single game (172 vs. Penn State in 1969), his repeated requests to be sent in as a kick returner on special teams were ignored. "Rocco Pirro, the line coach, was the only member of the staff who took an interest in my situation," Allen says. "In 1972, when Ben wasn't playing me, Coach Pirro implored him, week after week, to put me in the game. It didn't happen, but at least Coach Pirro showed me that he understood the situation. We remained friends after that, and he gave me a good recommendation when I tried out with the Ottawa Rough Riders."

On November 18, 1972, Allen spent most of the game on the sidelines watching the Orange take a 43–12 shellacking from the University of West Virginia in Morgantown. Thus ended Schwartzwalder's first losing season at Syracuse since 1949, and thus ended Allen's career as a student athlete at Syracuse. Things hadn't gone the way he expected. Allen had played some great football for the Orange, but the promise of his athletic potential was not reached, suppressed by obstacles off the field.

Greg Allen tells the story in his own words:

> I was born in Newark, New Jersey, and grew up nearby in Plainfield. We were a strong Christian family: mom, dad, my two brothers, my younger sister and me. My parents taught us all the meaning of personal integrity and the importance

of moral accountability. They exhibited in life every charac-
teristic they stressed to us in words. Their example played a
key role in my decision to boycott. When I was in the deciding phase of what to do, I asked my father for advice. He told
me I would have to make my own choice, but that I should
remember that this decision would affect me for the rest of
my life, so I had to be prepared to take responsibility for it. In
the end, I did what I thought my father would do. I joined the
boycott because it was the right thing to do.

Sports had always been important to me, and I had what
I considered an excellent athletic record in high school, competing in track as well as football. I ran the 100-yard dash in
9.7 seconds, which was pretty good for a kid running on a
cinder track in those days. I won the county and state sec-
tional championships in the event, and I'd placed third in the
Eastern States. As a junior and senior at Plainfield, I was a
member of the state championship teams in the 440- and
the 880-yard relays. My speed and my good balance helped
me excel in football, and I spent a lot of time in the gym lifting. My high school team went undefeated my senior year.
I got hurt my senior year and missed a couple of football
games, which prevented me from making the all-state first
team, but I received my share of honors, including recognition by local organizations as the team MVP. I was a good
student with strong SAT scores, and so I was recruited for
both football and track by some excellent schools, including
Purdue, Michigan State, Boston College, Colgate, Rutgers,
Colorado, and Syracuse.

My decision to go to Syracuse was based on a couple
of factors. I remember watching Jim Brown on television as
a youngster. It was a formative experience for me. I became
intrigued by the possibilities of playing college football and
then going on to play in the NFL. I paid attention to the careers
of great Syracuse players—Ernie Davis, John Mackey, Jim
Nance, Floyd Little, and Art Baker. I heard stories of Bernie

Custis in Canada. To me, Syracuse was a good academic school with a terrific reputation in football and, most importantly, it was a place where African Americans could succeed. When I received my letter of interest from Syracuse, I was ecstatic. But I would say the real clincher was the campus visit. That's when I met John Lobon; we were both recruits. We were taken around campus by John Godbolt and Alif Muhammad, who was known then as Al Newton. It was a good weekend for me in many ways, but the most significant thing that happened was that John Lobon and I became instant friends. He has been my best friend ever since, going on half a century. The last event on the agenda that weekend was a meeting with the coach—the legendary Ben Schwartzwalder. John asked me what I was going to say to him. I told John if he decided to come to Syracuse then so would I. He came right back at me: "If you're coming, Greg, I'm coming too." So in that spirit of friendship and mutual respect, we committed to Ben.

The value of John Lobon's friendship became apparent to me soon after I arrived in Syracuse. We were having our first meal at the training table with the varsity. There was a tradition of the varsity players hazing the incoming freshmen by making them do things like take off their shirts and flex their muscles, hold hands and sing their high school alma maters, or even strip down and hug one another. Ridiculous juvenile stuff like that. Well, John and I were sitting together and we agreed we would go through the hazing like everybody else, but we wouldn't let them get either one of us to humiliate the other. So, when our turn came, we refused to strip down and hug each other. We just refused to do it. Of course, this was not received well by the varsity players. They told us we were "marked men," implying that there would be unpleasant consequences for us. But what was most important to me and to John is that we stood our ground. We were willing to face the consequences for keeping our self-respect.

In our first scrimmage against the varsity, we were put on defense. I was playing cornerback and John was middle linebacker. They ran a play right at John. They gave the ball to Alif, the best running back on the team, and John met him in the hole. Alif went down with a "thwack." It was one of the toughest hits I had ever witnessed and it became the defining moment for our freshman team because after that any fear we might have had of scrimmaging the varsity dissipated. I also learned something very valuable. I would only be a "marked man" if I submitted to the idea of being a marked man—and I didn't. I was ready to play football with anyone on any level.

The next major moment for me as a freshman came when we were all competing for positions. One of my personal priorities was to play offense. I was competing for the starting wingback position. I was doing well and felt I had an excellent chance of winning the position. We were having two-a-day practices, and during the morning session Jim Shreve, the freshman coach, told me to go down and work with the defensive backs. I told him I didn't want to play defense and that when I was recruited I was assured I would be playing on offense. He told me to go down and work with the defense anyway. I did as he said, but I wasn't really giving it my all. The defensive back coach saw it. He approached me and said, "I can tell you really don't want to be down here." As I was walking off the field, he told Jim Shreve he was sending me back over to offense. Shreve turned to me and said, "What's the problem, Allen? You afraid to hit?" I said, "No coach. In high school I played both offense and defense. I was a starting defensive back for two years. I'm not afraid to hit." Shreve gathered the team around and told us what was scheduled for the afternoon session, but before we cleared off the field, he said, "Wait, before we break, we're going to try one more thing." He wanted us to do a one-on-one drill, something we used call "bull in the ring."

He circled the team up and told me to go into the middle. He selected the four biggest backs we had. Each would try to run through me with the football. I knew the time had come for me to step up and prove that I could play defensive back if I wanted. The first back came at me, and I pancaked him. I hit the next guy so hard he fumbled. I drove back the third guy from the point of contact. I hit the fourth one with all I had and we stalemated. I got a roaring cheer from my team-mates. Coach Shreve came over to me and said "Where did you learn to hit like that?" I said "Coach, I told you I could hit. I'm not afraid to play defense. I just prefer to play offense." I ended up as the starting wingback on the freshman team and had a very good season.

During the off season, I worked out regularly, lifting, running track, and playing basketball. I even made the first team All-Intramural basketball team as a freshman. Going into spring practice in 1969, I was sixth on the depth chart at the wingback position. Being down so low on the list didn't upset me. I was used to being on top in high school, but so was just about every guy on the Syracuse team. I knew I had to prove myself to earn a top spot on this team. By the spring intrasquad game, I had worked my way up to second team. I started at wingback for the Blue Team ("B" squad) in the game against the White Team ("A" squad). I did well in the game and when spring practice ended I was solidly the second-team wingback and I was an alternate for the first team. I could see, without exaggeration, that I was the fastest runner on the entire football team. I went home for the sum-mer and worked out intensely.

I came back to school in excellent shape, ready to go. When I found out that the first-team wingback had quit school because of some personal issues at home, I was sure I would move up to first-team wingback. That was not the case. The fourth-team tailback was moved to first-team wingback. I couldn't understand it. I went to my position coach and asked why I wasn't moved to first team. I'd earned second-team status just ten weeks ago, and there hadn't been any scrimmages or practices since. He told me that "Steve" had been taking courses in summer school and had been working out and learning the plays. "Coach, it seems like I'm being penalized for not having to go to summer school." He didn't really have any answer. He just said, "Steve is the starter, but you'll get a chance to play."

I was very disappointed, and what made it worse was that there didn't seem to be any rhyme or reason to it. I was a 19 year-old kid with an athletic scholarship at the same school that Jim Brown and Ernie Davis had gone to. Should I have guessed that I was being made a victim of a racial quota system? I just told myself to suck it up and prove them wrong. I practiced every day like it was game day. Now we are two weeks away from opening day against Iowa State, and Steve gets into some type of trouble and is dismissed from school. Once I heard that, I was beyond all doubt that I was going to be the starter. Incredibly, they moved the reserve fullback to first-team wingback. I couldn't believe it! Then, to add insult to injury, they asked me to help him learn the wingback assignments so he would be ready for the game.

I went up to my position coach again. "Coach, what's going on? How come you refuse to let me start?" He told me they wanted to go with "experience." I said "I know he's a junior but you were going to let Steve start, and he was a sophomore just like me. So I don't understand this thing about experience." His reply showed me he wouldn't discuss what was really going on. "Look, Allen, that's the way it is, and if you don't like it you don't have to play at all."

I was tempted to quit but I had come too far. I was a just few seasons away from possibly realizing my lifetime dream of playing in the NFL. I remembered one of my father's mantras, "Don't ever quit; finish what you start." I made up my mind that I was going to prove the coaches wrong. In my first varsity game, I got some playing time against Iowa State and I made several key runs, including one that set up the winning touchdown and another that got us a critical first down late in the fourth quarter and helped us put the game out of reach. But it didn't seem to make any difference to the coaches. The following week, against Kansas, I still wasn't a starter.

The third game of the 1969 season, a road game against Wisconsin, was pivotal in a lot of ways, but the most important thing was that I came away from it knowing beyond any reasonable doubt that the problems I was encountering did not have to do with my abilities on the football field. It was all about race.

Because of injuries to some of the white players, three African Americans—Alif, John Godbolt, and me—started in the backfield. It had never happened before and we got together before the game and made a pledge that we were going to play so well that the coaches would have to play us together from now on. I'll skip the play-by-play, but Syracuse won the game 43–7. It was the team's biggest offensive output in years. We scored 20 points more than the team put on the board in any game that year. All three of us scored touchdowns, a total of five altogether. I think we each gained more than 100 yards on the ground that day. I carried the ball in on the longest Syracuse touchdown run from scrimmage in three years.

It wasn't good enough.

The following week we played Maryland, and only Alif started. John Godbolt and I were moved back to second team. I started just one more game in 1969, the season finale against Boston College. Even though Wisconsin and BC were my only two starts that year, I finished second on the team in total rushing yards, pass receptions, pass receiving yardage, and total yardage, and I was first in kickoff and punt returns. At one point, I was the number one punt returner in the nation; no opponent would even kick the ball in my direction. I set an all-time Syracuse record for most punt-return yardage in a single game against Penn State, which was ranked number one in the nation at the time.

I tried to tell myself that at least I was getting a decent amount of playing time and that I was carrying the ball. But getting a chance to play wasn't my goal. I wanted to be number one, a starter. If I hadn't been producing, okay, I'd understand. But I was doing the things that were necessary. I was earning that privilege. I was working hard, making sacrifices, and I was getting results. I was outperforming others, yet they were being rewarded and I was being kept back. I was beginning to understand that the playing field wasn't level. Even so, I told myself that's no reason to quit. I decided to embrace the unfairness, squeeze the energy out of it, and turn it into an opportunity to grow and succeed.

When the season ended, I worked out all winter, running and lifting, getting ready for spring practice. I even competed in several indoor track meets and qualified for the IC4A [Intercollegiate Association of Amateur Athletes in America] championships in Madison Square Garden. I didn't win, but that was okay because the track work helped me improve as a football player. I was focused on two things: football and, of course, academics.

In high school, I had been one of a few students in an advanced biology group, which allowed me to take a freshman college biology course my senior year at Plainfield. As part of the program, I had an after-school job in the pathology department of a local hospital. I enjoyed the work and thought seriously about a career in pathology. When I registered for classes as a freshman at Syracuse, I already had credit for freshman bio and this allowed me to take an advanced course, which required several lab sessions each week. When I informed the coaches that I needed to be excused from some practices to attend the labs, they said

I couldn't do it. They told me to take different courses and they even told me pursue a different major. They treated me as if the "real" reason I was in college was to play football, and everything else had to fit in with that. I didn't know what to do, so I went to see Alif. This was one of the many times he helped me sort things out. Alif really became like a big brother to me. With no real academic advisors, we all helped each other as much as we could. But by helping each other, we could see that we were facing problems that the white members of the team didn't have. We came to realize that we had to do something to get better academic advising than we were getting from the football staff.

We also realized we needed more academic help in the form of tutoring. For example, several of us were taking the same math course and we tried to help each other work through it. I remember coming back from dinner one night and seeing several white ballplayers who were being helped by tutors. I asked them how they were able to get that kind of help, and they told me the coaching staff arranged it. But when I asked the coaches for tutoring, they just told me to study harder, and if that didn't work they would consider getting me help. When I told some of the other black ballplayers about this, some said they had asked for tutors and gotten the same answer. This string of unequal, unfair experiences got us talking more and more to each other about how to handle things and still play ball. Through it all, we kept coming back to the idea of a black coach. If we only had someone we could talk to, someone in a position to talk to the other coaches, someone who would be a serious advisor and an advocate for us, we believed we could work through these problems. This seemed like a reasonable and workable solution to us.

I remember seeing the depth chart at the beginning of spring practice in 1970. There I was, first-team starting tailback. I was extremely excited, but at the same time I was concerned about the impact this would have on John Godbolt, who had been starting tailback in 1968. I had a tremendous amount of respect for John. I remember my first impression of John. Physically, he seemed to me to be the epitome of a running back. "Here is a guy who will be a pro one day!" I told myself. In terms of character, John was probably the most mature of all of us. He talked to me during my freshman year about how important it was that I got my degree, and I could see how hard he was working towards his. So I had mixed emotions about replacing him. Starting tailback at Syracuse was a coveted position. Because of the many great players who had held it in the past, your chances of being taken seriously by pro scouts were greatly increased. You still had to excel, but you had this extra assurance that you had their attention. One of the sad things about competing for a position under a biased quota system is that success, no matter how well deserved, can only come at the direct expense of another athlete. John Godbolt was not benched in 1969 because of me; he was benched because of the coach's failure to put the best team possible on the field, without regard to race.

I remember standing next to Ben during practice one day. Richard Bulls, who was a freshman then, took a handoff and ran into the wrong hole. Ben yelled, "Al, that's the wrong hole." Coach Shreve turned to him and said "That's not Al, that's Bulls." Ben replied, "Well, they all look alike." What was significant about this exchange is that Ben did not look at Shreve, when he said it, but looked at me—right in the eye.

I was very excited when I heard that Floyd Little was coming to spring practice in 1970 as a coach. He was a role model for me and for many of the guys, and he was one of the reasons I'd chosen Syracuse. After the first couple of days of spring ball, we found out that Floyd really was not there to coach us, but was in town to take care of other business, and he would just be with us for a few days. Before he left, Floyd pulled me aside in the locker room and told me he wanted to talk to me. I sat down with him and he told me that the coaches thought I really had promise, but that I needed to be careful about who I was hanging around with. He said they were concerned about me getting too involved in campus politics and all the "black stuff." I told him what I had told Ben: I wasn't involved with anything to the point where it would interfere with my playing. He told me he was just "passing along the message," adding that I shouldn't miss out on the opportunity that Syracuse was giving me. "Thanks," I said. "I won't."

Later that day, all the black players met and we discussed what had happened. It was clear that Floyd wasn't really joining the coaching staff and that we had been deceived. Even if, technically speaking, his three days at spring practice qualified him as a "coach," he was not acting as an advocate for us by delivering a message from the coaches about what kind of campus activities they wanted us to stay away from. That's when we started to discuss how to get the attention of the coaches and how to let them know we were serious about hiring a black coach. The decision to boycott practice really grew out of this. It wasn't an easy decision for any of us. Every one of us knew what role football had already played in our lives and the role it could play in our future. We were not the kind of guys who took missing practice lightly, no matter what the reason.

Dick Bulls, John Godbolt, John Lobon, D. J. Harrell, Bucky McGill, Alif Muhammad, Duane Walker, and myself were the core group of active varsity players who decided to boycott. There were three other African American students in the football program and we consulted with all of them. Everyone knew that Ron Womack had been victimized by the football program, which led to his being put on what amounted to permanent medical leave. Since Ron was not allowed to participate in spring practice, he could not boycott it, per se. But he was in full sympathy with us and we appreciated his support. Ron Page was in his second semester as a freshman in 1970. I spoke with him and explained what the boycott was about, but he decided not to participate. I also spoke to Robin Griffin, and he decided to join, at least for the short term. So eight of us decided not to go to practice until our requests were met or, at the least, actively addressed. Of the eight who boycotted, five were starting players with significant roles on the team.

It was only after the press got hold of the story that we really began to understand the enormity of the action we took, and then I personally started to realize what a major impact this was going to have on my life. It also became clear to me that there was no turning back. This proved to be especially important for me when I was approached by the coaches with an opportunity to turn my back on my friends and deny the truth of what we had said.

As the story spread, more and more people took an interest in what we were doing and offered to help us navigate through the historic events. There were other protests going on all over America at that time. Students across the country were protesting the war in Vietnam, including the fatal incident at Kent State, which happened in May, just weeks after we began our boycott. Student takeovers of administration buildings at Syracuse and other schools, from Berkeley to Columbia, were in the news on what seemed like a daily basis. During this period, several articles appeared in newspapers and magazines, locally and nationally. Our boycott was getting a lot of attention.

As we were going through all this, it was always our intention and hope that things would be resolved so we could go back to school and play football. I returned to my home in New Jersey and worked out all summer to get ready to play football. I remember reading an article indicating that Syracuse was only interested in bringing back a couple of the players who had participated in the boycott. The story turned out to be true, and I turned out to be one of those players who was asked back. I got a call in August inviting me to fall practice. It was welcome news, but at the same time it created an unwelcome dilemma. I knew our cause was just. I knew we were doing the right thing, not just to improve things for us, but for those who would come after. I confided my dilemma to my father. He said, "Son, I can't make this decision for you. Just remember, this is a decision that you will have to live with the rest of your life. You're going to have to make a man's decision." I understood him perfectly well. My parents lived by the credo, "Do what's right." I knew that I had to act on that for myself and for the good of others. Yes, my interests were at stake, but this was also about something bigger than me: change. What had been the way things were done, could no longer be the way things would be done. I felt like part of humanity, like my destiny was plugged into history and this was a chance to do something for the greater good.

But it still hurt. You see, I wanted to be one of those great sports legends that I read about when I was a kid. I wanted to inspire others the way they inspired me. I wanted to play in the NFL. I wanted to be rich and famous. I wanted to be in the Hall of Fame. I wanted celebrity and acclaim, and the rewards that go with those things. I wanted to be remembered as one of the greats at Syracuse University. I'm not ashamed of wanting those things. Dreaming of fame and fortune is part of being human. But so is knowing the difference between right and wrong. You learn just what kind of a human being you are when material desires come into conflict with moral judgment. While doing the right thing doesn't necessarily get you external or material satisfaction, it does offer you internal gratification and spiritual enrichment.

During the spring and summer of 1970, my roommate John Lobon and I constantly discussed what we hoped the final outcome of all this would be. Yes, we both wanted to eventually go back and play football and realize those dreams. But I learned a lot from understanding John's particular motivations. He wanted to do so many things for his mother, who he adored. He wanted to achieve the success that had eluded other members of his family because he knew she would share in his success. I believe it was our friendship and the brotherly bond it created that gave us both the strength to get through this period in our lives. This sense of brotherhood was evident in the relationships that we all discovered because making a commitment to a cause is making a commitment to the others involved in that cause. We each thought it was important that we all made it through and that we all graduate no matter what the final outcome of the football situation. That's why it hurts so much when we remember John Godbolt. John did not survive intact. His spirit was broken and, in my analysis, he went into a state of depression that we couldn't bring him out of.

I continued to work out during the summer of 1970 as though it was a certainty that I would be playing football that fall. When I returned to campus in late August, I found out that not everyone had received the phone call that I received. Just two of us had been asked back. I was shocked. It made no sense to me. All of us, every one as much as the other, had acted in protest of unfair treatment. To accept this solution—allowing two of us back—would mean agreeing to even more unfair treatment. We had all done the same thing. None of us believed the boycott was a "crime." So what sense did it make that two us were "pardoned" and six of us "punished"?

When we were all back together again in Syracuse that August we knew, based on the media's handling of the story, that we had to be more focused and committed than ever to a set of demands and principles. We had several helpful mentors and advisors during this period. Rev. Dr. Charles

Moody of the First Methodist Church of Syracuse and Syracuse professors Charles Willie and John Johnson were the
closest to us and the most deeply involved with us.[2] We were
constantly portrayed in the press as being manipulated by
others, but I think it's important to set the record straight on
that. We acted on our own volition. We knew what we were
boycotting for and we were capable of articulating our positions. Dr. Willie, the chair of the sociology department and
the first African American to become a tenured member of
the Syracuse faculty, and Dr. Johnson, Syracuse's first vice
president for minority affairs, were tremendously helpful to
us in dealing with the university bureaucracy and securing
our rights as students. They were invaluable when it came to
filing with the Human Rights Commission.

Alif decided to reach out to two African American football
alumni who we respect very much. John Mackey encouraged
us, but he was involved in negotiations to bring together the
NFL and AFL player associations as the two leagues moved
toward merger. We got a tremendous boost when Jim Brown
agreed to get directly involved. Jim's role was inspirational
and crucial to our cause. There we were, faced with a powerful iconic figure in the person of Ben Schwartzwalder, who
was able to influence the press, the alumni, and members of
the administration. But now we had a powerful iconic figure
of our own in Jim Brown, and he was someone we could
trust to be fair. Jim came to Syracuse and took the time to
get to know us individually and collectively. He bonded with
us and, without making specific promises, tried to help us
as best he could. We didn't just meet with Jim; we hung out
with him. He even challenged us athletically. He challenged
each of us to one-on-one basketball, and even though we
were just students and he was a Hollywood movie star, he
collected on his winnings. We didn't mind paying a bit.

I remember meeting with Jim, just the two of us, like
it happened yesterday. He kiddingly told me I wasn't the

biggest back he had ever seen but evidently I must have some talent because the coaches told him specifically that they wanted me to return to the team even if the others didn't. Of course I was glad to hear that, but I knew that returning without the others was out of the question. I wouldn't do it. I couldn't do it. We were in this together to the end. "What's more important to you, an NFL career or the boycott?" Jim asked me. I told him the principles behind the boycott were more important to me than either of those things. He gave it to me straight, telling me that if we continued the boycott, an NFL career was not likely to be an option for any of us. I told Jim I was willing to take the risk. He smiled the Jim Brown smile and said "Good." We shook hands.

That meeting with Jim was meaningful to me in several ways. For one thing, there was no doubt in my mind that Jim knew the lay of the land at both Syracuse and the NFL. He knew we wanted to go back and play and he was hoping for the same outcome. But I needed to hear a realistic assessment about the likely consequences of what I was doing. It was a gut-check moment. It prepared me for whatever was going to happen and strengthened my resolve. He helped me grow up that day.

Although the African American students at Syracuse were relatively small in number, their support for the Syracuse Eight was monumental, and we very much appreciated it. They reached out to us and offered to help in any way they could. They let us know how much they cared and how proud they were of us for taking a stand. Without their support and encouragement, the whole thing would have felt unbearable. Many white students supported our cause as well, showing up at rallies and at Archbold Stadium on game days to demonstrate in support of us. They invited us to speak at various sororities and fraternities, which allowed us to tell our side of things directly to people, without being "filtered" by Ben's friends in the press. We found the people who attended these events were far more open to what we had to say than anyone reading the newspapers or watching local TV would have thought. Faculty members, black and white, were involved throughout. I've already mentioned the special relationships we developed with Charles Willie and John Johnson. But there were others. Michael Sawyer, professor of constitutional law at the Maxwell School and one of the most respected people on campus, encouraged us and gave us the benefit of his views. Some professors opposed what we were doing and made no secret of it, but they seemed to be in the minority. We even had supporters in the athletic department, and we knew how risky that was for them, given the power Ben wielded over there. Roy Danforth, who had recently become head basketball coach, was never anything but friendly, as was his assistant, a young graduate student named Jim Boeheim. Roy and Jim greeted us when they saw us on campus and they even talked to us while just about everyone else in the athletic department gave us nothing but the deep freeze.

I can't say enough about the Syracuse African American community. They backed us in every way, and to this day I feel a debt of gratitude to them for the warmth they showed us, which dates back to before the boycott. From the day we arrived, we were welcomed and adopted by the community. At a time when we could not be sure whether we would be served if we went to dinner at a restaurant in town, we were always treated like celebrities by Henry Ben, the proprietor of Ben's Kitchen. This was especially important on Sunday evenings, when the campus dining halls were closed. I personally have to acknowledge the Harlow family. They treated me like I was a brother-in-law long before I married their sister, Sirena. They extended that same degree of kindness and encouragement to all of us. They were my family when I needed someone to talk to or be consoled.

After the chancellor had appointed a committee to investigate our allegations, we tried to make our lives as normal as possible. But it was a "new normal" for us. We were in an unfamiliar position. We had never spent a fall without football and we had never been without the structure that football gave to our lives. We knew we had to keep working toward our degrees. We made a pact: whatever the outcome of the boycott, we were going to leave Syracuse with our degrees. And the importance of that was magnified by another factor. We knew if we didn't stay in the school, the draft was a real possibility. It almost became a reality, even though we did stay in school.

That fall, John Lobon and I both received draft notices. My mother called me at school and told me that someone she knew who worked at the local draft board called and told her my draft notice was being mailed. My mother told her I was still in school, and her advice was to have me contact the draft board as soon as possible. I learned that they had not received my student deferment form from the university. John and I went up to the administrative office to see why our forms had not been sent. When they pulled our records, our deferment forms, signed and ready to go, were still sitting in the file. They offered to mail them that day. I said, "No, thanks," and asked them for my form. I delivered it personally to my draft board in New Jersey. How did the perfectly legal and correct draft deferments of two members of the Syracuse Eight each manage to get left in the files when they should have been mailed by the university, as thousands of other deferments were? Was it a coincidence?

We also had some interaction with the white ballplayers during this time period. Most couldn't quite understand how we could put our concerns ahead of football and ahead of the team, and many of them really wanted to understand why we were doing this. Of course there were some who didn't want to understand. But even with the more reasonable guys on the team, there was no getting around the fact that the relationship between "us and them" had become strained. Alif and I were asked to appear on a community magazine show at one of the television stations in New York City. We were asked to summarize the issues and to describe what we hoped to accomplish in our boycott—all in a five-minute interview. As we prepared for the show, it astonished us to realize how basic and fundamental our requests were—and how complicated things had become. The issues that had motivated us to take action had become buried under all kinds of arguments about whether or not we even had the right to express ourselves without being treated like criminals.

As the season progressed, we of course followed the fortunes of the team. Most people thought we were rooting against Syracuse and that we were hoping they would lose every game. It wasn't so. We weren't even thinking about that. We were focused on the chancellor's committee and what their findings would be. Would it be a whitewash or would the truth come out? That was what interested us. Also during this time we met with other African American students to see if we could get involved in other campus issues, such as instituting a black studies program and creating a black student union facility. The fall of 1970, our first fall without football, gave us time to talk about life after football. Were we prepared if we didn't make it to the pros? We became more focused than ever on our educations and continued to encourage one another not to let anything interfere with graduation.

As the football season progressed, the team found its footing without us. They went on a five-game winning streak. By beating Miami in the final game of the year, Syracuse ended up 6–4 and Ben was named ECAC [Eastern Collegiate Athletic Conference] coach of the year. The press came to us for a statement. They were looking for an "in-your-face" moment, but we didn't bite. We simply said we were happy for the team and Ben. By this time, most of us had been interviewed by the commission investigating our allegations. We knew that their findings would be coming out soon. We knew their report would be crucial to proving our belief that we had done the right thing. That was the victory we wanted. The press seemed to think our goal was to prove to Ben that he couldn't have a winning season without us. That was never what the boycott was about.

When we learned that the committee report had described the way we were treated as "an act of institutional racism unworthy of a great university," we felt vindicated. We had taken an unpopular stand, been maligned by the press, and been disowned by many alumni and fans of the team. But there it was for the world to see: thoughtful, intelligent people had taken the time to investigate our claims and they concluded that we had spoken truthfully.

We all agreed that this wasn't a time for the kind of celebration we might have had after winning a big game on the football field. The stand we took wasn't about us and it wasn't about immediate rewards. It was about remembering those who had endured the humiliations of racism before us and about those who would not have to endure those humiliations in the future. We were elated, but in a sober way. We had closed a chapter in history and made something better possible. We had changed, and now athletics at Syracuse could change and collegiate sports across the country would change. The university was already changing it, and we had helped that process along, too. This was more than we thought was possible when we started out, and in that sense the meaning of the boycott had changed. People who knew nothing about us or about what we faced had called us ungrateful malcontents. The report proved them wrong. We were activists in athletics. We honored the moment of that recognition and still do to this day.

What we didn't realize was that the struggle we had chosen to participate in was not over in our lives. There would be more dues to pay. Despite our vindication, we knew that what we had done would be viewed as little more than an act of rebellion. Jim Brown was right when he predicted the NFL's reaction. We had gained the advantage of becoming capable, principled men prepared to make our way in life, but in the process we had permanently sacrificed any chance of playing professional football.

That's not to say I didn't keep dreaming about it or that I didn't continue to make every effort to make the dream come true. The Dallas Cowboys were interested in me—until someone found out I was one of the Syracuse Eight. The process went further with the Ottawa Rough Riders of the CFL. I signed a contract with Ottawa and even received a signing bonus. I was supposed to play as a wide receiver and wingback on offense. Before I reported to camp, the head coach, Frank Gotta, sent me a letter saying he wanted to know if I would also spend some time at cornerback since one of their defensive backs was still recovering from knee surgery. He pointed out to me that since the league only allowed them to keep fifteen Americans on the roster, my chances of making the team would increase if I played more than one position. I agreed to try out at defensive back as long as the decision of whether or not to keep me on the team would be based on my ability to play on offense. He agreed to that in a letter, and that satisfied me. As we began preseason drills, I initially worked out with the receivers and worked a little at wingback. I was the fastest athlete in camp. After about two weeks, I began playing as a defensive back, and it went very well. I was made the starting defensive left corner and played three exhibition games at that position. According to the agreement we'd made, I was still supposed to go back to offense. But I was okay with the change, since I was starting and it seemed to guarantee that I would make the team. The head coach had nothing but praise for me. In a newspaper article, he said I had speed, I could play multiple positions, and that I was the best athlete in camp that year. Shortly after that article came out, someone spoke to the coach about me and notified him that I was one of the Syracuse Eight.

Usually when a player gets cut, he goes out to the fieldhouse and finds his locker empty. When that happens, you know it's time to go see the coach and start packing. My experience was different. I got a call from my position coach to come to the head coach's office. I was fine with that. I assumed they wanted to talk about my contract or move me back to offense. When I arrived at the office, the head coach told me they were letting me go because they were going in another direction. I asked him what that meant and he just repeated, "We are letting you go." Of course I was puzzled. I reminded the coach of his comments in the paper and I reminded him of our agreement about my status with the team being based on my offensive skills. He said it wasn't contractual and he wasn't bound by it. I exploded and began to tell the coach what I thought about his decision. As I was leaving my position coach told me that he tried to convince the coach to keep me but I had some "baggage" and there was nothing he could do. I didn't realize until a couple of weeks later what was really behind his decision. A coach who had been recruiting me to play semi-pro ball in Hartford, Connecticut, had been up there in Canada at the Ottawa camp. He told me it was my Syracuse Eight history that scared the coach. I knew it was all over.

For years, I had a recurring dream: the coaching staff at Syracuse would call to tell me they knew I had been wronged, and invite me back for one more season of eligibility. I would accept, but there was always a problem: I couldn't find my locker; my equipment was missing; I'd put on my uniform, but couldn't find may way through a maze of tunnels. I would wake up in a sweat and rethink the "what if" all over again.

Ben was a product of his time, and I understand how it molded his thinking. He accomplished some great things in his life and I acknowledge and respect him for his achievements. I leave it to historians and ultimately to God to judge him on the events surrounding me and the other members of the Syracuse Eight. For myself, I feel the committee said all that was necessary in its report. They confirmed the conditions we dealt with, and agreed those conditions had to change. I would have abdicated my moral responsibilities to leave it for others to do that. Instead, I lived up to the legacy my parents provided for me.

Greg Allen graduated from Syracuse University in 1973 with a bachelor's degree from the S.I. Newhouse School of Public Communications. He holds a graduate certificate in sales and marketing management from Syracuse, as well as executive training certifications from Duquesne University and Northwestern's Kellogg School of Management. Allen began a thirty-three-year career with the Liberty Mutual Insurance Group in 1977, rising through the ranks of the company to managerial leadership positions in Cleveland, Phoenix, and Chicago. At the time of his retirement in 2009, he was regional manager of Liberty Mutual's Midwest Division. Allen has maintained his connection to sports throughout his life, serving as general manager of a semi-pro football team and as head coach of youth teams in football, basketball, and baseball, wherever his work has taken him. A deacon in the Second Baptist Church of Elgin (Illinois), he gives his time to a wide range of outreach activities, including prison ministry, male chorus, soup kitchen, and youth mentorship. He is active in alumni affairs at Syracuse, serving as a member of the School of Education's Board of Visitors. Greg and Sirena Allen live in Algonquin, Illinois. They have three grown children, Tamika, Damian and Monika, and four grandchildren, Arianna, Alaina, Evan and Bryce.

9

Richard Tyrone Bulls
(1951–2010)

Dick Bulls was born in Hartsville, South Carolina. The youngest of seven children, he came North with his family in 1958, settling on Buffalo's Lower West Side, a multiethnic working-class neighborhood where Native Americans, African Americans, and European Americans have lived in proximity since before the Civil War. During Bulls's teenage years, the neighborhood had a large influx of Puerto Rican immigrants and was thought to be the most ethnically diverse area in Upstate New York. "My dad was a farmer who grew up in the backwoods country down South, and he wanted us to live in a city with different kinds of people," Bulls said. Making the transition from a segregated rural school to Buffalo public schools with unusual ease, Bulls expressed an early aspiration to study chemistry. But after his father's death in 1962, his hopes of becoming the first in his family to attend college were increasingly tied to his winning an athletic scholarship.

An honor roll student at Grover Cleveland High School, Bulls was a star athlete in both baseball and football. At age 18, he had a tryout with the New York Yankees and was offered a minor league contract. He chose not to sign, hoping instead to attend college on a scholarship. A two-time Buffalo all-city fullback, he received full-ride offers from Syracuse, Holy Cross, and the University of Buffalo, and received offers of (nonathletic) academic scholarships from Case Western Reserve and the University of Georgia.

23. Richard Bulls at the Chancellor's Award Ceremony, 2006. Photo courtesy Stephen Sartori, Syracuse University.

"I chose Syracuse because it was a school I always dreamed about," he said. "I was still thinking about becoming a chemist, and I knew I could get the education there, and the football team was big time—Division I. There were other reasons too. Joe Ehrmann had played for Riverside High, maybe five miles down the road, and he was making it at Syracuse. As a kid from Buffalo, I could relate to that and I could see the way people respected him for it. What really clinched the deal was how impressed I was with the black teammates when I met them on my visit to Syracuse. They were mature, serious guys. I wanted to be around people like that."

Rocco Pirro, Syracuse's offensive line coach from 1952 to 1973, recruited Bulls. Pirro had played professional football for the original Buffalo Bills of the All-America Conference during the late 1940s, and was a well-known figure in the area, especially to the parents of recruits during the 1960s. "Rocco told me that my best shot at the pros was playing for a team like Syracuse, which had produced so many great black players," Bulls said.

When he enrolled in Syracuse, Bulls was surprised to find he was the only black freshman in the football program, and wondered how that was possible at a place that had produced so many famous black stars. He was also disturbed by the problems that the more experienced black players were facing. "I started hearing about the treatment of some of the athletes, as I got to know them. Greg Allen and Al Newton [Alif Muhammad] had experienced some of the inequities directly. I would say that a lot of my motivation to take part in the boycott developed through my kinship with the other Syracuse Eight players. I saw the injustices they suffered. It was less about my own personal experience, since it was my first year there. I saw the pain they were going through. Travel arrangements and accommodations for road games weren't fair. They didn't get the kind of tutoring that they needed. They had to make sure the classes they took were approved by the coaching staff. Some classes were discouraged and forbidden because they would take too much time away from football. That was all so disappointing to me. I was playing football to get an education, not the other way around." Bulls also remembers being let down by the way he was treated by the coaching staff after injuring his knee during freshman year. "I didn't expect to be babied or anything like that, but it didn't seem like the coaching staff cared about our well-being. When I was hurt in practice and couldn't perform, I felt like I was being discarded."

Rattled by all he had gone through during the boycott, Bulls completed the courses he was taking during the fall 1970 semester and withdrew from Syracuse. "I am proud to this day that I was part of the boycott and that I stood up for what was right," he said in 2006. "But I was just a kid back then, and all the hostility and coldness and bad feelings that we experienced from some people told me something about the world that made me want to be close by my family."

Returning home, he hoped to transfer to the University of Buffalo and start taking classes again the following fall. He had been heavily recruited by UB just two years earlier, and believed his chances were good of getting at least a partial athletic scholarship there. Those hopes vanished on January 18, 1971, when the university made a surprise announcement that it was dropping intercollegiate football. According to the *Buffalo News*, "The difficult part was the timing. There was no discussion, no warning, no chance to try to raise money to save the sport."[1]

It was still possible in those days to find a job in the banking industry without a college degree, and Bulls set his sights in that direction. "Most tellers didn't have but a high school diploma, and a lot of the banks were trying to bring on more neighborhood people at that time," he recalled. He was hired by Manufacturers and Traders Trust (now known as M & T Bank) and began working in the company's financial services division. In 1975, he accepted a job at Banker's Trust Corporation in New York City and eventually specialized in international loans. By 1980, he had risen to a supervisory position at Banker's Trust, responsible for a staff of 75. Returning to Buffalo in the 1990s, Bulls moved into the telecommunications field, serving for a decade as a credit manager and financial analyst for Northern Telecom Finance Corporation. He later worked for the Buffalo office of Advance2000, advising businesses on the purchase and maintenance of high-technology office systems.

In 2006, when the members of the Syracuse Eight were invited by Chancellor Nancy Cantor to come to campus to receive the Chancellor's Medal, Bulls was in poor health and his physician urged him not to make the trip. "I said, 'Doc, this get-together has been waiting for 35 years. No chance I'm missing it.'" He felt that way until the end of his life, leaving instructions that the pages of a magazine article about the Syracuse Eight be taped to his casket so people attending his funeral could read about the events of 1970. "This is what I want people to remember me for," he said.

Richard Bulls died of a respiratory illness on May 21, 2010. He is survived by his daughter Kelli; grandson Tariq Bell; sister Rena McIver; and brothers, Estrice and Bobby.

10

Ronald J. Womack

Ron Womack fully supported the statement of grievances by the Syracuse Eight and would have liked to join his friends and colleagues when they boycotted spring football practice in April 1970. However, that was not possible because he had been removed from the team a year earlier as retribution for stating his own grievances. He was, and has remained, so much a part of the group that he is sometimes referred to as "the ninth member" of the Syracuse Eight. "Ron was the first casualty of our common struggle," said Duane Walker. "His removal from the team was the beginning of the end of 'business as usual' for us."

A lineman who played both offense and defense in high school, Womack played freshman football at Syracuse in 1967 and joined the varsity as a defensive tackle the following year. As the 1968 season wore on, he found himself sharing his position with a player who clearly was not performing at the same level he was, and so went to see Coach Schwartzwalder about why he had not been awarded first-string status at the position. Not long after, he was placed on the injured list for a long-term condition that the coach knew of when he recruited Womack (and for which the team doctor had been treating him since his arrival on campus). Declared "unfit" for athletic competition, Womack's name remained on the injured list and he never played another minute of football for the Orange.

Forced to give up the game he loved—and his lifelong aspiration to play pro football—he forged a path to a successful career in a difficult profession as a teacher of children with emotional and behavioral disorders. "My athletic scholarship had given me access to the

24. Ron Womack, no. 67, in SU uniform, 1968.

educational system, and as long as I maintained my grades, they could not legally take that away from me," he says. "So I learned I could do something else in life besides play football." Needing at least a C average to continue receiving his scholarship benefits while on the injured list, Womack was a Dean's List student for six consecutive semesters while completing a double major in Elementary Education and Special Education for the Emotionally Disturbed at Syracuse University's School of Education. After receiving his bachelor of science degree in 1971, he pursued graduate studies in educational psychology in Minneapolis at the University of Minnesota, adding a master's degree to his credentials. Womack settled in the Twin Cities area and has been teaching English, math, and study skills to special-needs students for almost half a century.

Considering the difficulties Ron Womack faced in getting his own education, his story is as unlikely as it is inspirational:

> I was born and raised in Charleston, West Virginia, a small southern city in which most people were poor, including my family. My father, Howard Womack, was a coal miner and my mother, Catherine Womack, stayed at home and raised the ten of us—eight boys and two girls. I was the sixth child. When I was eight years-old, my father died from lung cancer. He was forty-three and had been inhaling coal-mine dust for twenty years. I was the oldest of the male children living at home, and my mother told me I was now "the man of the house." I took this very seriously, internalizing my responsibility for the well-being of my family. Two years later, my mother died of a heart attack at age forty-one. Her sister came to live with us as our guardian, but she was verbally and physically abusive. I ran away from home repeatedly. At age twelve, I was placed in a foster home. I lived with an older black couple. It was a very loving and caring foster home, but I never forgot my attachment to my real brothers and sisters.
>
> Through all this turmoil, I did well in school, in both academics and sports. I went to Stonewall Jackson High School. The school colors were red and gray—the colors of the Confederacy—and the school had just been integrated the year before I got there. Racial tensions were high, but I was on the Honor Roll for three years and I was active in sports competition all year long. I was an all-conference football player and I twice received honorable mention for the West Virginia All-State Team. As a senior, I was voted Best Lineman by my coaches and teammates. I wrestled during the winter months in the heavyweight class, and made it to the

state tournament. In the spring, I threw the shot put for the track and field team.

In 1967, just before graduation, I received the Thomas Hornor Award as Best All-Around Scholastic Athlete. This is an extremely prestigious honor in West Virginia, and I was the first African American ever to win it. The community just wasn't ready for it. The coach sent me to pick up the trophy at some trophy shop. I didn't realize it at the time, but they usually had a banquet with newspaper coverage, and the reason they had me go get it like that was so nobody would know I had won it.

Brown University offered me a full academic scholarship, which was in no way tied to football or athletics. My high school guidance counselor discouraged me from taking it, telling me I was not smart enough to succeed there. I was encouraged instead to attend West Virginia State, a traditionally black college just outside of Charleston. Some of my white school teachers who had never made it out of the hills of West Virginia were resentful of me. I remember finding out that one of them lied about sending my transcripts out. I'll never be sure if I missed other opportunities.

A football scholarship was what interested me most, and I had offers from a lot of schools, including Syracuse, Ohio State, West Virginia University, and the three major military academies: Army, Navy, and Air Force. Syracuse made a strong play for me, and did it in a very personal way. Ben Schwartzwalder was born and raised in West Virginia and he knew my high school social studies teacher, Mrs. Janie Johnson. Early in his career, he had coached at a high school where she taught. Mrs. Johnson frequently invited me to her home so that Coach Schwartzwalder could call me on the telephone to tell me about all the great opportunities that Syracuse had to offer me. She had informed him about the deaths of my parents and other details of my family life, and Schwartzwalder knew how to make use of that information in ways that could get to me. "If you come to Syracuse, I will be like a father to you," he said. Those were his exact words; I'll never forget them. Mrs. Johnson, who would serve me a steak dinner at her house, assured me that Coach Schwartzwalder was a great coach and a person who would take great care of me.

I gradually narrowed my choices down to Syracuse and the Naval Academy. I was impressed by the quality of the academic and athletic programs at both schools. I have to say that I was somewhat discouraged from attending Navy once I discovered that as a graduating second lieutenant, I'd probably be leading troops into the Vietnam War. The war had been going on and on, and nobody seemed to know exactly what the goal was or how it would end. There were a lot of people in Charleston who considered themselves very patriotic. But no matter how patriotic people are, nobody wants to risk their life when they don't know what they're risking it for.

In the spring of 1967, while I was still a high school senior, I made a campus visit to Syracuse and met Ben Schwartzwalder in person for the first time. The coach was very friendly and congenial toward me and he repeated his promise to be "like a father" to me if I came to Syracuse. Coach told me I would be a great asset to the SU football team because of my speed and my thrust power—that's the ability to push back an oncoming lineman without using hands. He also said he knew I was a good player because I was from West Virginia, his home state. He told me I could always feel free to come and talk to him about any problems I might have because "my door is always open to you" and "we West Virginia boys have got to stick together." After I accepted the Syracuse offer, Mrs. Johnson contacted some people in the Charleston Downtown Business Association and convinced them that my scholarship was a good reflection on the community and that they should make sure

I represented the city in a positive way. The store owners donated about $500 worth of clothes so I could go up to Syracuse—Syracuse, New York—looking like a rich kid, and they gave me $400 of spending money. I even had a letter from the governor as icing on the cake. Some years later, after Mrs. Johnson died, one of her relatives thought I'd be interested in seeing some letters that she wrote to Schwartzwalder. She described me as "wistful buck negro walking through the halls of the school." She wrote, "Ronnie is an excellent student . . . my only concern is that Ronnie is a real African type with nary a drop of white blood. With those heavy Negroid features, he will have to go all the way to top or else he will stay at the very bottom."

When I got to Syracuse, I initially felt close to the coach, like I had bonded with him. During my freshman and sophomore years, he was very complimentary to me about my performance on the football field, and this added to my trust in him. But during my sophomore year, I was alternating in my position with another player, a white player, and I felt strongly that my performance, both in practice and in games, had been far superior to his. I couldn't figure out why I was being taken out for him. It just didn't make sense. So I went to see the coach, just as he said I should whenever I had a problem. I told him that I felt that I should be starting, first team varsity, instead of alternating with the other player, and I told him why. Schwartzwalder agreed that I was doing a "damn good job," and he told me to be patient and that he would look into increasing my playing time. I still trusted him, and during that meeting I spoke honestly to him about my belief that other black team members were not getting a fair opportunity to play. He told me to worry about my own issues and that it was up to him and the other coaches to make those decisions. The coach thanked me kindly for coming in and sharing my concerns. It had been a really cordial conversation, so I was totally shocked the next day when Coach Bell, who was also from West Virginia, came to see me and told me that he had heard that I had been "bitching" to the head coach about the black athletes not receiving fair playing time. He said to me, "Womack, when we recruited you, I didn't think that you would turn out to be a troublemaker." That was the beginning of the end for me. At the start of spring practice in 1969, I was called in by Dr. Pelow for an examination. Based on a medical condition that I had since before I came to Syracuse, and which he knew was under control, he declared me medically ineligible to play football at Syracuse, even though I had played the entire 1968 season without any problem. Given what Coach Bell said to me, I felt this was a blatantly racist act to punish me by excluding me from the team for what I had said. I believe Coach Schwartzwalder did this to shut up an outspoken black athlete who he perceived to be a "troublemaker." Looking back, I also think that by doing this to me he was sending a message to every black player on the team. He didn't want to hear one word from any of us about our playing time or our position assignments or about the depth chart, because there was no way he was going to admit to setting up racial quotas, which was exactly what he was doing. He knew it was wrong, and so he just wasn't going to discuss it. He let us all know, "If you bring up the subject, you are gone."

Allen Sullivan, a graduate student who had been acting as a mentor and spokesman for us, felt heartbroken by what happened to me. He told me he wished I hadn't gone in to talk to the coach. I had made a political mistake. By being so up front about my concerns, I had identified myself to them as a ringleader and they decided to get rid of me. I had known Al Sullivan since my first semester and I trusted his judgment. He had helped me register after the coaches had advised me to take all gym courses, even though I told them I had no intention of majoring in phys ed. Sully explained to me that all those courses would do for me is keep me eligible to play football, but that I would never be able to graduate with them.

We had all been told that football was the one area in life where there was no discrimination because the coaches want to win and they'll always use the best player. We were young and naïve enough to believe it. Racism existed in football, just as in every other area of society. They didn't want D.J. [Dana Harrell] to play quarterback. They didn't want too many blacks on the field at the same time. They always had Spoon [Duane Walker] guard the best pass receiver, but no matter how well he did, his name was never mentioned in the press. They didn't want a team "dominated" by blacks.

Other things were happening during 1969 that were only indirectly related to football, but had a strong influence in increasing the animosity that the coach seemed to be developing toward black athletes. Most of the black football players at Syracuse, like black college students all over campus and all over the country, started growing mustaches, pork chop sideburns, beards, and large Afro hairstyles. The coach did not like any of this and he "requested" that we cut off facial hair and get short haircuts. We refused to do that, and I think that was a turning point. He started seeing us as "militants" or "black militants." It's as if disobeying him wasn't just disobeying him—it made you a political radical. I believe we were only football players to him, and he didn't see us as black college students or think about where we were in our history. We became active in various student groups that were confronting the administration about black issues, such as proposals for an African American studies program, a cultural center, and a black student union. There was nothing unusual about that. We got involved because we believed in those things. But I don't know if the coach ever considered that. He thought we were just rebelling against him.

Things heated up in February 1969, when black members of the football team joined with other Syracuse students in refusing to stand during the playing of the National Anthem at a home basketball game. The point of this was to protest racism in the football program and elsewhere on campus. Schwartzwalder threatened to suspend us from the team for our actions. Of all the students on campus, black and white, who participated in that, the black football players were probably the only ones who were threatened with consequences for exercising our right to free speech. The following month, the black athletes joined with five other black groups to form a unified organization to represent all the black students on campus. It was known as Project Spearhead. The New York Times ran an article about it with a picture that included some of us. After that, the coaches harassed us openly and labeled us as militants and troublemakers.

These increasing problems between the coaching staff and the black athletes are what led us to request the hiring of a black assistant coach. Had that been done in 1969, I believe much of the damage to the individuals involved and to the Syracuse football program could have been avoided. But instead the request was ignored until after the boycott of spring practice in 1970. I think that proves what we all believed at the time: it was necessary for black athletes to take action or we would continue to be ignored.

To fully understand what was going on with the Syracuse football team, it helps to understand what was happening nationally, and how that was reflected on campus. President Nixon's decision in May 1970, to send U.S. troops into Cambodia expanded the Vietnam War, and this brought a wave of anti-war demonstrations across the country. The Kent State University demonstration was part of this, and when four unarmed students were shot dead there by the Ohio National Guard, it prompted mayhem in Syracuse and other campuses. There was no way of knowing whether it might happen here next. Students barricaded campus roads. The Daily Orange called for a student strike and that emptied out the classrooms pretty quickly. David Ifshin, the student government president, led a sit-in at Chancellor Corbally's office. One of the demands, believe it or not, was that Syracuse University pay $100,000 to the Black Panther Defense Fund to bail Bobby Seale out of jail! Remember, the black student athletes were asking for things like tutoring and better medical care. Unfortunately, a lot of people just lumped all the students together as dangerous radicals. Needless to say, Syracuse did not bail Bobby Seale out of jail. The occupation of the chancellor's office lasted for twenty-four hours, and the demonstration ended quietly. But the administration had enough of this kind of thing and announced the cancellation of the final six weeks of classes. So all these things were happening and, in the middle of it, eight African American student athletes were accusing Coach Ben Schwartzwalder of discriminatory practices and staging a boycott of spring practice. People who were "fed up with student radicals" might not know anything about why the Syracuse Eight had refused to come to spring practice, but they knew they were against those "militant black radicals." Our actual issues got lost in the larger politics.

The black athletes had endured many broken promises and disappointments prior to 1970. We had requested a black assistant coach a year earlier and Schwartzwalder had promised to hire one. Our purpose in making this request was to get somebody on the staff who we could relate to and who was sensitive to our needs and understood our issues. When Floyd Little came to spring practice for a couple of days and Schwartzwalder told us that Little's visit had fulfilled his promise to hire a black coach, we took that as a blatant insult. The situation was made worse when an article appeared in the newspaper in which Little criticized the black players' attitudes. He hadn't talked with us and we thought he was obviously just echoing Schwartz-walder's opinions. That whole farce was the straw that broke the camel's back. We were dead serious about needing a coach we could trust and we believed the entire team would be better off. But he had treated the whole thing like a joke. It was clear that some kind of an action was necessary to get the point across.

Because of the broken promises and because we were experiencing increasing harassment from the coaching staff, we decided to approach our problems in a more organized and professional manner by putting our needs and demands in writing. We were helped in this by Allen Sullivan, who was studying for his doctorate in sociology. He had already established mentorship relationships with some of us, even before the crisis began. We also received advice and guidance from Rev. Dr. George Moody; Dr. John Johnson, a Syracuse professor who became the university's first Provost for Minority Affairs; and Norman Pinkard, a member of the Syracuse area Human Rights Commission. We owe them all our thanks, but in my estimation, Allen Sullivan provided the greatest assistance in helping to articulate the demands of the black athletes.

I had been devastated when I was unfairly declared ineligible to play in the spring of 1969, so I could easily empathize with what the Syracuse Eight players were going through in 1970 as it gradually became clear that they would not be able to rejoin the football team. I knew their hurt went deep, because my hurt went deep. I came to Syracuse believing I could one day play pro football and it was my goal to achieve that. It wasn't that I craved having riches and luxury. I had grown up in tough circumstances, and the prospect of not having to think twice about spending money on the things that my family needed and that I needed was an irresistible goal. Everything that happened in my first two years in college seemed to be taking me closer to that dream. I had excelled as a defensive nose tackle for the freshman team, and as a sophomore on the defensive line. I was able to dominate the senior offensive and defensive linemen on the varsity, some of whom were heading for the NFL (and some of whom became big stars in pro football). By the end of my sophomore year, I was confident I could play in the NFL. When I went to see Coach Schwartzwalder about why I wasn't getting the playing time I thought I should get, I had two things in mind: 1) I wanted to protect my possibility for a pro career by getting the kind of playing time NFL scouts would expect of a good prospect; and 2) the coach had repeatedly urged me to come talk to him about any problems I might be experiencing. I never anticipated the outcome that meeting brought. During the boycott of 1970, I had nothing to fear by involving myself and supporting it. For me, the damage had already been done and I was still suffering the pain. The time had come for me to do everything I could to help right these wrongs, both for the sake of the current black athletes, who were my friends, and for those who would come after us.

After promising to treat me "like a son," Coach Schwartzwalder completely ignored my needs and interests. After promising to hire a black coach, he completely ignored the interests of the black athletes as a group. With the help of Allen Sullivan and Dr. Johnson, I learned an important lesson about power, money, and politics. Ben Schwartzwalder had too much power. He was supposed to be under the regulation of the Athletic Board of Directors, but all they did was support him due to the money he generated for Syracuse through the football program. Even though the black athletes had legitimate complaints, the coach had money and power on his side. In the end, the coach had even more power than Chancellor Corbally, who was supposed to be his boss. Schwartzwalder kept his job, while Corbally left. The most ironic thing was this: Schwartzwalder demanded the right to punish the black athletes for failing to respect his position and the power that came with it, but all the while, he failed to respect the chancellor's power over him. I think the coach violated the university's institutional order in a far worse way than the black athletes did.

I was grateful to Chancellor Corbally for appointing a committee to assess the legitimacy of our complaints, and I was satisfied by their report, which confirmed the practice of institutional racism in the Athletic Department. One of the most sensitive and conciliatory things that Corbally did was to sit down with Allen Sullivan and John Johnson to establish protection, in writing, for the scholarships of the black athletes who participated in the boycott, regardless of the outcome of the crisis. Even though we were entitled to those scholarships as long as we kept our grades up, Corbally knew how Schwartzwalder operated by this time, and that it would be necessary to take special precautions. I remember during the year after I was declared medically ineligible, Ben would come up to me whenever he'd see me and threaten to snatch my scholarship and give it away to someone who deserved it. It made me feel like a targeted man. But I would just tell myself that they've already taken my football career and there's no way I'm going to let them take my education, too. The chancellor was not able to exercise his rightful power over the Athletic Department because money and politics were aligned against him. But at least he was able to make sure that the university's legal and moral obligations to the education of the black athletes were not compromised.

The coach acted like he was at war with us, and he manipulated the white players on the team to take that same attitude toward us. He got them to believe that the black players' boycott was an attack against not only the coaches and the football program, but against them. Some of the white athletes did not understand why we were complaining.

Some felt that all the athletes were being mistreated, so what was so special about us? I think the racial aspects of our mistreatment were invisible to them. They didn't have to try to convince the coaches that they really were qualified college students who were capable of taking difficult courses. They didn't have to taste the bitterness of knowing that no matter how well they performed on the field, it might never be good enough because of this other factor—the color of their skin. There were a few white athletes who understood why we had to take a stand and they secretly supported us; I say "secretly" because the coach took any disagreement with him as an attack against him, and he retaliated.

During my senior year in Syracuse, I married LaShella Sims, a high school friend from Charleston, and a month later we adopted my twelve- and thirteen-year-old brothers. They were both victims of my aunt's abuse and needed a loving home. I received my bachelor's degree in 1971, becoming the first member of the Womack family ever to graduate from college. It would be less than truthful to deny that I entertained thoughts of trying out for an NFL team. The closest I came was in 1972. I started serious training to get into shape with the idea that I might make it onto a Canadian league team and use that as a stepping stone to the NFL. But I hurt my ankle while training and I did not like the pain. Back in my playing days in high school and college, I would have simply ignored it. But I had a different life now, with different obligations to myself and others. I turned my attention back to teaching students with behavioral problems.

The loss of football and the ordeal of the boycott inspired me to greatly improve academically and professionally. My focus and my concept of self-worth shifted from my physical prowess to my intellectual prowess, and I put that to good use. I earned my master's degree in educational psychology. I even pursued a doctoral degree, completing all the requirements except for the dissertation. I suppose that's a roundabout way of saying I didn't complete my PhD, but I did continue to learn more and to advance in my field. My love of education and my desire to become better at what I do have guided me to a successful forty-year career as a Special Education Teacher of Emotionally and Behavior Disordered Students and certified Director of Special Education Licensure in the State of Minnesota. Thus, I pass on knowledge to youth, just as knowledge was passed on to me by others, including my mentor, Dr. Allen R. Sullivan, and Syracuse professors John L. Johnson, Charles Willie, George Moody, Michael Sawyer, Robert McCauley, Peter Knobloch, and West Harris. I must admit that I take special joy in teaching athletes the importance of being student athletes rather than athletes who happen to be playing sports while they're enrolled in school.

After completing work on his doctorate, Allen Sullivan went on to a distinguished career as a teacher, scholar, and professor of education. He served in administrative positions for several major school systems, as well, retiring in 2005 from his post as assistant superintendent for student development and advocacy in the Dallas Independent School District. Recalling his role in the African American football boycott at Syracuse, Sullivan said, "When I think about the Syracuse Eight, the first person I think of is Ron Womack. He had a medical issue that Schwartzwalder knew about all along, and then used as a pretext to get him off the team because he didn't like hearing Ron speaking the truth. Ron was the first to go. You might call him the 'Syracuse One'—and the Syracuse Eight followed. My family and I became very close to Ron and I was very happy to see him become an outstanding teacher in the St. Paul schools. We were all very proud of him. I look at what he and the others have achieved and I'm proud to have played a part in their lives."

A special education teacher for more than forty years, Ron Womack is a member of the faculty of Highland Park Junior High School in St. Paul Public Schools. In 2006, he was honored, along with Rosa Parks, by the district during Black History Month for his outstanding record of active citizenship leading to change. "I'm still in the business of change, but I'm changing student behavior and academic skills," Womack says. "That's my lifelong challenge." After adopting and raising his two younger brothers, William and Quinten, Womack started a family of his own with LaShella Sims. Their two children, Howard Womack and Catherine Womack, both live in Minneapolis.

11

Dana Jon "D.J." Harrell

During the late 1960s, Dana "D.J." Harrell was the only African American member of the Syracuse football team who hailed from outside the Northeast. "I grew up in an all-black community in Indianapolis," he says. "I had a loving family, everything I needed, and most of what I wanted. My parents, Kenneth and Betty Harrell, both worked in government as career civil servants. I attended Catholic schools, and even though my father was not a Catholic, he participated in the sports programs as a volunteer parent. He was a kind of unofficial athletic director at my grammar school, Holy Angels, coaching football and track, and he brought in friends to coach basketball and baseball. He put special emphasis on track, because his philosophy was, 'If you can run, you can play any sport.' Our parents taught us 'sound mind, sound body' and my entire family was athletic. My three younger sisters all ran track and my mother volunteered as a women's track coach. She was also quite a tennis player."

In 1963, Harrell enrolled in Brebeuf Jesuit High School, which had opened just a year earlier. Its founder, Father William Schmidt, envisioned the school as a germinating center of academic and athletic excellence. Unhappy with the de facto segregation that was typical of both public and Catholic schools in the Indianapolis area, Father Schmidt made a personal mission of assembling a student body that, as Harrell put it, "looked the way America looked." Harrell thrived there as a student athlete, lettering in football, basketball, and track. During his senior year, the basketball team went 17–1, and he was member of the one-mile relay team that won the Indiana state championship. But it was Harrell's performance on the football field that

25. D.J. Harrell at Chancellor's Award Ceremony, 2006. Photo courtesy Stephen Sartori, Syracuse University.

really stood out. He quarterbacked the Brebeuf Jesuit Braves to an undefeated (10–0) season in 1966. Football is a team sport, but the enormity of Harrell's personal accomplishment is highlighted by the fact that he was leading a predominantly white team during a period when there was still widespread belief that whites would reject the leadership of an African American quarterback, no matter how talented he was. "I graduated with the longest winning streak in history by a black quarterback playing for a predominantly white team," Harrell says. "I also learned at an early age that I could work with people of all races."

Harrell recalls how he landed at Brebeuf and went on to college at Syracuse:

> Jesuits have a reputation for being good businessmen, and Father Schmidt, to whom my family and I will always be indebted, was no exception. When he went looking for students who would attract attention to the school that he was

building, he didn't head for the science fair. He approached my dad at a Catholic Youth Organization championship football game. My school, Holy Angels, was an all-black team and we were playing for the CYO championship against St. Christopher's, an all-white team. It wasn't by happenstance that he showed up at this game to urge my dad and some of the other parents to consider having their kids take the entrance exam for Brebeuf. St. Christopher's beat us that day, but Father Schmidt ended up with the six best players on both squads. We all became teammates in high school and we had quite a run.

I was a sophomore in 1964, the school's first varsity football year. We were all sophomores and juniors because the school hadn't been around long enough to have any seniors yet. We got our socks knocked off; didn't win a single game. But we figured things out after that and we came back with two consecutive undefeated seasons. The year we didn't win a game, I played safety and was a backup quarterback. My junior year, I played safety, ran back kicks, and was backup quarterback again. I was first-string quarterback my senior year, and we went undefeated for the second season in a row.

Football had emerged as my ticket to a college education, but I knew that a black high school quarterback didn't have much of a chance of becoming quarterback at a predominantly white school. Indiana is Big Ten country, and I could see what was happening at those schools. Most would recruit a handful of black athletes each year, but the quarterbacks were usually converted to defensive backs, running backs, or wide receivers. There were exceptions. Michigan State, for example, won the Big Ten title in 1966 with Jimmy Raye at quarterback. But that was a rare exception.

I received scholarship offers from Syracuse, Indiana, Wisconsin, Wyoming, and a few others. I do remember one thing. All the schools that recruited me, except Syracuse, told me right up front, "We want you here, but you'll have no chance of becoming quarterback." I had my doubts about whether I'd really get a shot at it at Syracuse, but then again, there was no way to be sure. Syracuse was the school of Jimmy Brown and Ernie Davis. Maybe anything was possible. When I got to Syracuse, I was converted to a pass defender almost immediately. Let me emphasize that I was not really surprised when that happened. It was something that most schools did at the time.

I didn't know anything about the black quarterbacks who had played for Syracuse in the past, so that didn't figure in my decision. Nobody ever mentioned Bernie Custis to me when I was being recruited. Maybe they didn't want to get my hopes up too high or maybe they just didn't know who he was. It wasn't until I got to Syracuse that I found out that Custis had played there back in the late 1940s. Two of my teammates, Ed Phillips and Tony Gabriel, told me about him. Custis had coached them in high school up in Canada. In fact, Coach Schwartzwalder was able to recruit them because of his relationship with Custis. I had never heard of Avatus Stone, either. He was the other black quarterback who had gone to Syracuse. But his name only came up when the coaches warned us, "Don't be like Avatus Stone!" He had gotten in some kind of trouble for dating white women back in the 1950s.

But I had plenty of reasons for wanting to go to Syracuse, mostly having to do with the great alumni: Jimmy Brown, the greatest football player ever came from Syracuse; Ernie Davis, the Heisman winner; three-time All American Floyd Little; John Mackey, the greatest tight end to play the game; Jim Nance, Art Baker, and so on. I can remember watching Syracuse play on TV when I was kid. They would just roll over opponents—and it was the black athletes that were doing it. I was a young kid in the Midwest, and I can tell you that just the fact that it was Syracuse, New York, meant something to me. Taking all that together, I thought to myself, "If I'm at Syracuse, I'm in the best place possible." I remember my father taking me aside at one point and telling me to stop telling all these other recruiters that I wanted to go to Syracuse.

I had been a strong safety in high school and I knew how to play the position, and I got used to playing the position again during my freshman year at Syracuse. The following summer—the summer of 1968—I stayed on campus and an incident occurred that became a turning point in race relations on the football team, even though it didn't start as a racial thing. Along with some other members of the football team, I had a summer job working on the grounds crew at Archbold Stadium. One day, some of the white ballplayers were fooling and spraying each other with a garden hose; you know, horsing around. I wasn't part of it. I had just finished my lunch and I was sitting there nearby, on the side. It just so happened that I was the only black ballplayer there. Then they pulled the old trick where the hose is pointed at one guy, and he knows to duck down so the guy behind him gets it—and that's me. I didn't see it as anything racial. I just thought they were messing with me. But the aftermath of it was another story. I asked them to stop, but that just made them do it again. Then one of them walks up to me, and with the nozzle of the hose maybe two inches from me, blasts me right in the face. It escalated into a fight and, well, I whipped his ass. Then two or three others—and these were big guys, athletes, football players—came at me. So I grabbed an axe handle to defend myself. I just put my back up against the wall and said, "Okay, come get it." It hadn't started as a "let's get the black guy" thing. But in the end, it went down to everyone as a fight between one black guy and a bunch of white guys. It played out as a racial thing.

Coach Schwartzwalder called me in and he asked me why I picked up that stick. I said, "Well, you know these are big dudes, offensive linemen," and I told him that the first time I just said to them, "Come on, guys. I'm not in it." I wasn't mad or anything. I understood it was a joke. But then they did it again, and so I started resisting. And when the others tried to corner me . . . well, I wasn't going to let that happen either. Here's the problem. The coach didn't make a real effort to find out what happened. He wasn't interested in the facts. The coach's response was something like, "They're your teammates and we can't have this type of stuff going on with the team." I said, "Coach, I was just sitting there, minding my own business." But that didn't seem to matter to him.

I don't know whether the coach spoke to the white players who started the whole thing, and if he did speak to them, I don't know what he said to them. They were obviously mad at me about what happened, because they sent Tony Kyasky, the team captain, to talk to me. I think by now it had all become a question of ego for those guys, because the way people talked about it was "the one black guy had taken all of them in a fight." There was a definite split in the team about whether I was right or wrong, or they were right or wrong—and the split was along racial lines. It wasn't originally about that and it didn't have to play out that way. But instead of getting to the bottom of what happened, the coach just allowed it to develop along those lines.

Having a black coach on the staff would have been very helpful in resolving that situation. All of the black ballplayers could see that, and we made that point to Coach Schwartz-walder. The white ballplayers didn't have any interest in the "black coach" issue; most of them didn't understand why it would matter. There were other things we advocated that they knew were in their interest, but even on those issues, they felt that we shouldn't have gone outside the athletic department. That was their mentality and that was the mentality of football in those days. The relationships that players have with coaches today are very different. It's more of a business relationship now. In those days, it was like you had been recruited into the army. Believe me, football was like the military in those days. You go up there, and if the coach wants to change this or move you there, that's what you do. You obeyed orders.

It's a mistake to think that the white ballplayers, across the board, hated the black ballplayers, or anything like that. It wasn't like that at all. There were white guys we got along with. But even most of them disagreed with the boycott. I remember, during the middle of it, some of my white teammates said things to me like, "Dana, what you said was right about medical treatment and what you said was right about poor academic advisement. But you don't go outside the family." That was something they really didn't like. They believed that no matter what the problem, everything should be and could be taken care of in-house.

In our experience—in the experience of the black players this was just not true. We knew that most of the things in the football program that we wanted to change were things that were going on all over the country. But we couldn't just leave it at that. We couldn't just say, "Well this is wrong, but it's wrong everywhere." Instead, we said, "No, no, no, this is Syracuse. We can't just ignore this. Too many good things have happened here. This is the place where Ernie Davis won the Heisman. We're not going backwards. We've got to have something better." I don't mind telling you right now that I love Syracuse University, and I've always loved Syracuse University. But my answer to my white teammates in 1970 was this: "When the family is not working right, if you want to survive and you want to make things better, you've got to get help. When you can't fix things from the inside, you may have to go outside." That's where I'm coming from. I think the story of what we went through in 1970 absolutely needs to be told.

Dana Harrell did not play intercollegiate football again after the boycott. He graduated from Syracuse University with a BA in history in 1971. The recipient of a Ford Foundation fellowship, he remained at the university and earned a master's degree in public administration from the Maxwell School of Citizenship and Public Affairs. Moving to New York City, he began his life's work in the real estate industry as a leasing representative for the Port Authority of New York and New Jersey, where his responsibilities included leasing space to retailers at such facilities as the original World Trade Center complex, the Port Authority Bus Terminal in Midtown Manhattan, and LaGuardia, JFK, and Newark airports. While working for the Port Authority, he attended New York University Law School, earning a JD degree in 1979. Harrell was admitted to the bar in New York the following year.

In 1980, Harrell took a position with Equitable Real Estate Investment Management. Over the course of the next two decades, he rose to the position of senior vice president, managing a $1.3 billion portfolio of office and industrial assets in the Northeast. A sampling of his high-profile mixed-use projects for the company includes 500 Park Avenue in New York City (1984), Rowes Wharf in Boston (1987), and the Mellon Bank Center in Philadelphia (1990). When Equitable Real Estate was acquired by Lend Lease Real Estate Investments in 1997, Harrell became a principal in the new corporate structure. In 2004, he founded Harrell Associates Boston, a consulting firm providing a variety of commercial and legal services to land developers, community development corporations, investors, and other components of the real estate industry. In 2008, Massachusetts Governor Deval Patrick appointed Harrell as Deputy Commissioner for Real Estate Services in the Commonwealth's Division of Capital Asset Management.

Harrell, who lives in Milton, Massachusetts, is an adjunct faculty member at Bentley University in Waltham, where he teaches courses in the finance department. He has lectured to academic and professional audiences in a variety of settings, including the MIT Center for Real Estate and the Society of Real Estate Appraisers. Active in youth football, he has served as president of Boston Raiders Pop Warner, Inc. His wife, Michelle "Jean" Harrell, whom he met and married while the two were students at Syracuse University, is a professor of early childhood education at Roxbury Community College in Boston. Their daughter, Alva, graduated from Syracuse University in 2011.

12

Clarence "Bucky" McGill

Bucky McGill was born and raised in Binghamton, New York, about an hour's drive south of Syracuse. Binghamton's small black community, numbering less than 3 percent of the population, was mostly concentrated in the downtown area along Susquehanna Street, but McGill, the youngest of three children, grew up on the city's East Side, a few miles away. "We were the only African American family in the neighborhood," he says. "We were a single-parent household headed by mother, Hattie Jones, the hardest-working person I've ever known. She retired from her job at IBM years ago, but even now, in her nineties, she works full time and gets up to go running every day at 5:30 a.m. I'm sure I got my athletic toughness and my work ethic from the example of my mother's boundless tenacity." McGill's affectionate memory of childhood extends beyond his immediate family. He got along well with the neighborhood kids, mostly descendants of Italian and other European immigrants. His Hispanic neighbors included the Gonzalez family, whose youngest son, Bobby, became head basketball coach at Seton Hall University. McGill's mother made sure he had opportunities to socialize and find friends in the black community as well. "Race didn't seem to be an issue for me when I was growing up," he says.

McGill's status in the neighborhood as a star athlete, beginning in Little League baseball and blossoming into a multisport career at Binghamton North High School, was no doubt a factor in his easy socialization, but he resists the stereotype of a one-dimensional jock. "Athletics were fun, but I was involved in all kinds of things," he says. "In high school, I was elected vice president of the student

26. Bucky McGill with Nancy Cantor and Art Monk at Chancellor's Award Ceremony, October 2006. Photo courtesy Stephen Sartori, Syracuse University.

council and sergeant-at-arms of my senior class. I was one of only three black students in a graduating class of two hundred, but I was voted 'most popular boy.' My experiences were basically good, clean fun. There was no racism to speak of. It wasn't part of my life." Ironically, perhaps, the Binghamton of McGill's childhood hardly exists any more. The three public schools he attended—North High, East Junior High, and Thomas Edison Grammar School—have all disappeared, victims of consolidations and closings as the city's population has declined. North High's home football field, the scene of some of his fondest memories, still stands, but it's now the home field of Binghamton Central High, North's old archrival.

McGill recounts his athletic career and the events that led to the Syracuse Eight players' boycott in 1970:

> I started playing Little League baseball for Hall's Printing when I was ten, and I was a pretty good first baseman. I

still remember the thrill of going 4 for 4 and hitting two home runs in the game that won us a championship. I liked baseball, but I wasn't getting anywhere with my skills. By the time I got to high school, I was, as they say, "all field, no hit." I spent a season in centerfield for the junior varsity at North, but my batting average was so low that I decided to pursue other interests. I couldn't be without a sport in the spring, so I joined the track-and-field team in my senior year as a shot putter. I was mediocre, at best.

I did better in basketball and became captain of the North varsity as a senior. We had a great season that year. They called us the "Cinderellas" because we had limited talent, but we made up for it with lots of heart. We went all the way to the Southern Tier Conference Western Division Championship before losing to Ithaca High in overtime. At 6 foot 3, I was the shortest center in the conference. As much as I enjoyed it, my only real talent was rebounding, and that was because I loved to bump people in the paint. That will take you only so far in basketball, which according to the rule book is supposed to be a "noncontact" sport.

When it came down to it, my claim to fame—and my ticket to a college education—was football. After playing tight end on the JV, I played both offensive tackle and defensive end for the North High varsity. We went undefeated in my senior year, 1966, and won the Southern Tier Conference championship. We were a very strong team in a lot of ways. Eight of us, including me, were selected as all-conference. We were not only good football players, but, for the most part, we were even better students. Six of us received football scholarships, including Gary Farnetti, who went to Harvard, and Richard Allman, who went to Cornell. Another member of the team, Jerome Simandle, received an academic scholarship to Princeton; he became an attorney and was appointed a federal judge. They talk about Jerry as a possibility for the Supreme Court. We were all from low- to middle-income families and took great pride in our accomplishments, both in school and on the football field. I was mainly recruited by the U.S. Naval Academy, the University of Wyoming, and Syracuse. I committed to Syracuse for a number of reasons. For one thing, Jim Brown was my childhood idol and I wanted to follow in his footsteps. For another, Jim Shreve, who recruited me for Syracuse, made a positive impression on my mother, which was not an easy thing to do. And, of course, Syracuse was close to home, only sixty-five miles away from my family and friends. Everything about it seemed right for me.

I owe a lot to my coaches at North High School. They were fine men who influenced my approach to sports—and to life—in a positive way. They were the kind of coaches who considered overall development of their students as part of their job. Jim Howland, the head basketball coach, was a quiet, pensive person with a dry sense of humor. He was completely devoted to winning, without any of the negative characteristics that sometimes can go along with that. The assistant football coach, Don Klein, had a raspy low voice, and he always seemed ready to pounce on you if you made a mistake. But we didn't fear him; that wasn't his way of motivating us. We learned from him and we tried to please him by avoiding mistakes. Jim Weinman, the head football coach at North, was both a thinker and a hustler. He was always coming up with ways for us to improve our game and get the competitive edge. It's important for me to mention my high school coaches, all of whom were white, because later on, when the Syracuse Eight asked for a black coach, some people misinterpreted that as meaning we couldn't or wouldn't work with white coaches. It wasn't about that. I'd always had white coaches, and I'd gotten along fine with them and respected them. We felt we needed a black coach on the staff at Syracuse because we were being treated unfairly based on race and we believed we could trust a black coach to understand what we were going through and to speak up or advocate for us to the other coaches. When I came to Syracuse, I had high standards for what I expected of coaches, and because of Syracuse's reputation, I expected even more of the coaches. Ben Schwartzwalder represented a stark change from what I was used to. I knew that things would be different in college, but little by little I realized that it wasn't just a question of style. That's especially true in the area of character building. It's hard to look up to people as role models when they think nothing of deceiving you.

NCAA rules were different back in 1967, when I arrived in Syracuse. As freshmen at a Division I school, we were not allowed to play on the varsity. Instead, we had a separate team and we played our own "frosh" schedule. Jim Shreve, who recruited me the year before, was coach of the Syracuse freshman team. He acknowledged that I was a hard-hitter and very quick, and I became starting defensive end for the team. I felt like I was off to a good start.

The highlights of playing on the freshman team were not so much the games against freshman teams from other schools as the intra-squad practices in which the frosh defense got to scrimmage with the varsity offense. It was a big deal for us because the varsity offense had some pretty impressive players, including Larry Csonka, the fullback who had already broken rushing records at Syracuse and was on his way to a great pro career with the Miami Dolphins, and wingback Tom Coughlin, who would eventually coach the New York Giants to two Super Bowl victories. I particularly admired Tommie Coughlin because he was an Academic All-American, and I knew how tough it was to get those kind of grades while playing D-I football. As defensive end, I would line up head-to-head with him. Most of the time, Tommie would go in motion before the snap, and the hand-off went to Larry. It was easy to hit Larry because he tended to run straight ahead. But knocking him off his feet was a whole other problem. He was able to lean his body so far forward while running that all his force was concentrated low to the ground, making it very tough to upend him. But I was tackling Larry Csonka and the other varsity backs. I didn't feel like a high school kid anymore; I felt like I was playing big-time college football.

Ron Womack, Duane Walker, and D.J. Harrell were with me on the freshman defense in 1967 and we all looked forward to those scrimmages with the varsity. It brought out the best in us; we all just seemed to shine. We liked going up against the top players because we liked being challenged and we knew it was a way for us to get better. I had a pretty idealistic view of what it meant to be a college football player. When I saw someone perform in a superior way, I respected him for it and thought I could expect the same.

But I was learning that it didn't always go that way. For example, a reporter for the Binghamton Press, my hometown paper, attended practice and wrote this about me in the Sunday sports section: " . . . former North High defensive end Bucky McGill made a lasting impression in his first . . . scrimmage against the varsity. The agile 210-pounder shifted past an initial line block and threw a crashing forearm that mowed down the blocking back who happened to be the 230-pound Orange captain and All-American candidate Larry Csonka." I was just a freshman and Larry hardly knew me. Up to that point, he seemed friendly enough, but after the article came out, Larry gave me the distinct feeling that he did not care for me. I don't think it was a racial thing, but it just wasn't the way I thought teammates should react to each other. Maybe it just shows how green I was, but I felt disappointed. Looking back, that was nothing compared to the kind of let-downs I would experience while playing for the varsity over the next two years.

I began to see indications of racial problems in the football program after joining the varsity as a sophomore in the fall of 1968. When I returned from summer vacation, my black teammates told me the story of how a group of four white players had attacked D.J. while working on the grounds crew in Archbold Stadium. In my experience, fist fights and flare-ups of that type between teammates were a common occurrence, but it was also common for the guys who were fighting to become friends after it was over. I can remember getting into a fight back in middle school with a white classmate, Lawrence Brown. It was a pretty tough fight, nonracial in nature, and afterward we put it behind us and became friends "forever." The full impact of that incident reached me when Lawrence was killed in Vietnam, and I felt the pain of his loss. I had nothing in my background to prepare me for a violent racial situation like the one D.J. had faced.

Another indication of possible racial problems on the football team was the way D.J. was treated concerning his playing position. D.J. played safety in the pass defense, but as I got to know him, I learned that he had been a highly successful high school quarterback in Indianapolis. Now that we were both on the varsity, it was clear that he would never get any kind of fair chance to compete for that position. To me, that was racial bias, pure and simple. I believe the recruiters and the coaching staff intentionally misled D.J. about his chances of playing quarterback at Syracuse. As D.J. has said, at least the other schools that were recruiting him told him flat out that he wouldn't get a shot at quarterback. It's a pretty cold thing to lead a kid on about something like that when he's making a decision about his career. In retrospect, I know that college recruiters often make false promises to high school kids. This is an unfortunate part of college athletics. But there was an undeniable racial aspect

in D.J.'s case. Quarterback is a leadership position on a football team and in the late 1960s, even with many teams now
integrated, there was a widespread racist belief that blacks
were not capable of that kind of leadership. D.J. had proved
his leadership ability by quarterbacking a racially integrated
high school team to a 10–0 record. Refusing to even give
him a chance to show what he could do as quarterback was
unfair to him and unfair to the team.

A third indicator of racial bias was the personal attitude
that the coaching staff showed toward me and other African
American students. They warned us not to date white girls
at Syracuse and they told us again and again not to emulate
Avatus Stone, an alum who dated white co-eds back in the
early 1950s, maybe fifteen years before any of us came to
Syracuse. I think this was especially painful to me, because
I had grown up in a multiracial family. Were they telling me
that something was wrong with my family? Beyond that, I
was from Binghamton, New York, an hour down the road.
Interracial dating was never an issue there. Why was it such
a big issue here? What were they implying in these warn-
ings? Were they threatening to take away my scholarship
based on who I dated? And who the hell was Avatus Stone,
and what did he have to do with me? These questions made
me more aware—and more wary—of my environment as I
began to play for the varsity. I lost a certain innocence about
the relationship of sports and race. I realized that, yes, Jim
Brown and Ernie Davis had gone to school and played football here, but this was not "the promised land" I had imagined. Somebody needed to tell Ben that it wasn't the 1950s
anymore, but nobody could tell Ben anything.

As our awareness grew, we realized there was no one for
us to turn to in the athletic department, and so we depended
more and more on each other for support. In that sense,
we became the Syracuse Eight because we had to. Intense
friendships grew out of our shared adversity, and I consider

all of those who participated in the boycott to be my lifelong friends.

I was particularly close with John Willie Godbolt, and I cannot forget the life-changing effect that the boycott and the events surrounding it had on him. I first met John in 1967. We were assigned as freshman roommates and continued to room together throughout our college football careers. He was not like anyone I knew up to that point in my life. He was a polished young black man, always neatly dressed, shoes shined, hair trimmed, and so on. He constantly checked his face in the mirror, and was always fixing his clothes or adjusting his look in one way or another. He wasn't vain or conceited, just always very conscious of his appearance, which most people found striking. He was about 6-foot 1 and 205 pounds. His upper body was chiseled, and his thighs and buttocks were exceptionally large. He ran in fast choppy strides with low knee action, and was capable of extremely quick cuts in either direction. He could stop and start on a dime. Along with Greg Allen, John had the best sprint times on the entire team.

John was a striking person in other ways too. He had a lighthearted spirit which expressed itself in his person-ality. I remember this peculiar high-pitched laugh he had. You'd hear it whenever he won at anything. It didn't matter what—a sprint, slap-boxing, an eating contest, you name it. In tackling-and-blocking drills, Ron Womack and I were often faced with the challenge of beating a blocker to get to John and tackle him. John's remarkable ability to make quick, sharp cuts in a very small space made taking him off his feet very difficult. He'd do a couple of his 90-degree cuts and all we could tackle was air while listening to that high-pitched laugh trail off in the distance. I remember one time when Ron did manage to get his hands on John during one of those drills. Ron hit him really hard and brought him down. John responded almost immediately with one of his rhymes, which he composed in the style of Bundini Brown, Muhammad Ali's trainer: "Ron's short and squatty, and doesn't love nobody."

John took real interest in the people around him, and I appreciated him very much for the interest he showed in me. If something was wrong, he could see it in my face, and he wanted to do something to help, even if it meant self-sacrifice. John brought all these positive traits with him from Connecticut in 1967, and it was so sad to see him so drastically changed by 1970.

I tearfully remember the days leading up to the opening of the 1968 football season. We were scheduled to play Michigan State in East Lansing on Saturday, but when the travel list was posted on Thursday, my name wasn't on it. I would not be making the trip. It hit me like a punch in the gut. I left the locker room and cried all night. The team was set to leave for the airport early Friday morning. As John prepared to head out, I pretended to be asleep. The sun wasn't up yet and our dormitory room was still dark. As John was about to leave, he said to me, "I'm sorry," and then shut the door behind him. I cried some more. As soon as I could, I called my girlfriend in Binghamton and asked her to come to Syracuse. I took a hotel room and hid there with her until the football team returned. That was a highly emotional event and I'm thankful it was the only time that it happened to me. I made all future travel squads and started at left defensive end all of my junior year. But I never forgot that morning. I had never heard a man tell another man "I'm sorry," and it had special impact on me during that low point in my self-esteem. By expressing his empathy for me, John showed me he had reached a higher level of maturity than anyone I knew of my own age. Like me, he had grown up without a father, but he hadn't let that stop him from becoming an honorable and sensitive man. I promised myself I'd get there, too.

I always had the feeling that Ben didn't like John, and I was not sure why until I heard Ben say that John reminded him of Jim Brown. That may sound like a paradox. Why would a football coach dislike a player who reminds him of one of the greatest football players ever? The context for Ben's comment was important. He had been urging John to run through tacklers (in the style of Larry Csonka) rather than around tacklers (in the style of, say, Gayle Sayers). If you had ever seen John run with the ball, you'd know that by making this suggestion, Ben was attempting to change John in a fundamental way. I realized that what Ben didn't like about Jim Brown and John Godbolt was that while both wanted to learn from the coach, neither would allow Ben to tamper with what they knew were their core natural talents. John knew he was at his best when he was evasive, avoiding collisions rather than creating them. To tell him to do it the other way was like telling him to stop being John.

During an intrasquad scrimmage in the fall of 1969, Tommy Meyers, who later played for the New Orleans Saints, tackled John, injuring John's knee so badly that he had to leave the field. I remember the play. It was a wide-right pitchout. John took the pitch and tried to run right through Tommy. To do that successfully, John should have run low. But he never ran low; it wasn't his style. As a result, his legs were completely vulnerable and Tommy made the logical play. We—the black members of the team who would become the Syracuse Eight—witnessed this debacle and wondered why John hadn't side-stepped the tackler, as we had seen him do so many times in similar situations. Later that day, when we spoke to John, he confirmed our suspicions. He was trying to satisfy Ben by doing it Ben's way. I took it as a sign that John's spirit was being broken. To understand how things had come to that, it's necessary to look at an earlier incident that was a pivotal moment for all us.

In October of 1969, a few weeks prior to John's injury, we had traveled to Madison for a game with the University of Wisconsin Badgers. I think Wisconsin was ninth in the polls that week and we were tenth. It was a memorable game for a number of reasons. Ben broke his rule of not playing more than two blacks at the same time on offense because of injuries to white players. John Godbolt, Greg Allen, and Alif Muhammad played together in the backfield for the first time—and we won big. It was a raucous game that included an all-out fourth-quarter brawl between the two squads, with dozens of football players going at it. We were wearing special Orange helmets that season with the number 100 emblazoned on a blue football to commemorate the centennial anniversary of Syracuse University, and helmets figured prominently in the fight. Our teammate Tom Smith, an African American senior who played on the offensive line, was hit in the head with one and had to keep an ice pack on the huge bump he had during the flight back to Syracuse. I'm happy to say that Tom survived the blow and eventually became a Superior Court Judge in New Jersey. Joe Ehrmann lost his helmet during the fight, but got it back forty years later, sender unknown, when it arrived at his office in a UPS box. That was my first experience in a brawl where the benches were emptied in the middle of a game, and I have to admit, despite the violence and injuries, it was big fun for a nineteen-year-old kid to be involved in a melee like that. But the most memorable thing that happened that day occurred after both the fight and the game were over.

The brothers on the Syracuse football team had reason to be happy that day, and we couldn't hold back our joy. We had witnessed three blacks in the same backfield playing most of the game—something we did not think we would ever see—and we won the game 43–7. It was the most points Syracuse had scored in a game in more than two years. John Willie had rushed for two touchdowns, Al for one, and Greg had gone 63 yards to take one in. During this jubilant moment, as we were walking off the field together, Ben comes over to John and says, "Don't be too happy. It's a short walk from the parlor to the outhouse." John's body language just went limp. I'd heard Ben use that line before, but all I could do was wonder why Ben would say such harsh and hurtful words at a time like that. We had just won an important game that would move us up in the national rankings. We had won the game Ben's way—with an overpowering running game. Didn't Ben take any satisfaction or pride in that? Or was the race quota more important to him than the success of the Syracuse football team? If there was any doubt, the answer came soon enough. The following week, John and Greg both saw their names drop down on the depth chart, as if the Wisconsin blowout had never happened. By doing this, Ben had placed John in a desperate situation. John had so much riding on his football talent. He had performed at his peak, but it was to no avail. Ben's negative reaction to the Wisconsin victory indicated that there was nothing John could do to get a fair shake from Ben, the one person who held the most power over his chances of playing pro football.

Despite all this, I continued to concentrate on my game and improve as a defensive end. During the 1969 season, not one opposing player ran around my left end all season long. In the Syracuse–Penn State game that year, I made key blocks that would spring Greg for his record-breaking punt return yardage. Some say that the 1969 Penn State, which went 11–0, was Joe Paterno's best. It had such great future NFL stars as Franco Harris (fullback, Pittsburgh Steelers), Lydell Mitchell (halfback, Baltimore Colts), Mike Reid (defensive tackle, Cincinnati Bengals), and Jack Ham (linebacker, Pittsburgh Steelers). We were beating Penn State 14–0 and we had the ball with about three minutes left in the game. Unfortunately, we lost the game 15–14 due to fumbles. It was a disappointing loss, but I took pride in my performance. After the game, I briefly met Franco and Lydell outside Archbold Stadium, before they boarded their bus back to Penn State. They complimented me on my football skills and confirmed that it was part of their game plan not to run towards my defensive side, which also included Joe Ehrmann at defensive tackle. After hearing that from two of the best college players in the country, I was sure I was headed for the NFL. I was even written up in the New York Times that day: "On defense, Bucky McGill . . . played a fine game for Syracuse."

One time I accompanied John on a visit to his home in Bridgeport, Connecticut. He lived in Father Panik Village, a crime-ridden, poverty-stricken public housing project. I hadn't grown up rich, but I'd never seen anything like that place. There was broken glass underfoot everywhere you walked. I was amazed and fascinated by what I learned about John's life on that short trip. Although still a teenager, he was the patriarch of his family. All the members of the family, immediate and extended, came to him for advice and decision-making. Nothing was done without his approval. Back in Syracuse, he was a college student and a member of the football team, living like the rest of us. But he had a whole other life in Bridgeport, including two daughters, Lorraine and Sabrina, and all kinds of people depending on him for things. He was an impressive man with adult responsibilities, making adult decisions. I was just a year younger than him, but I was still a kid who had never experienced anything like that kind of accountability. I have always wondered what happened to John's daughters. I hope that they will read this book and know how much their father loved them. He wanted to give them everything a pro football career would make possible. It didn't happen, and the stress and psychological damage he experienced robbed him of his concept of fatherhood. John had the talent to play in the NFL and was doing everything necessary to get there. But when he was systematically robbed of the opportunity to succeed, it was more than he could cope with. Unfortunately, like many college football players, he did not plan any career options outside of football. When the promise of pro football fell apart, he didn't know what to do. There's a lesson in John's story for all young athletes: Develop every talent and skill you have. The thing you love most may not work out—and that may be through no fault of your own. For all the toughness it takes to be an athlete, anything from an unexpected injury to a hostile coach can force you out of the game. You've got to be prepared to achieve success in another way.

As his football dreams began to wither away, John was transformed right in front of my eyes. He became a recluse. His speech became slurred. He began to mumble and to laugh spontaneously at what appeared to be nothing. He repeated phrases that didn't seem to make any sense. He had always looked so sharp, but now he began to appear unkempt. He started missing classes. He would stay in the dorm room with the shades drawn, sometimes sleeping all day. I had never heard of "clinical depression" at that point in my life, but I'm sure he was suffering from it. I wasn't the only one who noticed his emotional and mental deterioration. We, the Syracuse Eight, were always serious about our schoolwork and the boycott underlined more than ever the importance of getting our educations. John's faltering classroom attendance worried us and worried all his friends. We knew he couldn't continue in school this way much longer. He had always been there for the people around him, and now we all wanted to help him. There just didn't seem to be anything we could do.

It has always puzzled me—and disappointed me—that so many of Ben's former white players and coaches will not admit to Ben's flaws, to this very day. Anyone who spent time with Ben knew, for example, that racial and ethnic slurs were basic to his vocabulary. I remember how Ben liked to tell his World War II stories to the players, usually on the Friday night before an away game. He told those stories to all the players during the years I was on the varsity, and he would continuously use terms like "Polocks," "Krauts," and "dirty Japs." It was just basic to his vocabulary. Maybe if that was all there was to it, I could understand their position. But I don't see how they can overlook Ben's actions toward us. No one forced Ben to place a quota on black players, especially during the late 1960s, when other Northern schools were scrapping quotas and segregated Southern schools were admitting blacks for the first time. Those who deny that a quota even existed cannot explain why Ben broke up the backfield that gave the team its best offensive performance in two years, and instead went back to a lineup that never once, before or after, scored even half the points that John Godbolt, Greg Allen, and Alif Muhammad put on the board that day in Madison, Wisconsin. If nobody could make Ben's diehard "fans" admit there was a quota back then, even as it was happening right before their eyes, maybe it's not so strange that nobody can convince them of it now. People sometimes remember things the way they want them to be.

I was shocked in 2012, forty-two years after the boycott, when I was shown a petition signed by all but four of the white players on the team demanding that none of the Syracuse Eight be allowed to return to the football team. While it has come out that many of them were pressured by the coaches to sign that document, I still feel betrayed by some guys who I thought of as friends. Even if those players who considered issues such as ending racial restrictions on positions and hiring a black coach to be "black issues," they should have at least stood with us on the medical care issue. What member of that team, white or black, would deny that medical care was poor? None of us knew at the time that the team doctor had no background in orthopedics or any other area related to contact sports, but everyone did know that Dr. Pelow was not the man to see if you got hurt. When new players joined the program, the upperclassmen told them that right away. Those who didn't take that advice found out the hard way. It is my current understanding that Pelow was schooled as a gynecologist and that Ben hired him because the two played golf together.

And what about academic counseling? I was a full-time student at Syracuse University, majoring in history and minoring in math, and my academic advisor was Joe Szombathy, an assistant football coach whose specialty was defending against the run. Believe it or not, here's what I had to do in college in order to make sure that I was keeping up with the requirements to graduate in my major: I would print the courses in pencil that I was told to take by the coach on a form that the coach, as my "academic advisor," had to sign. After getting his signature, I would erase these courses and fill in the courses my major required in ink, and then turn the form in at the registrar's office. During my sophomore year, after officially declaring as a history major, the courses required by my major were set automatically and the advisor could not alter the form to make me register for irrelevant courses. These are not wild accusations or paranoid fantasies. These were the facts for African American football players and, I've been told, for some white players too during this period. By making all these conditions public, we demonstrated our commitment to improving the athletic department in ways that would benefit all student athletes.

In September 1970, D.J. and I were asked by the other members of the Syracuse Eight to go to Houston for the opening game of the football season against the University of Houston. Our task was to scout the team's first game without us. Houston had some great offensive stars, such as running back Robert Newhouse, tight end Riley Odoms, and wide receiver Elmo Wright, and I had been looking forward to going up against players of that caliber until it became clear that Ben was not going to let that happen. D.J. and I attended the game, which was played in the Houston Astrodome. Spoon Walker always covered the opposing team's best receiver, and there was nobody to adequately take his place. Syracuse lost big that day. D.J. and I had bought seats that were right above the visiting team exit, and as our former teammates and coaches passed by underneath, they looked up our way and glared at us. We glared right back. Years later, I learned that our presence at the Astrodome led Ben to believe that we were being financed by some "black militant" group because, he figured, how else could we afford to make the trip to Houston from Syracuse? If Ben had asked me, I would have gladly told him the answer to that question. We borrowed the money from Henry Ben. Henry and his brother, Roy, owned Ben's Kitchen, a soulfood restaurant in Syracuse that was friendly territory for the Syracuse Eight. D.J. and Al both worked there and all of us ate there regularly. Ben's restaurant was an important link in the loving bond we developed with the local African American community in Syracuse. They treated us like family and supported us every inch of the way. Henry Ben loved us so much that he displayed a big picture of six of the Syracuse Eight in football uniforms in his restaurant for more than fifteen years.

The home opener against the University of Kansas was set for the week after the Houston game. By this time, I was coming to grips for the first time with the reality that I probably would not play college football again. It was a bitter blow, but I took some satisfaction in that I had accomplished two things: I had stood up for what was right and I was going to complete my education. If I had chosen to accept the athletic scholarship offered to me by the University of Wyoming, I probably wouldn't have been able to do both.

When fourteen African American players told the coach they intended to wear black arm bands in a game against Brigham Young University to protest the racist policies of the Mormon Church, they were not only thrown off the football team, they were thrown out of school. Those Wyoming football players were ousted from school on October 18, 1969, the same day as the Penn State–Syracuse game that was such a big day for me.

After graduation in the spring of 1971, I still believed I had a chance to play pro football. With the help of Jim Brown, Pat Summerall, and John Wooten, I made contact with the New England Patriots and signed an agreement to participate in their summer rookie camp. What I didn't know was that the Syracuse Eight controversy wasn't over. It was still raging on in the mind of Ben Schwartzwalder. He had gotten his way and kept us from playing for Syracuse after the boycott, and he had kept his job despite the report of the Chancellor's Committee on Racism. But it wasn't enough for him. He was one of football's grand old men, and he let it be known to the pro football world that the Syracuse Eight were to be treated as outcasts. When I got to the New England rookie camp, I was asked to try out as a linebacker, even though my position was defensive end. I did not know linebacker terminology, and could not understand where I was supposed to go and what I was supposed to be doing. Even though I had never asked for a tryout as a linebacker, they told me they felt my conversion to linebacker would take too long and said goodbye. But I wasn't ready to give up yet. Alif, Duane, and I played semi-pro football for a couple of seasons with the Triple City Jets, a team based in my hometown, Binghamton. The TC Jets had a working agreement with the New York Jets, which guaranteed TC players a tryout with the NFL team. When we arrived at the Jets' camp at Hofstra University out on Long Island, all the players who were scheduled to try out lined up and Head Coach

Weeb Ewbank called out the names. When he got to us, he said, "Aren't you the boys from Syracuse who caused all the trouble?" We went through the drills that day, but the coaches didn't even bother to write down our times. It was their way of letting us know that we were just going through the motions. The time had come for me to put football aside. I moved to Washington, DC, and began graduate work at Howard University.

I would be remiss if I did not thank the African American students of Syracuse University and our brothers and sisters in the Syracuse black community for their assistance, support, and advocacy during the trying times of the boycott. Without the kindness they showed us and the many favors they did for us, our efforts might have drained us of all energy and sanity. I also want to express my appreciation for the late Dr. John Corbally. As university chancellor during the boycott, he didn't always side with us, but he treated us with the respect that we were denied by the athletic department, and he made sure we were given the opportunity to finish our studies and graduate without financial or political pressures. I also must thank Syracuse University's Chancellor Nancy Cantor, for recognizing us, reconciling with us, and allowing us to tell our story. Ours is one of the many true stories of athletics, politics, and race in America that older black athletes must tell so that all young athletes can benefit from hearing.

Bucky McGill graduated from Syracuse University with a bachelor's degree in history. He also holds a master's degree, received in 1975, from Howard University's School of City and Regional Planning. He has worked for the Commonwealth of Virginia's Department of Juvenile Justice for more than thirty years, joining the department as a classification and compensation manager, and serving today as Workforce Transition Coordinator, responsible for the transition of youthful offenders into employment, training and/or school upon their release. His lifelong commitment to at-risk youth in Virginia includes service on a wide range of committees, commissions, and councils. He is an usher and fundraiser for the Holy Rosary Catholic Church and maintains his attachment to sports by coaching boys basketball at Benedictine College Preparatory High School in Richmond, where he lives with his wife, Evelyn. They have two grown sons, Askia and Evan, and a grandson, Zahkee.

13

Abdullah Alif Muhammad

Abdullah Alif Muhammad, so named since his conversion to Islam in 1975, was born Al Newton Jr. in 1949 at the former Chelsea Naval Hospital, near the mouth of the Mystic River overlooking Boston Harbor. His mother, Georgiana S. Reid, was from Portsmouth, New Hampshire, a descendant of one of the first African American families to settle in the town. "When I'm asked where my family is from and I say, 'New Hampshire,' people often say to me, 'Oh, come on, man, where are you *really* from?'" Muhammad says. "They expect black people to come from the South, and my family background is partially from the South—my father was born in Malone, Texas—but my mother and grandmother were both born in New Hampshire." While working at the Portsmouth Naval Shipyard in the late 1940s, Georgiana Reid met and married A. L. Newton Sr., a naval chief petty officer who had been decorated for his service in combat on a submarine in the Pacific during World War II. The couple had two sons, Al Jr. and Robert, but their marriage ended in divorce when both children were young. "After my parents separated, my father relocated to New London, Connecticut, near the Groton submarine base, and he remained a part of my life," Muhammad says. "My brother and I moved with my mother to her family's home in Portsmouth. The household was very matriarchal, run by my grandmother, mother, and aunts. I was raised Baptist." In 1961, Georgiana Reid took a job in Boston and moved there with her sons.

Academically and athletically gifted, Muhammad won acceptance to the Boston Latin School, one of the nation's premier public schools, but was forced to withdraw when his mother's remarriage

27. Al Newton, Jr. (Abdullah Alif Muhammad),
no. 39, in SU uniform, 1969.

resulted in the family moving to a home outside the city limits. "I could have gone back to Boston Latin, but since we now lived in Cambridge, I would have had to pay tuition to go there, and that was out of the question," he says. Faced with choices of which high school to attend in Cambridge, he was urged by Mike Jarvis, then a student at Northeastern University (and later a nationally prominent college basketball coach), to attend Rindge Technical School, Jarvis's alma mater, even though Rindge was mainly a technical vocational school with only a small "college-bound" cohort.[1] "Mike told me I would be valued at Rindge and that I would get all the attention I needed as a student," he says. "His argument was, 'It's better to be a big fish in a small pond than a fish swimming in an ocean because nobody will take you for granted.'"

Following Jarvis's advice, Muhammad enrolled in Rindge and thrived. A straight-A student with a promising talent for mathematics, he served as class president each of his four years and was inducted into the National Honor Society. His academic and social achievements won him recognition from organizations across the city and across ethnic lines, including the Jewish War Veterans Award for Brotherhood and a scholarship from the Catholic Youth Organization. In sports, he captained Rindge's varsity football team (playing fullback on offense, linebacker on defense) and its baseball team (playing catcher and outfielder). He also competed in track and field (short-distance sprints and shot put). As a senior, he received the Walter Brennan Award as Rindge's outstanding scholar-athlete in 1966.[2] "I was the first in my family to graduate from high school, and every effort was made to prepare me for college," he recalls. "I participated in a program at Tufts University which was designed to prepare working-class kids to fit in at college. I internalized this as a responsibility. I even remember getting a part-time job on Friday nights as a way of keeping out of trouble on the weekends."

An ideal candidate for admission to college at a time of expanding opportunities for African American students, he received inquiries and offers from Princeton, Columbia, Yale, Tufts, Boston College, Holy Cross, the U.S. Naval Academy, and Syracuse. "Harvard was interested, but even though I was a National Merit Scholarship finalist, they wanted me to take a year at Deerfield Academy before enrolling," he explains. "Deep down, my first choice might have been MIT Ever since I was a kid, my Uncle Asa, a great storyteller who had a way with words, had somehow put it in my head that I was going to become a civil engineer. 'Build bridges!' he used to say, and of course MIT was the place for that. The problem with MIT was that they didn't have a football team or football scholarships."

Muhammad chose Syracuse for a number of reasons. Academically, the university offered an unusual program that gave students an opportunity to complete two bachelor's degrees in a five-year period, one in engineering and one in a liberal arts subject of their choice.

Muhammad describes his decision to attend Syracuse University, his experience there, and the path he followed when it became clear that his future would not include a professional football career:

> That five-year program was a big part of the attraction, but I was also moved by my perception of Syracuse as a black athlete's heaven. We all know the famous names on the list: Jim Brown, Ernie Davis, Jim Nance, John Mackey, Floyd Little. My nickname was "Big Al" in those days, and I used to think, "Maybe Big Al belongs on that list, too." I remember meeting Floyd Little for the first time at an awards ceremony in Boston. He greeted me by saying, "Big Al, how are you?" Wow, I couldn't believe it. How did Floyd Little know my nickname? Amazing! I remember something that happened on my first campus visit that also affected my decision. I was taken over to a dorm to meet some of the student athletes, and when I got to Dave Johnson's room, he was studying calculus. Calculus! Seeing him with that calculus textbook was like a dream come true. I also remember Dave saying to me, "Come to Syracuse not because of us or anything we say about the place, but because you want to come." That was straight talk and I liked it.
>
> Freshman year is a time of adjustment for most students, and that's exactly what it was for me. I had a lot to adjust to: college football, college classes, being away from home, and all the freedoms and responsibilities of college life. With so many new things to deal with, it wasn't always easy for me to fully understand what was going on around me or to judge things clearly in terms of right and wrong. Some aspects of the football program seemed wrong to me, but then I'd think, "Maybe this is just the way things are done in college." For example, it didn't seem right to me that so many guys who had come here were being reassigned to

different positions before they even had a chance to compete for the positions that had won them their scholarships. None of the recruiters had ever mentioned anything like that. I kept wondering why we had four fullbacks. I asked the coaches about it and they told me it was a good thing. If I had gone to Notre Dame, they said, I would have had eight fullbacks to deal with. Was that really true? College football was exciting, but there was something that made me worry about the way things were done.

There was nothing worrisome about meeting new roommates and making new friends, some of whom became my lifelong friends and members of my extended family. I went home with people for weekends and holidays and I got to travel the country to places I'd never been to before: Binghamton, Bridgeport, Brooklyn, Harlem, the Bronx, Indianapolis, and Charleston, West Virginia. It wasn't exactly the grand tour of Europe, but these were exotic places to me. With the friends I made, I was exposed to all kinds of new ideas and culture. I discovered the power of diversity: every new perception becomes a new resource for understanding something else. I did things I'd never done before. We—the guys who became the Syracuse Eight— did more than just play football together. We collaborated together on all kinds of things. We produced a talent show, The Overdose, and it was a powerful and desperately needed social event for people of color on the Syracuse campus. We created the Ernie Davis Memorial Basketball Tournament. Our team, the United Society Team, consisted of athletes and artists. We were responsible for organizing and founding the African American Cultural Center. I know that today Syracuse students are involved in projects all over the city, but back then off-campus activities were rare and they were almost considered taboo. I got involved in something called Project 70, which gave me an opportunity to tutor and mentor youth in the inner city. It was my first experience with teaching, which eventually became an important part of my life, and it opened up all kinds of doors to community folks. The older sisters who worked in the university dining halls saw what we were doing in the community and they began to invite us to Sunday dinners in their homes. This was more than a nice gesture, as the dining halls didn't serve dinner on Sundays and we were expected to eat out. We were students and money was tight, and when we did go to restaurants in Syracuse, we didn't always know whether we would be served. We discovered one restaurant where we were always welcome: Ben's Kitchen, a 24/7 soul food joint. I worked there for a time. It was more than a restaurant for us and for the black community in Syracuse.

I remember returning to school in the fall of 1969, my junior year. We had intense preseason practices—two a day, morning and afternoon—where you just eat, breathe, and sleep football. The black players, including me, had participated in a student protest that winter at a home basketball game, and I was told we were going to a have a team meeting to discuss racial issues on the SU football team. Sitting there at the meeting, I was singled out by Coach Ben: "Big Al, do we have any racial problems on this team?" Mind you, the coach had done this before. This seemed to be his MO. The star black athlete is asked that question in front of the team and he responds, "I don't have a problem, coach!" Naturally, the coach concludes out loud, there is no problem, and so we get back to football. This was done to show the other black players that if they thought they were experiencing some kind of race problem, it was just inside their heads. But that was not going to happen again, not this day, not this time, not with me! When Ben asked the question, I responded, "Yes, coach. We do have problems. We feel we need a black coach on the team to deal with our issues and concerns."

I have vivid flashbacks of certain things the coaches said to us that helped push us to finally take action in the spring of 1970:

"On our team you're a football player first, and black, Negro, or anything else you want to be, second." If that was true, why were we treated differently from the white players in terms of what positions we could play and how much game time we were given? If the white coaches couldn't see the contradiction in that, we needed a black coach who could.

"Remember: It's a short walk from the parlor to the outhouse." This was a mean-spirited remark that was reserved for black players who had achieved something on the football field. It was a way of telling us that merit didn't count and there was nothing we could do that would improve our situation. If the coaches didn't understand that singling out black players that way was a form of psychological cruelty, then we needed a black coach who could point that out to them.

"Don't be like Avatus Stone!" At first, I didn't even know who that was. When I found out that he had been on the team years ago and was supposed to be some kind of womanizer who got into all kinds of trouble, I realized that they had turned this guy into some kind of evil folklore figure as a way of warning us that we had to follow their rules in how we conducted our social lives, even if what we were doing was perfectly legal and none of their business. They didn't explain who Avatus Stone was, so we would ask about him and hear all kinds of exaggerated stories of terrible things he had done and how this or that had happened to him as a result. When I later found out that his big "crime" was dating white women, and that he had graduated from Syracuse and played pro ball in the Canadian league, it made me even angrier to think of how they had taken an alum and turned him into a stereotype as a way of scaring us to exert more control over us. If the white coaches couldn't speak straightforwardly to us about issues of personal conduct, maybe a black coach could.

"You can't take an honors calculus class—you're a football player!" When they told me that and advised me, instead, to take Techniques of Basketball in summer school, did they know they were damaging my chances for graduating? Did they know they were damaging my development as a person? Did they know they were disrespecting me as an individual? If they didn't see that, maybe a black coach would.

In the spring of 1970, Marvin Gaye was risking his career at Motown by recording "What's Going On?" instead of the formula pop songs that had made him famous, and we went to spring football practice expecting to see the African American coach we had been promised. There he was—Floyd Little. And three days later, there he wasn't. Gone. Another broken promise. Another slap in the face. Disrespected again. That was the last straw. It was time for us to find out "what's going on." We had to do something, but what could we do that could not be ignored? How could we stand together on principle for justice and equality? Our answer: the football boycott of 1970.

Instead of responding to the real problems we brought up—including some issues that affected the white players too—they played the race card, turning what we did into a black versus white thing. That was really deceptive and wrong! We had functioned well as a team until that point, but instead of building on that, they made it impossible to continue together by pitting the white players against us. Ben seemed to think that he was strengthening the team by ignoring these problems and by ostracizing anyone who wouldn't ignore them. But the opposite was true. He weakened the team by peeling us away from the other players and turning us into enemies. If Ben had taken the need for a black coach seriously, the boycott probably would have been avoided and the 1970 team might have been a contender for a national championship. Ben didn't want to listen to us, but it may have been possible for a mature, capable black coach to sit down with him behind closed doors and iron out at least some of the problems. I remember thinking this, and then thinking how strange it was that a bunch of twenty-year-old kids were trying to get a sixty-year-old man to act like an adult.

In the summer of 1970, when Chancellor Corbally told Ben to get on with it and hire a black coach, the papers made a big deal of Ben's trip down to Florida to consult with Jake Gaither about finding a suitable candidate. What the papers didn't report was that more than a year earlier, Sully and D.J. went down to Florida and tried to recruit Jake, himself, to come up to Syracuse and take the job. They knew that it was a lot to ask of a man of his accomplishments to take an assistant coaching job, and even if Jake agreed, they would still have to convince Schwartzwalder to offer him the job. But they thought Gaither might be persuaded because his presence might have a significant and lasting impact on conditions for black athletes at Syracuse and at other northern schools. It was also true that of all the possible candidates in the country, Gaither would be the one that Ben would have the most trouble saying no to.

When Sully and D.J. met with Gaither, they told him, "We want a coach who can be a role model and a mentor. We want somebody who can stand up for black student athletes and advocate for fair treatment." Gaither said, "You've got to be kidding me. There's no coach alive who can do all those things. You need more than a coach. You need somebody like a Jackie Robinson who's going to go up there and put up with all kinds of abuse to get things done." Gaither was no fool. He understood what they were asking. But he was retiring after a long and successful career at Florida

A&M and this wasn't the kind of job for someone who had just decided that his working days were over. A year later, Ben went to A&M to ask for a recommendation, and Jake gave him Carlmon Jones, who was anything but a Jackie Robinson. Maybe the reason he recommended Jones was because there weren't any Jackie Robinsons around, and he figured if someone was going to get a good assistant coach's job up in Syracuse, it might as well be one of his former players. I had nothing personal against Jones. But he wasn't the guy we needed. He didn't seem to have any sense of what the situation was for black players at Syracuse or what he might do to make things better. That made him Ben's guy for the job. Considering what we had sacrificed to get a black coach hired, it was a real disappointment. I'll go further than that: it was another slap in the face.

I remember, after the boycott, I had the option to be red-shirted and play another year of football for Syracuse. Another year on the team might have helped my chances to turn pro, but I decided to just focus on school and graduate. Considering how Greg was treated by Ben when he returned to the team after the boycott, I probably made the right decision. I had always looked at my football scholarship as a means of going to college, and while I wanted to play pro football and thought I deserved the chance, that was never my life's goal. I wanted an education, and if I also got to play in the NFL, all the better.

I switched majors twice in college. I had such a good football season in 1968, my first year on the varsity, that I opted out of the five-year engineering program to study business administration. It seemed only logical for me to prepare myself to deal with all the millions of dollars I'd be making in the NFL. It didn't take me long to discover that managing money was neither my passion nor my strong point, and soon after that, the burden of all those millions seemed less than inevitable. I finally chose to major in communication. I studied television, radio, and film production. I found a balance in it for my technical skills and my need for creative expression.

Even as my visions of football glory were disintegrating in front of me, I remember thinking how fortunate and blessed I was to get to know the African American Syracuse football alums who supported us during the boycott. I was able to meet Jim Brown and spend time with him. I worked out with Jim Nance of the Boston Patriots. I spent a week as the guest of John and Sylvia Mackey at their home in Baltimore. I met Art Baker, John Brown, and others. I missed a season of football, but I had a pretty good season of life in return. Interacting with accomplished people gave me new confidence to take charge of my life.

I also met Buddy Young, one of the pioneering African Americans in professional football. Buddy was just 5 feet 4 inches tall, but he had what it took to become a star running back for the University of Illinois in the 1940s. He played pro football for ten years, mostly with the Baltimore Colts, and gained more than 1,000 yards a season five times. He was also one of the first African Americans to become a pro football league executive. As director of player relations for the NFL, he was one of a very few who took an interest in the way teams were informally blacklisting college players who had been labeled as "militants" and "radicals" for their civil rights and anti-war activism in the 1960s. Buddy and his people worked behind the scenes to negotiate a tryout for me with the Cleveland Browns. I reported to the Browns' camp in the summer of 1971, but, unfortunately, I failed the physical because of a damaged knee. Buddy then helped me get treatment. Through his influence, Dr. Anthony Pisani, the team doctor of the New York Giants, performed surgery on my knee.

At this point, I was living in Syracuse and working at WCNY, the local public television station. My boss, a guy named Bill Underwood, took me under his wing and taught me television production. He made my life hell and I called him every name in the book, but in truth this was one of the best things that ever happened to me. I was forced to learn everything at a professional level. I was a cameraman, sound man, lighting man, floor director, technical director, and producer. These skills served me throughout my life, both as a television producer and a teacher. I was also working during this period as a manpower training officer for the Upstate New York Urban League. There wasn't really time for football, but I still had a bit of it in me and I made time for one last shot, courtesy of my friend, Bucky McGill.

Bucky, who had moved back to Binghamton, was playing football for the Triple Cities Jets in the Empire Football League. Through Bucky, Spoon Walker, Dave Johnson, and I connected with the TC Jets and started commuting down to Binghamton nights and weekends. Conditions were terrible. We were getting something like $100 per game, and after practices, we'd have to drive all the way home to Syracuse—more than sixty miles—just to get a shower! But there was a purpose to that misery. The TC Jets were a farm team for the New York Jets, and by playing for the TC Jets, we were guaranteed a tryout with the New York Jets at their preseason camp. The big day came, and I will never forget it. Head coach Weeb Ewbank was calling out the names on his list to see who had shown up for a tryout. When he came to us, he yells out, "Newton! McGill! Walker!" and then, barely hesitating, he adds, "Aren't you the boys from Syracuse?" Those words and the way that he said them are engraved in my memory; I knew my football career was over. We stayed for the tryout, but we knew they were just going through the motions with us. All hope of ever playing in the NFL left me. When we got in the car to drive home, I turned my back on football. Bucky had come to the same end with football after the Jets camp, and when he told me he was enrolling in graduate school at Howard University, I decided I'd move down to DC with him and make a new start. I packed my things in a U-Haul truck, picked up Bucky in Binghamton, and we headed for the Beltway.

My plan was to try to get a job with WETA, the public television affiliate for Washington, DC. They had just built a brand new broadcast center in Northern Virginia and they were advertising about fifty jobs in the trade papers. Somehow, I didn't manage to get one. But I did find a job at WTOP, the CBS affiliate in DC. I became associate producer and director of a live Monday-through-Friday half-hour show called Harambee. The title is a Swahili rallying cry, sometimes translated as "Pull together, everyone!" It was one of the only daily black community affairs programs on American commercial television at that time.

Sometime in 1974 or so, I was out for a walk in Washington when I noticed the inscription on a building as I was passing by: The African American Center for the Study of Life and History founded by Dr. Carter Woodson. I said to myself, "Now here I am a college graduate, a National Honor Society member, and a National Merit finalist. How can I know enough to be all that and not know about this place?" That chance experience was an awakening for me. I realized that I had acquired certain pieces of knowledge and I had learned to do certain things, but there was no rhyme or reason to what I knew. I lacked an organizing principle, a basis for assigning value to knowledge. I began looking for something to fill that void, and my search led me to Al Islam. I began to read the Holy Qur'an. As with most if not all religions, there were different organizations within the religion with different ways of viewing the world. I had issues with The Nation of Islam and their "white man is the devil" philosophy. So I came to Al Islam through the teaching of Wallace D. Mohammed. He showed me a broader view that made sense to me. I studied three to four hours every day in preparation to reconnect and make my Shahadah (Oath, Pledge, Covenant). I had the privilege of making the hajj, a pilgrimage to Mecca, in 1980 and again in 2003.

My thinking became very different about all kinds of things, including things you might not immediately associate with religion. For example, I had started my own television production business, and I was renting both a store-front office and an apartment. I began to question that. "Hey, I'm paying two rents; this doesn't make sense." So I gave up my apartment and moved into the store front. I slept in the basement and had my office on the first floor. At that point, youth from the neighborhood started coming in and I showed them films. I had all kinds of films in the office because I had a production company and I would get them for free from clients and associations. The films were always pushing something. They could be pushing the dairy industry, or promoting automobile safety, or whatever. Showing those films to youth and talking with them about the films taught me something about the nature of education. The form of education—learning how to enjoy learning—is the most important gift a teacher can give to students, and it can be accomplished with just about any subject matter. I discovered my vocation as a teacher. I had been wronged as a young man and I had been hurt, but I was not damaged. For that I thank our Creator, the Merciful Benefactor, the Merciful Redeemer.

Alif Muhammad returned to his native New England in 1977 and has been working ever since as a math teacher, instructional technology specialist, and staff developer (that is, a "teacher of teachers"), writing new curricula and introducing innovations to faculty at public and charter schools in Cambridge and Boston. A lifelong student as well as teacher, he holds a master's degree from New Hampshire College and has enhanced his professional assets with advanced course work at six universities, including Harvard and MIT Among the leadership positions he has held are Dean of Freshman Academy for Boston Public Schools (1993–95); Executive Director and Academic Coordinator of Technical Vocational Education for Cambridge Public Schools (1995–2000); and Technology Integration Specialist for the Boston Renaissance Charter Public School (2000–2004). In recent years, Muhammad has expanded his efforts as a teacher and educational innovator to reach students of every age and type. A member of the faculty of Springfield College's School of Human Services, he has also taught mathematics to adult education students and preschoolers. Since 2007, he has served as an instructional coach and professional development facilitator in the Massachusetts juvenile justice system, introducing techniques and technologies to teachers at thirteen schools of the statewide system. Muhammad's wife, Janean, is a case manager for Early Head Start, working with low-income parents. Married in 1977, Alif and Janean Muhammad live in the Hyde Park neighborhood of Boston. They have seven grown children, Nadirah, Raushanah, Sahirah, Quadir, Mujihad, Marzuq, and Wadi, and three grandchildren, Tahira, Saida, and Kamal.

14

John Lobon

Born in Hartford, Connecticut, in 1950, John Lobon, his fraternal twin brother Ronald, and older sister Josephine were raised by their mother, Lucinda Lobon, who migrated to Hartford from Montgomery, Alabama. Lobon spent much of his childhood growing up in Bellevue Square, a 500-unit public housing complex near downtown Hartford. While the difficulties of life in a public housing project are often given a great deal of attention, Lobon speaks of another side of that experience. "The importance of community was something you learned from your elders at an early age," he says. "Many of us embraced those concepts and became good citizens because of it." Lucinda Lobon, a domestic worker who often worked a second job for a caterer, eventually moved the family to the city's North End. As a teenager, Lobon worked for the same catering company to help out with expenses.

"I used to ask my mother why we couldn't make a trip to her home town down South," Lobon recalled. "She would tell me that we couldn't go because I wouldn't understand the environment down there. She said she feared for my safety if I tried to go downtown to a department store, or have a hamburger at a lunch counter or go to the movies, or do any of the things I did all the time in Hartford. I'd ask her why, and she'd say, 'Because of the hate.' After a while I understood. I have never visited my mother's birth place."

Lobon showed affinity and talent for athletics as early as grade school, participating in Midget football, Peewee basketball, American Legion baseball, and other organized sports. As a student at Weaver High School in the Hartford public school system, he started

28. John Lobon with Chancellor's Medal for Extraordinary Courage, 2006. Courtesy Wallace Black Jr., W.B. Photography.

at center on offense and middle linebacker on defense for the football team, and he played first base for the baseball team. During Lobon's three seasons of varsity football (1965–67), Weaver was a dominant, nationally ranked high school power, losing a total of just three games in that period. Named co-captain as a senior, Lobon was selected as center for the all-state team after helping Weaver to an undefeated season and the 1967 Connecticut state championship.

Lobon recalls the factors that influenced him to attend Syracuse and reflects on the struggles he faced in 1969 and 1970:

I owe a lot to my teachers and coaches at Weaver, but the one who inspired me most was my math teacher, Curtis Manns, who was black. To some people it may sound like a cliché today, but he told me that I could be anything I wanted in life and that had a powerful impact on me. I located him many years later and thanked him for his advice and support. In football, Ted Knurek, the head coach, and Philip Kearney, the line coach, gave me every opportunity to prove my abilities and improve my skills. They were white, and the student body was majority white at that time, but "black and white" was not an issue to my coaches. I will always be grateful that they judged me by my ability. I would learn how valuable that was just a few years later.

Other than family members, teachers, and coaches, the person who had the greatest long-term impact on my life was Walter "Doc" Hurley. He had made history at Weaver by lettering in football, basketball, baseball, and track in the same year. He went to college at Virginia State University, a traditionally black school in Petersburg, but he came back to Hartford and was a middle school teacher when I was a student at Weaver. He was committed to helping any kid who would listen to him, and he helped send a number of students to Virginia State on scholarships. He organized a basketball tournament as a way of raising scholarship money and that grew into the Doc Hurley Scholarship Foundation, which I have been involved with for more than thirty-five years. In 1968, after Dr. Martin Luther King was assassinated, there was, of course, tremendous anger and shock. Students were gathered out in front of the school and it looked like there might be some kind of riot. The administration called Doc Hurley to come over and help. He stood at the school entrance and addressed the crowd, saying, "We are not going to destroy our school." There was a park across the street and everyone moved over there and people demonstrated their anger by speaking and singing. No one was hurt. The school was not vandalized.

I thought about the possibility of going to Virginia State or another historically black college, but I was inspired by Dr. King's "dream" to cross other boundaries, to enter territories that required further exploration. I wanted to create pathways for others to travel. I believed that attending a white university was the crossing of one of those boundaries, and I believed it all the more after the boycott. I graduated from Weaver with a B average in the top third of my high school class, and I received letters of interest from Syracuse, Michigan, Purdue, Colorado, and UCLA. Eddie Crowder, the head football coach at the University of Colorado, visited me at home and met my family, and I went out to Boulder for a campus visit. Jim Shreve, the freshman coach, recruited me for Syracuse. It came down to Colorado or Syracuse, but there was a lot in Syracuse's favor. After all, it was Jim Brown's school, and it had a great reputation. The location was important, too. I was very close with my mother and I didn't want to go too far away from home. I felt I should be nearby in case she needed me; I grew up poor and that's just how we were. What closed the deal for Syracuse was meeting Greg Allen, who made his campus visit the same time I did. We related very well and really got to know each other. Even though it was just a two-day period, by the end we felt like we were old friends. That meant something to us, because we were leaving home and going off to a strange place. Prior to our final interviews with the coaches, Greg and I discussed what we were going to do. We made a pledge to each other that Syracuse would be our choice.

When people ask me about the football boycott of 1970, I tell them, "If you want to understand what happened in 1970, look at 1969." The civil rights struggle and the Vietnam War were coming together in the public mind. Change was taking place in society and it was happening on all fronts. It was obvious that something had gone wrong with the society, but it was not obvious how to fix it. Television and the mass media were putting these tremendous problems right in front of people all day long, and yet society did not want to face the fact that something had to be done, that there had to be change. For me and for my friends, for the Syracuse Eight, I believe the main issue was that we were trying to be recognized as individuals. To the coaches, we were "blacks" or "black militants," or some kind of "others," but we were individuals and we were not treated with the respect that individuals expect to be shown. I wanted to say to them, "Look at me for what I am—a human being—and let's go from there."

I'll give you an example of what I mean. Today, most people who know something about the history of football know that black athletes were considered incapable of playing quarterback in those days because quarterback was considered a "thinking" position. Warren Moon and others changed a lot of minds on that subject in the 1980s, but even Warren Moon had to play six seasons in Canada before an NFL team would give him a chance. Not that many people realize that quarterback wasn't the only position blacks were considered incapable of playing. There were two other positions they said blacks couldn't play: middle linebacker and center. Well, I had played them both in high school and I made the all-conference team in both positions and I was even all-state center when I was a senior. Syracuse recruited me to play on defense, but after I got to freshman camp, the coaches asked me to move over to offense and play center for the freshman team because the center they recruited was too short for the position. Let me explain. The quarterback was tall, and in order to take the snap from this short center, he had to crouch over and that slowed him down a step once he got the ball. I'm about 6-foot 2, and the coaches knew I had played center in high school, so they made me the center on the freshman team and, for what it's worth, we won all five of our games. I had done a good job and most of my teammates believed I would get a shot at the center position on the varsity. That did not happen. It didn't matter to the coaches how I had performed. Center was not a position they would allow a black man to play on the Syracuse varsity at that time. I started my sophomore year at defensive end, and the coaches treated me as if they had never even seen me play center. When I asked about it, they just said, "A returning senior is playing that position." That was true. But there were plenty of examples of sophomores and juniors who were out there competing with seniors for starting positions. That's a basic part of college football; you have to earn your position every year. Those who understand those times will understand the real reason they wouldn't give me a chance at playing center. There was no sense in arguing with them. They were the coaches and their word was final.

I'll tell you another thing. When I was on the freshman team, an opportunity also came up for me to play middle linebacker. We were scrimmaging against the varsity and the freshman middle linebacker was either hurt or he didn't show up for practice that day, so they put me in to substitute for him. Alif, the varsity fullback, was the team's leading rusher, and I made a tackle on him that shocked everyone who saw it—the freshmen, the varsity, the coaches, and whoever else might have been there. When we huddled up for the next play, one of my teammates told me that my nose was bleeding. Feeling like a tough guy after making that hit, I just wiped away the blood and called the next defensive set. I understood that Coach Schwartzwalder was a creature of habit, and if he thought something was a fluke—like me taking down Alif—you could bet that he would call the exact same play again just to prove to himself he was right. That's exactly what he did. He called that play again—and the result was the same. Alif respected the ability I had shown by saying it was a good tackle. But I never got a chance to play middle linebacker again at Syracuse, not in a scrimmage or a game. Greg, who was with me on the freshman team, called that scrimmage "a defining moment" for the team and for us. That was reconfirmed by others when we had a 1968 Syracuse Freshman Football Team reunion in 2002.

Even now, some people claim there was no official policy of quotas that kept black students from playing certain positions. Of course it wasn't written anywhere, and if anyone had bothered to ask any of the coaches, none of them would admit that such policies existed. It's hard to say whether they even discussed these things among themselves. It was just a given. They didn't need to explain to each other why a guy with my record couldn't get half a chance to try out for center or middle linebacker on the varsity; or why a guy with D.J. Harrell's record couldn't get a shot at the quarterback job; or why the three best running backs on the team, the most effective backfield combination we had, couldn't be sent in together to get the job done on offense. But the coaches knew the reason and we knew the reason, and that's why we had to do something about it. That kind of discrimination had to end, not only for us, but for every kid who came to Syracuse after us.

Things got difficult during the boycott. We supported each other and we got support from people on campus and from the black community in Syracuse, but we also caught hate from some people, and hate is something that can get to you. Hate is something that can wear you down over time. I made a call one day to my mother and talked to her about what was going on and the kind of environment I was living in, and especially about the hate. I said to her, "I don't know how much more of this I can take. I don't want to be a disappointment to you by dropping out." That issue weighed heavily on me, because I was the first one in my family to attend college. She responded by saying, "Then come home." My mother's brother, my Uncle James Rose, came into the house while we were talking and she put him on the line so I could talk to him about it. I told him what I was going through and he responded that if I want to come home he would drive up to Syracuse and bring me home the next day. Their words revived me. They took me from a sense of weakness to a sense of strength that gave me the ability to move forward with a sense of pride. They had let me know that if I chose to come home, I would not be considered a failure, because doing what you believe is the right thing is not failure. From then on, I felt I had support back home from my family, my friends, my community, my high school classmates, and my high school teammates.

The experience changed me from a young man to a man. The norm was, "You become a man at the age of 21." But I learned that when you take an action that has impact on your life, on your future, and on the well-being of others, that can give you good reason to call yourself a man. Your actions are more important than your age. I made a pledge at a church service held at the African American Culture Center, which the black student body had established on campus, to move forward with the boycott, to act as one with my teammates, and I stated to the congregation that I was doing this so those coming after us might avoid going through what we were going through. It changed my life. I began a journey of purpose and self-respect, and a commitment to creating opportunities for others.

The boycott of the football season took place during the fall of 1970, my junior year. We were assured by Chancellor Corbally that we would keep our scholarships and that there would be no retribution against us, but it turned out to be not that simple. Two unexpected roadblocks were thrown in my way. Either one of them could have prevented me from completing my education.

During the spring semester of 1971, my junior year, I got a phone call from my mother telling me I had received a letter from the Selective Service Board requiring me to report to the board in New Haven the next day, and that it came with a one-way train ticket from Hartford to New Haven. I was being drafted. How could that be? I was a full-time student and I had a student deferment. I went to the office of the Dean of Men, which was in charge of this, and I found that they had not sent my deferment to my draft board. No one in the office could explain why, but they told me the best way to deal with it was to get the deferment notice to the Syracuse draft board, which would then inform the New Haven draft board of my status. They offered to mail it for me, but I said "No thanks," and I took the deferment notice over there myself and delivered it by hand. This was not just some random mistake that had happened to me. Greg and some of the other members of the Syracuse Eight ran into the same problem that semester. None of us had any trouble getting our deferments before the boycott, but now, for some unexplained reason, the paperwork hadn't been mailed to our draft boards by the deadline. It was no coincidence. I feel it was an attempt to remove me and the others from school as payback or punishment for participating in the boycott. And it was more than just some prank or slap on the wrist. Getting drafted in those days almost certainly meant you would be in Vietnam in a matter of months. There is no proof of who was behind this, so I won't make any accusations. But obviously it had to be someone with considerable power at the university.

The harassment didn't end there. In the fall of 1971, when I went down to the Dean of Men's office to get my student-aid package, just as I had done in previous years, I was told that I had two incomplete grades in history courses and that I had to complete these courses immediately before I would receive my scholarship for the coming year. History was my major and I didn't remember having any incompletes. Here's what had happened, to the best of my knowledge: Back in the spring of 1970, following the expansion of the Vietnam War into Cambodia, all classes were suspended at Syracuse and finals were canceled. Most students received a grade of "Pass" and I assumed that applied to me. Nobody said anything to me about "Incompletes." But it appears that the athletic department had the option of rejecting "Pass" grades and demanding regular grades for students on scholarship, based on the academic requirements that came with athletic scholarships. Did the athletic department demand regular letter grades for all the white members of the football team? I had no way of knowing at that moment. But fair or unfair, I needed to complete those courses before I could get my aid package and register for classes. If I didn't, my scholarship would be voided and, since I didn't have any other way of paying my tuition, that would be the end of my college career. I spoke with the two history professors, explaining the situation, and they gave me assignments. I would have to turn in a ten-page term paper for each course. I completed both assignments over the next two weeks and got credit for both courses. When I returned to the Dean of Men's office to pick up my aid package, the dean called me in to have a talk. He asked me if I was physically injured. I told him I wasn't. Then he asked me if I was at Syracuse on an athletic scholarship. I stated that I had an athletic scholarship, but that I wasn't playing football because I had not been asked to join the team that year. He then told me that I had to play football and that the coaching staff was waiting for me at Manley Field House. I didn't see how this could be possible, because the season was halfway gone and I had never received any kind of notice, written or any other way, from the athletic department or the team. Looking back, it appears probable to me that the football coaches were betting that I wouldn't be able to clear up my incompletes and would have to drop out. That would free up my scholarship so they could give it to someone else. After that didn't work out the way they planned, they probably decided that if I was going to get my scholarship, they might as well get something for the money by having me play. I went down to the field house and, just as I'd been told, they were expecting me. I said my hellos and was told to go get my equipment. I was given Number 90 even though I had previously had Number 53. The fact that they had given away my old number was evidence that they didn't think I'd ever be back. I may be one of the only players in the history of the Syracuse football team who wore two different numbers for the varsity.

I went to practice and none of the players seemed to have any problem with my being back, even though they told us during the boycott that the white players were so against having us come back that they would refuse to play. It was October, and more than half the schedule had already been played. I had seen the team play and I knew they were weak at defensive end, the position I played before the boycott. That might have also had something to do with their sudden willingness to have me back on the team. A few days later, Coach Carlmon Jones came to tell me that they wanted me to make the trip with the team to the University of Pittsburgh for the game that weekend, but I would just be running down the field on kickoffs. There was something wrong with this entire situation, as far as I could see. First they don't want me on the team at all and they don't even invite me to practice; then they want me on the team, just as if nothing ever happened; and then they tell me I'm only supposed to run down the field on special teams, which is something any player on the bench can do. So I asked Coach Jones, "Why would you want me to make the trip just to run down on kickoffs? Why would you want me to make the trip at all, when I've just had one day of practice after a year and a half off?"

Years later, it was suggested to me that one reason they might have wanted me to make that trip is that the report of the Chancellor's Committee on Racism had showed how the coaches would sometimes exclude black players from road trips as a way of not allowing us full playing time and preserving the quotas. Maybe they now thought they had to watch themselves on that issue. But I wasn't thinking about that back then. I just wanted to concentrate on getting my schoolwork done and graduating. I told them I wasn't in favor of making the trip and they agreed. That weekend, while the team was away in Pittsburgh, I decided that playing football was not in my best interest. I chose not to attend practice on the Monday following the Pittsburgh game.

Back during the boycott, Coach Schwartzwalder said missing practice was a good enough reason to drop someone from the team. But later that Monday evening Coach Jones came to see me at my dorm to ask what I was going to do. This time he wanted to know if I going to play football in the upcoming home game against Boston College on Saturday. He told me it was going to be a nationally televised game and they needed me to play on defense, not just run down the field on kickoffs. I decided I would play after all, mainly because it would give my family a chance to see me play college football on television, and after all that had gone down why not let them have some satisfaction from that? On game day, the announcers didn't know who I was for a while because my name and number were not even on the program. My family had a few laughs over the confusion, because they knew who I was, even with my new number. I was glad they had the chance to see me on TV because I knew it made them proud. After almost a year and half of not playing football, and with less than a week of practice, I started at defensive end against Boston College. It was the eighth game of the 1971 season. We lost by a score of 10–3, but we didn't give up a lot of points and I had played pretty well. After the game, I was approached by a pro scout and he told me he thought I would be drafted by an NFL team. That gave me some incentive to remain with the team. There were three more games left on the schedule and I played defensive end in all of them, and we won all three, beating Navy, West Virginia, and Miami. But the scout who encouraged me to think I would be drafted turned out to be wrong. I wonder if he would have said that to me at all if he had spoken to Coach Schwartzwalder about me first.

After I finished school in Syracuse, I moved back home and found a job at the Mechanics Savings Bank in Hartford. I still had the desire to play football, so I tried out for the Hartford Knights, a semi-pro team, and began practicing with them that summer. One day, the head coach, Nick Cutro, told me that someone I knew was coming to town and he wanted to have a meeting with us the next day. "Someone I knew" turned out to be Greg, who had just been released without a contract by Ottawa of the CFL. Nick, who had been an NFL scout for the Jets and the Browns, had obviously been contacted by somebody about us, because he told us, "If you guys are hoping that playing for Hartford this season will be a stepping stone to a big-league team, there's no need to try out. Both the NFL and the CFL consider you guys to be militants and troublemakers and they will not allow you to move up to the next level. You guys are black-balled." Any hope I had of playing pro football was gone, right then and there.[1] I ended my football career when I was traded to the Western Mass Pioneers for the season.

I do not harbor bitterness toward Syracuse University for what happened to us. I didn't just play football for Syracuse, I got an education there and I met lifelong friends there. I have even rooted for Syracuse's sports teams, and living in Connecticut, I've taken flak for it because of the Big East rivalry, especially in basketball, between UConn and Syracuse that went on for decades. After I saw all the positive

changes that took place in the program, I became support-
ive of African American student athletes attending Syracuse.
I was delighted when Dwight Freeney, who played middle
linebacker for Bloomfield High, chose to attend Syracuse.
Look at it this way: I wasn't given a chance to even try out
for middle linebacker at Syracuse, but I like to think I made
it possible for him to have that chance, and he became one
of the greatest linebackers in the school's history. He had
34 quarterback sacks while playing for Syracuse, which is
a career record that still stands there, and he was selected
as All-American at middle linebacker in his senior year. He
went on to become an NFL star with the Indianapolis Colts.
You don't hear much about African Americans not being
able to play middle linebacker anymore.

We all came to college with realistic hopes of playing
professional football and I felt I demonstrated on the field
that I had the ability to play at that level. When the boycott
began, Jim Brown warned us of the risk we were taking by
making our statement. Each of us, including me, decided
of his own free will to move forward with the boycott anyway. Making that choice has enabled me to stand tall and
to recognize that I am somebody and that I have a purpose
in life. My experience as part of the Syracuse Eight helped
me realize I would continue to encounter injustice for the
rest of my life and it gave me the confidence to compete at
any level, in any environment, in anything I have undertaken
since. We can only guess what our lives would be like if we
had done one thing instead of another. But I can say with
certainty that I'm satisfied that I did the right thing when I
had that opportunity at Syracuse.

John Lobon earned a bachelor's degree in history from Syracuse University and later augmented his academic credentials by completing
professional certificate programs at the New England School of Banking at Williams College and the National Association of Guaranteed

Lenders. Choosing a career in the financial services industry, he moved up the ranks from an entry-level job to become a regional manager with Connecticut National Bank. In 1984, Lobon redirected his financial expertise to the public sector, joining the State of Connecticut's Department of Economic Development. Beginning a long association with the Connecticut Development Authority (CDA) in 1992, he is today a senior vice president and senior financial officer with CDA, charged with managing its Urban Bank, commonly known as Urbank. Urbank's mission is the creation and retention of jobs in the state's major cities and distressed communities, with special emphasis given to providing small business loans to minority- and women-owned enterprises. Under Lobon's leadership, it has created access to capital for a wide variety of at-risk businesses, such as mom-and-pop groceries, car washes, and funeral homes, creating and retaining thousands of jobs in areas of the state that are most in need of them.

Lobon has kept his connection to athletics over the years through coaching high school and youth football teams and through a decade of service as a board member of the Special Olympics of Connecticut. In 2005, Governor Jodi Rell appointed Lobon to the Connecticut Commission on Human Rights and Opportunities, where he served a four-year term as commissioner. His civic engagements have been numerous and varied, and continue to expand. They include leadership roles as chairman of the board of the Doc Hurley Scholarship Foundation and board membership at Hartford's Knox Foundation. A member of the Bloomfield (Connecticut) Democratic Town Committee, his long list of extraordinary acts of citizenship were recognized in a citation of merit from the Connecticut General Assembly in 2007. Hartford, the city of his birth, proclaimed October 19, 2006, as "John Lobon Day" and Bloomfield, his adopted home town, declared its "John Lobon Day" on March 24, 2008. John and Pamela L. Lobon, an executive with Aetna Insurance, were married in 1971. They have a grown son, N'Gai, and a granddaughter, Najelena.

15

Duane "Spoon" Walker
(1949–2010)

Duane L. Walker led a quintessentially American life, making full use of his unusual combination of talents as an athlete, artist, and administrator to reinvent himself to meet whatever conditions life threw at him. Known as "Spoon" since high school, Walker told his college friends that he got the nickname because he "got the scoop" on everything and everyone in the neighborhood, especially the attractive young ladies. But D.J. Harrell heard a different story on a trip he made with Walker to Brooklyn during their freshman year at Syracuse. "I learned that his high school coach, John Jackson, gave him the nickname because he had such great hands." Harrell says. "He could really catch a football."

Born in Brooklyn in 1949, Walker was the second of four children of Roman Walker, a Pullman porter, and Albertha Hill Walker, a social worker for the City of New York. Native Floridians, the Walkers moved to New York during the 1940s, settling in Bedford-Stuyvesant, the sprawling string of African American neighborhoods that run through the heart of Brooklyn. Basketball, "the city game," was Brooklyn's game, but Walker, who liked to go his own way, excelled in baseball and football. "I was a catcher, and while I was in high school I was approached by the Cincinnati Reds. My dad was a little disappointed that I chose football over baseball. It was understandable. He loved baseball and lived in Brooklyn when Jackie Robinson played for the Dodgers. But for me, nothing compared with football. I felt like I was born to be a pass receiver. Beating

270

29. Duane "Spoon" Walker (right) with Duane Walker Jr. and Jim Brown, 2006.

your man off the line and pulling that ball down as it's coming over your shoulder—that was the greatest thing I could do in sports. Besides, my mom was all for football because it could get you a college education."

Walker entered Boys High School (now Boys and Girls High School) in 1964. The oldest operating public high school in Brooklyn, its famous alumni include an impressive array of writers (Norman Mailer, Isaac Asimov), musicians (Aaron Copland, Max Roach), visual artists (Man Ray, Langdon Kihn) and basketball players (Connie Hawkins, Lenny Wilkens). But as of 1964, only five Boys High alumni had ever managed to play even one game in the NFL. The only name among them recognizable to most fans is Allie Sherman, head coach of the New York Giants during the 1960s.[1]

Nevertheless, things seemed to be looking up for Boys football in the mid-1960s. Under John Jackson, Boys' first African American head coach, the Kangaroos had become a winning team, and Jackson was determined to see more of his players win college scholarships. In an effort to publicize the team, Jackson arranged for Boys to play a road game in 1966 against Altoona High School in western Pennsylvania, some 350 miles from Brooklyn. "Playing a game in Pennsylvania might not sound like much, but it was the biggest thing that ever happened to our football team," Walker recalls. "It was the first out-of-state football game that Boys ever played; it was the first night football game that Boys ever played; and for some of the guys, it was the first time they had ever even been out of New York City."

Coming into the Altoona game, Boys had been enjoying its best season in memory. The Kangaroos were undefeated, with blowout victories over three Brooklyn rivals in the New York City Public School Athletic League (PSAL) Division II: Erasmus Hall (38–6), James Madison (40–0), and Abraham Lincoln (40–26). The bubble burst that Saturday night, as the Altoona Mountain Lions crushed the Boys by a score of 79–12. Nevertheless, Walker, playing wide receiver, scored his fifth touchdown of the season. Boys returned to PSAL play after that and won all four of its remaining games to finish the season at 7–1, with a perfect record in the conference. Walker liked to call his team the 1966 conference champion, but that was "unofficial." No PSAL champion was crowned that year. A riot during a 1961 playoff game led to a moratorium on postseason play that lasted for nine years.

Walker reflected on the factors that led him to pursue an education at Syracuse University, and on the broader life lessons that came as a result of that choice:

> I was a good student in high school. I was a member of the honor society and I made the Boys High Scholastic Hall of Fame. I was prepared to go to college and I was prepared to play ball to pay my way. There were a lot of good players on our team, but I was the only one who had the kind of grades and SAT scores that interested the name schools. I started hearing from colleges while I was still a junior. Then I

made the all-city All-Star team as a senior and the recruiting was intense. I had letters from Penn State, the University of Iowa, Kent State, the College of William and Mary, the University of Cincinnati, and Southern Illinois. Coach Jackson was ecstatic about it. It was the kind of thing he was hoping for. I think one guy got a scholarship from Youngstown State in Ohio, but the other guys—the ones who got offers—were hearing from places that none of us ever heard of, like junior colleges in California. It's nothing against these places, it's just that we had never seen them play on TV or anything like that, so there wasn't the same kind of excitement. I remember, I got some letters from Southern schools—Alabama and Mississippi. I didn't even open those. My parents told me they didn't move all the way up to New York just to see me go down there and get involved in that mess.

The University of Iowa was the only school besides Syracuse I seriously considered. I wanted to major in English, and all my teachers told me that Iowa had a great English department. I also liked the idea of playing in the Big Ten because of the level of competition. Iowa sent an alum, Emlen Tunnel, to see me. He was the first black man to play for the New York Giants and he'd been in nine Pro Bowls. I didn't know anything about him; Coach Jackson had to tell me. Emlen Tunnel. I was impressed by everything about him—by the way he presented himself and how he talked about the school and by the fact that he lived up somewhere in Westchester, which I thought of as a place where rich white people lived. He told me that he had just finished writing a book, and that was like a dream to me. Even though I didn't pick Iowa, he sent me a copy of it— Footsteps of a Giant. When I read it, I found out that he played both offense and defense for Iowa, but that they only let him play pass defense and cover kick returns in the NFL. That turned out to be an important detail for me, but I didn't know it at the time.[2]

I went with Syracuse because it seemed right for me. Jim Brown was somebody we all looked up to and he went there. Even at Boys High, where basketball was king, everybody knew who Jim Brown was. Another thing: compared to Iowa and the other schools I was looking at, Syracuse wasn't that far [from home] and you could get there on the train. That mattered because my father was a member of the Brotherhood of Sleeping Car Porters and my family rode free. There was also something else. It was my senior year at Boys High and we were just about the best football team Boys ever had. There was a lot of school spirit. Coach Jackson told us football was on the rise at Boys and that if we got scholarships, if we did well in school and on the ball field, and remembered where we came from, one day football would be looked at with the same pride as basketball. And there was something on a much more personal level. The Syracuse coaches, Jim Shreve and Bill Bell, told me, with Coach Jackson sitting at the table, that Willie Smith, who graduated from Boys the year before me, had shown them a lot on the Syracuse freshman team and they expected big things from him. They said that if I came to Syracuse and showed that kind of talent, it would make two players in a row from Boys and they could develop a pipeline situation where Boys would be considered an "incubator" school, and it would help kids from my school get college scholarships to Syracuse. They told Willie the same thing and got him to contact me about it. They made it seem like going to Syracuse was doing the right thing.

After I committed to Syracuse, I made a couple of trips up there that summer and it was true, everyone was raving about Willie.[3] The season was about to begin and he was all set in the starting lineup as a defensive tackle, even though he was just a sophomore. It was nice getting away from home and going upstate in the summer, and I enjoyed going around together with Willie and Vaughn Harper [a Syracuse basketball player who was also a Boys graduate]. Let me tell you something about Willie Smith. Things were going so good for him that summer, but I saw how quickly someone's situation could change. It got back to the coach that Willie was dating white co-eds, and his football career went into a nosedive. I saw him go from starter to scrub to outcast in one season.[4]

It was very disheartening for me to see Willie, as good a ballplayer as he was, sitting on the bench; maybe more disheartening for me than for him. I say that because Willie said more than once that he had no great love for football. For him, football was almost like an embarrassment. He thought that the game was dumb and that it played into stereotypes that white people had about black men. He said the only reason he gave his time to it was because it paid for his education. Like anybody, Willie hated the fact that the coaches were snooping around in his personal life. But when he found out that they couldn't take the tuition part of his scholarship away over a thing like that, he didn't complain about losing his playing time. He was okay with it. You have to understand, Willie knew he had more than football going on for him. After he graduated, he went to Tufts Medical School. Last I heard, he was practicing medicine on the West Coast, somewhere up near Seattle.[5]

Things started going wrong for me on the first day of freshman practice. I walked out on the football field with all the other new guys and the first thing they did was to separate the offensive and defensive players. I was instructed to go with the defense and report to the coach in charge of the defensive backs. At first, I just thought it was some kind of mistake. Everyone in high school played both offense and defense, and I had been a defensive back for Boys. But that wasn't what got me the scholarship offers. I said to the coach, "Excuse me, I'm not a defensive back. I'm a wide receiver. Did you check my credentials? Do you know why I'm up here?" They just told me, "You won't be a receiver here."

Just like that! I couldn't believe it. How in the world had I given all of my time and effort and how had I gotten all of these accolades for catching the ball and scoring touchdowns? Then I come up there to be told on the first day that I can't play my position? That I can't even try out for my position? But that was it. I never got to catch one forward pass at Syracuse, unless you count the ones I intercepted. Just like that, they negated everything I learned from the people who worked with me and taught me the position and the fine points. I didn't know who to talk to. I would say to the coaches, "Please give me a chance." It's like they couldn't hear a word I was saying.

I was tempted to quit and walk away right there in my first semester. But I was a kid in a strange place and this was supposed to be my big chance in life. I didn't really know what would happen to me if I left the team. Would I be thrown out of college? I'd seen guys who came home after dropping out of college. I was all full of myself—big high school football star. I'd look at them and think to myself, "What's the problem with you? Ain't got what it takes?" I'd hear people say, "Hey, didn't he used to be . . . ?" I wasn't ready for all that at eighteen. I recall talking with D.J. one night in the dorm room about how angry and disgruntled we were about not being able to play our positions, and we talked about whether we should transfer to another school. The coaches used to come by and do a "bed check" on us. That night, while we were talking, I realized that Coach Shreve was eavesdropping, just standing there right outside the door. Man, what was going on in this place? Where was I?

In time, I began to accept my fate. If they are not going to let me play the position I was groomed for, I vowed to be the best defensive player on the team. I would make the best out of a bad situation. But the situation turned out to be even worse than I thought. Not only did I have to suffer the indignity of playing a position that was not my best, but I had to suffer the further indignity of playing behind individuals who were less talented than me and who were not performing at my level. It was like, "Okay, we'll let you play this defense position after we run out of white boys." That's when I learned about depth charts. You have a first-string, second-string, and third-string player at every position. I would see myself move up from third string to second string, and then some guy—always a white guy—who didn't make it at some other position would suddenly appear as the new second-string defensive back. And there I was, back to third. What killed me was that it didn't matter what I was doing on the field.

I had come to college to get an education—and I was getting more than I bargained for. The way to get ahead on the football team in the late 1960s was to be sponsored by boosters who gave money to the program, and all those boosters were white businessmen sponsoring white players. If a sponsored player was promised a place on the team, he'd get one, even if it meant being moved to a position he didn't know how to play. Coming out of a system where merit was the key to your playing situation, I couldn't believe this. I don't know how things were back in Jim Brown's day, or Ernie Davis's day, but, in 1967, winning was not a priority on Schwartzwalder's football team. It was about satisfying alums and sponsors, and one way you satisfied a lot of these guys was to show them that there was white control of the team. It was what these guys were used to, and they thought their whole world was being threatened in the 1960s. People say the race issue is diminished today and I believe it, but from what I see in college football, it's still about satisfying alums and sponsors.

Ben Schwartzwalder never came out and called us "nigger." I never saw it. Now you might think that's strange, because anyone who has ever been in his locker room knows he called the Italian ballplayers "grease balls"; the Polish kids "Polacks"; the Jews "kikes"; and on and on. He felt justified to do that for some reason and I think he just liked showing off to the white players what a colorful old red-neck bigot he was. I don't know, maybe he was jealous of all the doctors and lawyers and executives they were going to become. He treated them all the same way, insulting them all with that kind of talk. But he had a special way of insulting the black players. He insulted us with actions. The white guys got called those miserable, ignorant names; we just got moved down in the depth chart. We just got left home on the road trip. We just got put in the courses that didn't count credit for graduation. We just got told who we couldn't go out with on a Saturday night.

Just to give the full picture, I should mention that even though he would not use the word "nigger" to us, he had ways of getting at us with words. "You guys need to cut that frizz off your head." "We don't expect you to act colored around here; we expect you to act like football players." The truth is, I found it offensive—all of it. When he called a kid a "grease ball" or a "wop," you could see how he was hurting that kid, and it was disgusting to see a grown man using his position and his power to cause a teenage boy pain and humiliation. There's no good place for that in a school or anywhere else. The difference in the way he treated the black players was this: It wasn't enough to just insult us. He would do things that had negative impact on our lives. Lasting impact.

I remember in high school, Coach Jackson introduced me to Don Ross, the football coach at Virginia Union, a black college. Coach Ross asked who was recruiting me, and I told him. When he heard Penn State and Syracuse, he said, "Be careful about either of those two. They're old rivals. Beating each other can make the season for those teams.

One of them might want you on the team just so the other can't have you, and you could end up sitting on the bench or playing nothing but special teams the whole time you're there." I thought Coach Ross must be trying to recruit me for Virginia Union or something. Who is going to do a thing like that to a guy who can catch passes the way I do? I have no way of knowing if Schwartzwalder recruited me and put me on defense so I couldn't catch passes for Joe Paterno. But after seeing the way Schwartzwalder could talk and spit poison, I have no doubt he was capable of it.

There were all kinds of problems developing between blacks and whites in the football program, but if you looked at the problems one by one, you would see that many of the issues were not really about race. Medical treatment is a good example. That doctor didn't know what he was up to no matter what color you were. Or look at the sponsor issue. White players who had no sponsor were getting screwed out of positions the way black players were. I'm going to tell you something. The real difference between white and blacks on that team was that the black players were mostly progressive thinkers, mostly people who were willing to stand up for change when they were being bullied. The black football players were much more in line with what was going on with the mainstream of all the students at Syracuse. People were questioning all kinds of things in those days. The white coaches made believe they were army officers and a lot of these white guys just bought the whole thing and acted like they were army privates and had to take orders. A lot of them just didn't get the big picture of what was going on. While students from all kinds of different backgrounds were questioning U.S. foreign policy in Vietnam and the effects of racism on American society, some of these guys on the football team were still afraid to let their hair grow past a crew cut. I saw two white players get in a fight because one said he liked the Beatles and the other called him "faggot" for it.

Some of those guys got over it, and we can all thank God for that. Joe Ehrmann was Ben's boy back in college; I met Joe years later and he had totally turned around, 360 [degrees], in his thinking. Ray White was another one. I met him when I lived out in LA. But back then, Schwartzwalder knew how to crank up all kinds of racial animosities in these boys. He pandered to the bigots. He winked at them to let them know he was their guy. They were loyal to him, but he didn't have any loyalty or respect for them. He made fools of them in front of the administration and spoke about them to the newspapers like they were a bunch of wild thugs. "Oh, I wish I could let the blacks back on the football team, but those crazy rednecks are so violent that they might try to kill those guys." When it came to us, the song was always the same: "You've got to make a choice. You can be football players or you can be black, but you can't be both on my football team." Sorry, coach. Even when football was still an important part of my life, I never saw myself as a football player first. I saw myself as a member of a larger community who happened to play football.

I showed myself I could accomplish things under tough conditions. I had been thrust into a position I didn't want to play, and once I got my focus and concentration, I mastered it; I progressed to the next level. I was a letterman and a starter. My old high school coach, John Jackson, who had by this time become a coach at Dartmouth, kept an eye on how I was doing, and he told me that I was on the radar for several NFL teams, that I was a candidate to be drafted. So, with all that to comfort me, why did I throw it down the toilet to make a political statement? It was a difficult decision, but it didn't take me long to make it. When I looked into the faces of some of those coaches and saw the hate that flashed from those eyes, I knew I was doing the right thing by walking away from that. I walked away with my friends and with the support of my family. We were conflicted—all of us were conflicted—because we knew we were changing our lives. Some of us wanted it more than others, but all of us were used to having football as our ace in the hole. So be it. We were not going to report back until there was some change. It took me thirty-five years to be sure, but when Nancy Cantor, the first woman chancellor of Syracuse University, and Daryl Gross, the first African American athletic director of Syracuse University, invited me to come up to Syracuse and be their guest and receive an award, I knew some real changes had been made.

In June 1970, with spring practice behind him, and the unknown consequences of the boycott ahead of him, Duane Walker married Candee Parks, who was introduced to him by D.J. Harrell during a visit he made to Harrell's home in Indianapolis a year earlier. Alarmed by the deepening sense of alienation he had developed while in the football program, Walker turned from athletics to music to regain a sense of balance. A talented percussionist and vocalist, he had started playing congas with Syracuse jazz pianist Bobby Hamilton in his sophomore year. Following the boycott, Walker left school to perform, tour, and record with Hamilton. Critics have called "Dream Queen," a 1972 album recorded at Dell Studios in Utica, New York, the Bobby Hamilton Quintet's most evocative work. A remastered version was released on compact disc in 2011 by Superfly Records, a Japanese soul-jazz label. Hoping to develop a jazz-rock fusion sound in the mid-1970s, Walker formed a new group, Sail. He composed the title track and other songs on its 1976 album, "Steppin' Out on Saturday Night."

The economics of a musician's life being what they are, Walker held several day jobs during these years. One of his employers was the Syracuse Housing Authority, and his work there greatly affected him. "It was more than the steady paycheck and the health benefits for the family, although I'm not minimizing the importance of any of

To the Editor:

It was just a couple of days ago, that I walked across the chewed up grass and sod of ancient Archbold Stadium. I could faintly hear the echoes of pads crashing, the thud of helmets slamming into fleshy stomachs, as they bounced off the chipped and cracked stone bleachers, fading into the glorious legend, the saddening past of SU football. I back pedled; zigged and zagged across the field; heard the roar of the massive crowd as we went into the locker room leading Penn State's "great team" 15-0 (remember?), and for a moment, relived a part of my final year as a football player. I turned to face the mounted policemen, racing through the picket line. I heard the pop of tear gas canisters; the whirring of Sardino's "pepper fog" machines, and the choking, gasping gestures of the demonstrators. For a moment, I relived another part of my final year as a football player.

There are very few who remember, or care to remember the turbulent time during the black football players' boycott of 1970. Yet, that turbulence was an indication, a prophecy of the decline and fall of a mighty giant: SU football. There are those who look back upon those days (possibly even Coach Ben) and blame SU's current football demise upon it. That is not the case. SU's football program was dead then and had been dead for sometime. Its remains merely did not begin to stink until now.

The current concern over the poor shape of our football program is long overdue. There was no sudden downhill slide. There was no sudden breakdown in SU's recruiting program. There was no sudden dilapidation and aging of coaching strategy. The reason why the validity of the charges made against SU's football program was overlooked is simple: *they were made by black people.* The university committee which upheld the black ball players' charges of racism and suggested pertinent changes in the football program, was ignored. Why? It would be too much like right when upholding *the truth* if voiced by black people.

Yet, here we are, faced with what is sure to be the most saddening story in sports that we will ever have had the unfortunate privilege of being in the middle of. Syracuse had a great coach. Syracuse had a great University, but they never listened to *the truth* when voiced by black people. Recent problems between SA, the university and its black student body reflect SU's reluctance to deal with *the truth* when it relates to black people. No one could even conceive of Coach Ben's program being racist or unjust or outdated or a number of other things that it is, until it began to stink.

Will our society wait until everything dies and begins to stink before we try to change it? It might be too late for SU and its football team.

Duane Walker
Defensive Halfback
Class of '71

30. Letter to the editor written by Duane Walker, headlined "Dead Giant Begins to Rot," likely published in the *Daily Orange* in 1970.

that," he said. "There is great human satisfaction in helping to put a roof over somebody's head and in making sure that a mother with an infant has heat in the winter."

Toward the end of the decade, Walker returned to college and finished work on his bachelor's degree, graduating as an English major from Syracuse University in 1980. Diploma in hand, he was able to advance to an executive position with the Syracuse Housing Authority, and he set out on a new career path. Walker's talents in navigating political interests and negotiating agreements between municipal agencies and tenants gained him a national reputation. Over the course of the next twenty-five years, he held positions of increasing responsibility with public housing authorities in Los Angeles, Chicago, Detroit, San Francisco, and Las Vegas, culminating in his appointment as Commissioner of Public Housing for the City of Saginaw, Michigan. In 2008, Duane Walker was diagnosed with lung cancer. He died less than two years later. Greg Allen, Dana Harrell, Ron Womack, and Larry Martin, an associate vice president of Syracuse University, were among the pall-bearers at his funeral. Walker is survived by his wife, Sharon Joyce Roberts; three daughters: Kendra, Kera, and Ashley; and a son, Duane Jr.

Having remained a resident of the city longer than any of his Syracuse Eight comrades, Walker bore full witness to the decline of Syracuse football during the final years of Schwartzwalder's tenure and beyond. He wrote about it in a letter (illus. 30), a photocopy of which was found in his personal effects. Published under the headline, "Dead Giant Begins to Rot," the letter probably appeared in the *Daily Orange*, the student newspaper, sometime during the early 1970s (the letter is without documentation).

16
John Willie Godbolt
(1949–2012)

John Godbolt never recovered from the blows that were dealt him during his college football career. He lost contact with his family in Connecticut and eventually lost contact with his friends from Syracuse, including his colleagues in the Syracuse Eight. At some point, he lost contact with the talented and promising young man he had been. An investigation to determine his whereabouts was made during the preparation of this book. It ended in March 2012, with the discovery that he had died three months earlier, somewhere in the Miami area. The cause of death is unknown. Conversations with people who had known him in Florida revealed that they were unaware that he had been a college student or a football player, or even that he had grown up in Bridgeport, Connecticut. When asked, he listed his birthplace as Bridgeport, New Jersey.

31. John Godbolt (right) with Greg Allen and Al Newton before an SU versus Wisconsin game, 1969.

Notes

Bibliography

Index

Notes

1. A Context for Action

1. Silver medalist Peter Norman, a white member of the Australian Olympic team, was an outspoken critic of Australia's "whites only" immigration policy. He signified his support for the protest by wearing a badge for the Olympic Project for Human Rights, as did Smith and Carlos. Reaffirming their lifelong bond with Norman, Smith and Carlos traveled to Melbourne to attend his funeral. "Not every young white individual would have the gumption, the nerve, the backbone to stand there," Carlos said. Margaret Rees, "Peter Norman, 1942–2006," *World Socialist Web Site*, October 23, 2006, http://wsws.org/articles/2006/10/norm-o23.

2. Arnold Hano, "The Black Rebel Who 'Whitelists' the Olympics," *New York Times Magazine*, May 12, 1968.

3. Richard Hoffer, *Something in the Air: American Passion and Defiance in the 1968 Mexico City Olympic Games* (New York: Free Press, 2009), 222.

4. "Alcindor Shuns Olympics," *New York Times*, February 28, 1968.

5. In one of the few interviews Tommy Smith gave on the Mexico City protest, he described its purpose as an attempt at "regaining black dignity." See Vincent Matthews and Neil Amdur, *My Race Be Won* (New York: Charter House, 1974), 197.

6. Before 1970, only thirty-five San Jose State players had signed NFL contracts; just fifteen of them had played professionally for more than two seasons. (Source: *DatabaseFootball.com* Football Statistics and History Database, http://www.databasefootball.com).

7. In 1849, Brigham Young, president of the LDS Church (1847–77), banned interracial marriage and banned blacks from becoming members of the LDS clergy or receiving temple rites. These were reversals of practices dating to the founding of the Mormon religion by Joseph Smith. Young's racial policies remained in effect until 1978.

8. "Spartan Serves with Honor," *Washington Square: The Stories of San Jose State University*, Summer 2009. Although Jackson was widely criticized on campus in 1968 for participating in the protest, this profile of him forty years later in a San

289

Jose State alumni magazine asserts that his action "demonstrated the qualities of a future military leader." With his promotion to major general, Jackson became the highest ranking African American officer in the history of the U.S. Marine Corps.

9. On June 9, 1978, Mormon Church president Spencer Kimball announced he had received a revelation from God instructing him to confer priesthood upon any male church member "regardless of race or lineage." See "Black History Timeline," http://www.blacklds.org/history.

10. Clifford A. Bullock, "Fired by Conscience: The Black 14 Incident at the University of Wyoming and Black Protest in the Western Athletic Conference," unpublished collection on Wyoming history, Department of History, University of Wyoming, http://www.uwyo.edu/robertshistory/fired_by_conscience.

11. James E. Barrett, "The Black 14: Williams v. Eaton, A Personal Recollection," unpublished collection on Wyoming history, Department of History, University of Wyoming, http://www.uwyo.edu/robertshistory/barrett_black_14.

12. Clarence "Bucky" McGill, interview with David Marc.

13. Edwards gradually became known for collaborating with the professional sports establishment in pursuing greater participation for African Americans in the sports industry. Over the years he served as a paid consultant to Major League Baseball, the San Francisco 49ers of the NFL, and the Golden State Warriors of the NBA in recruiting African American front office executives.

14. Gregory George later became a career civil servant in New York City. He was appointed to the city's Civil Service Commission in 1954 and served as a commissioner until 1968.

15. Lou Bender, at age ninety-eight, was inducted into the New York City Basketball Hall of Fame, and he spoke about Gregory George at the induction ceremony, held at the New York Athletic Club on September 17, 2008. Bender died in 1999, just before his one hundredth birthday.

16. Willie Thrower signed, as a free agent, with the Chicago Bears and became the team's backup quarterback. In 1953, he became the first African American to take a snap from center in the NFL since the league rescinded its twelve-year ban on nonwhites in 1945. Warren Moon, in his induction speech at the Pro Football Hall of Fame, acknowledged Thrower for inspiring him to believe that a black quarterback could successfully lead a racially integrated football team.

17. Founded in Dover in 1891 as the State College for Coloreds, the school's name was changed to Delaware State College in 1947. It has been known as Delaware State University since 1993.

18. It is likely that Dr. Sol Bloom, an alumnus who recruited a number of African American student athletes for Syracuse during the mid–twentieth century, played a role in bringing Sidat-Singh to his alma mater.

19. "Equals to All persons: Minorities in SU's History," Syracuse University Archives exhibition description, September 2005, http://archives.syr.edu/exhibits /equal.html.

20. "SU to Honor a Pioneer—Wilmeth Sidat-Singh," Cuse.com, February 24, 2005, http://cuse.com/news/2005/2/24/sidat-singh.aspx.

21. Grantland Rice and John S. Martin, "'The Saga of Sidat-Singh' by Grantland Rice," *Syracuse Herald*, October 18, 1938.

22. Robert J. Scott and Myles A. Pocta, *Honor on the Line: The Fifth Down and the Spectacular 1940 College Football Season* (Bloomington, IN: iUniverse, 2012), 84–86. See also Charles H. Martin, *Benching Jim Crow: The Rise and Fall of the Color Line in Southern College Sports, 1890–1980* (Urbana: Univ. of Illinois Press, 2010), 34–35.

23. Sam Lacy was a tireless fighter for civil rights throughout his long and distinguished career as a reporter and editor with the *Chicago Defender* and other leading African American newspapers. He played a crucial role in covering and documenting the civil rights movement.

24. Scott and Pocta, *Honor on the Line*, 84–86.

25. Marty Glickman, *The Fastest Kid on the Block* (Syracuse: Syracuse Univ. Press, 1996), 51.

26. Luke Cyphers, "The Lost Hero: Wilmeth Sidat-Singh Was a Two-Sport Star at Syracuse and a Harlem Renaissance Man," *New York Daily News*, February 25, 2001, http://nydailynews.com/archives/sports/ lost-hero-wilmeth-sidat -singh-two-sport-star-syracuse-harlem-renaissance-man-article-1.906303.

27. In a Syracuse–Maryland game in November 2013, a four-minute onfield ceremony between the first and second quarters was held so that Maryland could officially apologize to Sidat-Singh. Sidat-Singh's family members were presented with a framed Wounded Warriors jersey with the word "commitment" on the back. Syracuse players wore Sidat-Singh's number, 19, on their helmets. An editorial in the *Syracuse Post-Standard* reflected on the ceremony, questioning whether the event was enough to right the wrong: "And—even though Maryland misspelled [Sidat-Singh's] name in a press release announcing the ceremony—it was due. . . . The color of his skin didn't prevent Sidat-Singh from taking the field. It was Maryland's overt racism and Syracuse's silent cowardice that prevented him from playing" ("One Small Step in a Long Journey to Repay Wilmeth Sidat-Singh," *Syracuse Post-Standard*, November 14, 2013). Sidat-Singh was also honored by Syracuse during a halftime event in 2005 when his Number 19 jersey was retired.

28. Glickman, *The Fastest Kid on the Block*, 53.

29. Cyphers, "The Lost Hero."

30. Pamela Grundy, *Learning to Win: Sports, Education, and Social Change* (Chapel Hill: Univ. of North Carolina Press, 2001), 263.

31. "Jim Crow in Athletics Hit by Duke's Action," *New York Ace*, October 29, 1938, 8. The story of the Wade telegram permitting Sidat-Singh to play in the 1938 Duke–Syracuse game was broken the previous day in the *Daily Worker* by sports editor Lester Rodney. Rodney's story, "Duke Yields on Sidat-Singh!," was picked up by the *Ace* and other African American newspapers across the country who saw it as a victory in the ongoing struggle against racial segregation.

32. "Sidat-Singh to Face Duke," *New York Times*, October 22, 1938.

33. Patrick B. Miller, "Sport as 'Interracial Education': Popular Culture and Civil Rights Strategies during the 1930s and Beyond," in *The Civil Rights Movement Revisited: Critical Perspectives on the Struggle for Racial Equality in the United States*, ed. Patrick B. Miller, Therese Frey Stegffen, and Elisabeth Schäfer-Wünsche (London: Lit Verlag Münster, 2001), 31.

34. Jim Sumner, "When the Rose Bowl Came to Duke," *Blue Devil Weekly* online, January 1, 2007, http://www.goduke.com.

35. In the mid-1930s, several all-black football teams were formed in an attempt to create a "Negro football league" on the model of Negro League baseball. But the enterprise never materialized. For an account of the plight on African American football players during the NFL lockout, see John M. Carroll's *Fritz Pollard: Pioneer in Racial Advancement* (Urbana: Univ. of Illinois Press, 1992). Pollard, who played in the NFL before the ban, coached the Brown Bombers, the most notable of the all-black pro teams.

36. James Naismith invented the game of basketball in response to a request from his employer, the YMCA of Springfield, Massachusetts, for a rigorous athletic team sport that could played indoors in a snowy climate during the winter.

37. The other starting players for the 1939 Syracuse Reds were all white. They included two of Sidat-Singh's Syracuse University teammates, center Mark Haller and guard Bobby Stewart. Forward John Bromberg, the team's player-coach, and guard Mike Sewitch were both members of Long Island University's 1938 national championship team.

2. Progress and Its Myths

1. Danny Biasone, who founded the Syracuse Nationals, is remembered principally as the member of the NBA Rules Committee who advocated the 24-second shot clock at every meeting from 1951 until 1954, when he was able to convince fellow owners to adopt it as a league regulation. Ironically, the shot clock increased the popularity of the game so much that small cities could no longer keep their franchises when big cities wanted them. The Nats became the Philadelphia 76ers

in 1964. Biasone was inducted into the Naismith Basketball Hall of Fame in 2000, eight years after his death.

2. Todd Gould, *Pioneers of the Hardwood: Indiana and the Birth of Professional Basketball* (Bloomington: Univ. of Indiana Press, 1998), 138.

3. Lloyd had previously starred for West Virginia State, a historically black public college.

4. Earl Lloyd and Sean Kirst, *Moonfixer: The Basketball Journey of Earl Lloyd* (Syracuse: Syracuse Univ. Press, 2010), 74.

5. Sean Kirst, "Sidat-Singh, A Name SU Ignores," *Syracuse Post-Standard* April 2, 2003, B1. Also see Thomas G. Smith's *Showdown: JFK and the Integration of the Washington Redskins* (Boston: Beacon Press, 2011).

6. With the Ivy Group Agreement of 1945, eight universities (Brown, Columbia, Cornell, Dartmouth, Harvard, University of Pennsylvania, Princeton, and Yale) committed to uphold common academic standards and eligibility requirements for football players, and to avoid issuing athletic scholarships. Their goal was to prevent commercialization of the college sport and to keep it "in fitting proportion to the main purposes of academic life" (Proposed Intercollegiate Agreement, 1945, accessed at the Univ. of Pennsylvania Archives online, http://www.archives.upenn.edu/histy/features/imagepenn/ivy1945.pdf).

7. Julius Franks (1922–2008) was born in Macon, Georgia, and grew up in the Detroit area. He graduated from the University of Michigan in 1947 and received his DDS degree from the UM Dental School in 1951. Setting up a practice in Grand Rapids, Michigan, he also gained prominence as a civil rights leader, playing a key role in establishing the rights of African Americans to freely purchase homes in "whites-only" areas of Grand Rapids.

8. Marty Glickman, *The Fastest Kid on the Block* (Syracuse: Syracuse Univ. Press, 1996), 51.

9. Kirst, "Sidat-Singh," B1.

10. James Roland Coates Jr., "Gentlemen's Agreement: The 1937 Maryland/Syracuse Football Controversy" (master's thesis, University of Maryland, 1982), 61.

11. Ibid.

12. The NAIB eventually expanded into the range of college sports and became the National Association of Intercollegiate Athletics (NAIA), whose membership includes many traditionally black colleges.

13. Ted Green, "A Lasting Moral Victory" Indystar.com, July 29, 2010, http://archive.indystar.com/article/20100606/NEWS/100729009/A-lasting-moral-victory.

14. Melvin Besdin, interview with David Marc.

15. "Kilpatrick Dropped from Hill Cage Squad," *Syracuse Post-Standard*, February 3, 1954, 14.

16. Jack Slattery, "Highlighting Sports," *Syracuse Herald-Journal*, February 9, 1954, 22.

17. Emanuel "Manny" Breland, interview with David Marc.

18. Abdullah Alif Muhammad, interview with David Marc.

19. Greg Allen, interview with David Marc.

20. See J. Thomas Jable, "Jim Brown: Superlative Athlete, Screen Star, Social Activist," in *Out of the Shadows: A Biographical History of African American Athletes*, ed. David Kenneth Wiggins (Fayetteville: Univ. of Arkansas Press, 2006), 243.

21. David L. Johnson, interview with David Marc.

22. Dr. Allen R. Sullivan, interview with Victoria Kohl, April 21, 2006.

23. Glickman, *The Fastest Kid on the Block*, 54–55.

24. Jable, "Jim Brown," 243; Marty Gitlin, *Jim Brown: Football Great and Actor* (Minneapolis: ABDO Publishing, 2014), 33.

25. John Carroll, "Jim Brown at Syracuse," *College Football Historical Society* 19, no. 2 (February 2006): 2, http://www.la84foundation.org/SportsLibrary/CFHSN/CFHSNv19/CFHSNv19n2a.pdf. Lyons, a professor of American studies at the University of Buffalo, is a Faithkeeper of the Turtle Clan of the Onondaga and Seneca Nations and serves as a member of the Onondaga Council of Chiefs. Simmons was rare if not unique among collegiate coaches in teaching his players about the roots of lacrosse in Native American culture at a time when most of his colleagues were either ignorant of it or loathe to mention it.

26. Joe Ehrmann, *InsideOut Coaching: How Sports Can Transform Lives* (New York: Simon and Schuster, 2011), 54.

27. David Marc, "Joe Ehrmann: Transformational Coach," *Syracuse University Magazine* 28, no. 3 (Fall/Winter 2011): 58.

28. Dr. David Bloom, interview with David Marc.

29. The Anti-Defamation League was founded in 1913 as part of B'nai Brith, a Jewish fraternal organization. The Norwich, New York, B'nai Brith Lodge was named in Sol Bloom's honor.

30. According to Manny Breland, one of the few black students to play basketball for Syracuse during the 1950s, "it's always been a mystery as to how Sidat-Singh got a scholarship offer from Syracuse back in the 1930s. I can tell you from firsthand experience that Lew Andreas had a biased attitude toward black people and probably would have opposed the idea, if he knew Sidat-Singh's real identity" (interview with David Marc). Bloom's involvement in bringing Sidat-Singh to Syracuse cannot be proved. An informal recruiter, he left no paper trail to follow.

31. William Haskins Jr., interview with David Marc, May 2, 2011.

32. Morris shared this recollection with Larry Martin, associate vice president for program development at Syracuse University, who related the story to David Marc.

3. The Rise of Syracuse Football

1. As quoted in Sal Maiorana and Scott Pitoniak, *Slices of Orange* (Syracuse: Syracuse Univ. Press, 2005), 12.

2. In *Jim Brown: A Hero's Life*, Mike Freeman writes, "In August of 1952 . . . after an intense argument with one of the Syracuse coaches in which he says he was called several racial slurs . . . Stone abruptly quit the team and signed with the Canadian Football League" (San Francisco: HarperCollins, 2006), 97. University records indicate that while Avatus Stone did not play football in his senior year, he remained a student and graduated in May 1953.

3. E. Culpepper Clark and Dan T. Carter, *The Schoolhouse Door: Segregation's Last Stand* (New York: Oxford Univ. Press, 1993), 19.

4. "When Buffalo Declined the 1958 Tangerine Bowl Because of Racism," *New York Times* (AP), November 15, 2008, http://www.nytimes.com/2008/11/16 /sports/ncaafootball/16buffalo.html?pagewanted=all.

5. Ibid.

6. John Robert Greene, *Syracuse University: The Tolley Years, 1942–1969* (Syracuse: Syracuse Univ. Press, 1996), 139.

7. Ibid.

8. The only consensus national college football championship teams from New York before 1959 were Cornell (1915) and Army (1944, 1945).

9. As quoted in Greene, *Syracuse University: The Tolley Years*, 133.

10. Ben Schwartzwalder, letter to Carl Schott, August 22, 1950.

11. Greene, *Syracuse University: The Tolley Years*, 196.

12. In an interview given at age eighty-six, Custis was asked if Davis had ever offered him a coaching position with the Raiders. He replied that over the course of decades Davis had offered him "countless jobs, but I have an issue with flying and haven't been on a plane in 41 years." The comment appeared in "Former Orange QB Bernie Custis Honored for Breaking Down Barriers," *Syracuse Post-Standard*, August 12, 2011.

13. Steve Milton, "Iconoclast, Quarterback, Educator—Custis Broke the Colour Barrier," *Hamilton Spectator*, August 11, 2011.

14. "Orange Coaches Gloomy as Colgate Drills Get Under way," *Syracuse Post-Standard*, November 13, 1950.

15. *Jet*, November 8, 1951, 46.

16. William Nack, *My Turf: Horses, Boxers, Blood Money, and the Sporting Life* (Boston: Da Capo Press, 2003), 284.

17. Joseph Lampe, interview with David Marc.

18. William Haskins Jr., interview with David Marc.

19. John A. Williams, "Portrait of a City: Syracuse, the Old Home Town," circa 1964, first published by *Syracuse University Library Associates Courier* 28, no. 1 (Spring 1993). *Holiday* magazine, the intended publisher, rejected the article. A typescript copy of the article is held by Syracuse University Library's Special Collection Research Center. Williams was Paul Robeson Professor of English at Rutgers University until his retirement in 1994.

20. Marla Anne Bennett, "Marginally Accepted: Policies and Practices Influencing the Enrollment of Black Students at Syracuse University from 1942 to 1969" (doctoral dissertation, Syracuse University, 1998), 203. UMI 9904235.

21. Mike Freeman, *Jim Brown: A Hero's Life* (San Francisco: HarperCollins, 2006), 81.

22. Eileen Brennan, "A Sad Farewell to 'Mr. Manhasset,'" *Manhasset Press* March 19, 1999, http://www.antonnews.com/manhassetpress/1999/03/19/news/molloy.html.

23. John Carroll, "Jim Brown at Syracuse," *College Football Historical Society* 19, no. 2 (February 2006): 2, http://www.la84foundation.org/SportsLibrary/CFHSN/CFHSNv19/CFHSNv19n2a.pdf.

24. As quoted in the Jim Brown exhibit, National Lacrosse Hall of Fame, http://apps.uslacrosse.org/museum/halloffame/view_profile.php?prof_id=35.

25. "Making History: Jim Brown Defeats Jim Crow in LAX," *Syracuse Manuscript* (Syracuse University's African American and Latino Alumni Newsletter), Fall/Winter 2011–12: 3.

26. As cited in Will Sullivan, "The Man Who Redefined the Game: Jim Brown," *U.S. News and World Report*, August 5, 2007.

27. Emanuel "Manny" Breland, interview with David Marc.

28. Carroll, "Jim Brown at Syracuse," 3.

29. Ibid., 4.

30. Ronald Womack, interview with David Marc.

31. David L. Johnson, interview with David Marc.

32. David Marc, "Garland Jeffries: Fearless Music," *Syracuse University Magazine* 28, no. 3 (Fall/Winter 2011): 56.

33. David Marc, "John Kellogg: Leadership Performances," *Syracuse University Magazine* 26, no. 3 (Fall/Winter 2009), http://sumagazine.syr.edu/2009fall-winter/alumnijournal/profiles/johnkellogg.html.

34. Roderick Boone, "At EFA, a Hoops Star, Too," *Elmira Star Gazette*, December 8, 2001, http://www.stargazettesports.com/ErnieDavis/ernie10.html.

35. To this day, the annual basketball media guides published by the university list the three forfeited games in 1957–58 as Syracuse wins.

36. Scott Pitoniak, "A Historic Moment 50 Years Ago Today," concerning the anniversary of Ernie Davis receiving the Heisman Trophy, http://suathletics.syr .edu/news/2011/12/6/FB_1206114105.aspx.

37. Rebecca Murray, "Floyd Little Interview," http://video.about.com/movies/ Floyd-Little-Interview.htm. The interview with Little took place on the occasion of the premiere of *The Express* (2008).

38. Marty Glickman, *The Fastest Kid on the Block* (Syracuse: Syracuse Univ. Press, 1996), 51.

39. Gary Youmans and Maury Youmans, *'59: The Story of the 1959 Syracuse University National Championship Football Team* (Syracuse: Syracuse Univ. Press, 2003), 37.

40. The career of Chester Carlton "Cookie" Gilchrist illustrates many of the obstacles facing African American athletes during the 1950s and 1960s. Gilchrist was a dominant player at Har-Brack High School in Western Pennsylvania. Receiving no academic support at school, he was nineteen years old and more than a year away from graduation when his high school eligibility ran out. With no possibility of attending college, Gilchrist went to a Cleveland Browns open tryout in the summer of 1954. To admit him to camp, the team had to get special permission from NFL commissioner Bert Bell. The Browns decided Gilchrist wasn't ready for the team, but they refused to relinquish exclusive rights to his services, effectively preventing Gilchrist from signing with any other team in the league. Rather than agree to a $10 per diem salary as a member of the Cleveland taxi squad, Gilchrist crossed the border to play in Canada, where he developed into a star running back with the Toronto Argonauts. The establishment of the AFL, which did not recognize NFL draft rights, opened the door for Gilchrist to return to the United States. Signing with the Buffalo Bills, he immediately established himself as one of new league's leading rushers—and one of its most outspoken players. When the AFL scheduled its January 1965 All-Star game at racially segregated Tulane Stadium in New Orleans, Gilchrist led a boycott movement, enlisting the support of all twenty-one African Americans on both All-Star teams. The AFL relocated the game to Houston. Gilchrist, the only player ever selected for All-Star teams in the NFL, AFL, and CFL, is also the only player ever to refuse induction into the Canadian Football Hall of Fame. He cited racism and financial exploitation as causes for his decision. Tim Graham, "Cookie Gilchrist Rumbled Right Until the End," January 11, 2011, http://espn.go.com/blog/afceast/post/_/id/24656/cookie -gilchrist-rumbled-right-until-the-end.

41. As quoted by Mark Palmer, "InterMat Rewind: African-American Mat History," February 27, 2008, http://www.intermatwrestle.com/articles/3568.

42. NFL 88 Plan, accessed at the NFL Player Care Foundation website, https://www.nflplayercare.com/88PlanOverview.aspx. John Mackey and the Center for the Study of Traumatic Encephalopathy at the Boston University School of Medicine, "20 More NFL Stars to Donate Brains to Research," Boston University School of Medicine website, http://www.bumc.bu.edu/busm/2010 /02/01/20-more-nfl-stars-to-donate-brains-to-research.

43. Jonathan Abrams, "From Patty Hearst to David Stern: Billy Hunter's Long, Strange Career," *Grantland* website, August 4, 2011, http://grantland.com /features/from-patty-hearst-david-stern/.

44. Abrams, "From Patty Hearst to David Stern."

45. Womack, interview.

46. Ibid.

47. Ibid.

48. D.J. Harrell, interview with David Marc.

49. Ibid.

50. John Robert Greene, *Syracuse University: The Eggers Years, 1969–1991* (Syracuse: Syracuse Univ. Press, 1998), 48.

51. Ibid., 49.

52. John Lobon, interview with David Marc.

53. Kevin McLoughlin, interview with David Marc.

54. Interview with Kevin McLoughlin, December 14, 2011. McLoughlin was reluctant to utter the words that he thought Schwartzwalder had stopped himself from saying. The interviewer asked, "Did he stop himself from saying 'nigger lover?'" McLoughlin replied affirmatively.

55. McLoughlin, interview.

56. Lobon, interview.

57. Greene, *Syracuse University: The Eggers Years*, 48.

58. Abdullah Alif Muhammad, interview with David Marc.

4. End of an Era

1. "Syracuse's Old Ben Going Strong at 61," *Daytona Beach Sunday News-Journal*, November 10, 1970, 7.

2. Pat Putnam, "End of a Season at Syracuse," *Sports Illustrated*, September 28, 1970, http://www.si.com/vault/1970/09/28/611240/end-of-a-season-at-syracuse.

3. "Syracuse's Old Ben," 7.

4. When Syracuse took the national championship in 1959, it was the first private college from the Northeast to earn that honor since the University of Pittsburgh turned the trick in 1937. Pittsburgh was the next to do it again, in 1976. Among public colleges in the Northeast, only Maryland (1953) and Penn State

(1983, 1986) have come out on top in college football since World War II. In the absence of national contenders, the region where college football was invented has become a place where tradition—Harvard-Yale, Army-Navy, Lafayette-Lehigh—suffices as the main attraction of the game.

5. American Football Coaches Association. "Amos Alonzo Stagg Award." *AFCA* website, accessed August 6, 2014, http://www.afca.com/article/article.php?id=StaggAward.

6. The Ben Schwartzwalder Papers are held by the Syracuse University Archives. The collection contains numerous letters of support from the public supporting Schwartzwalder's refusal to accommodate the Syracuse Eight in any way, despite the urgings of Chancellor John Corbally. For example, a letter dated August 26, 1970, stated that the writers wanted Schwartzwalder to know that they had just contacted the chancellor, telling him off for going over the coach's head by reinstating the black athletes who were causing trouble. Letters of support from alumni tended to use less vitriolic language, but were no less enthusiastic about Schwartzwalder's position concerning the protesting students. One member of the class of 1927 wrote to Schwartzwalder on August 25, 1970: "Your supporters . . . represent the responsible white element, not the demanding Black radical of dissent, riot, and revolution."

7. Joe Ehrmann, *InsideOut Coaching: How Sports Can Transform Lives* (New York: Simon and Schuster, 2011), 26.

8. "Jim Brown Fails in Mediating Role, Lashes Syracuse Bias," *Jet*, September 17, 1970, 54.

9. John Crittendon, "Schwartzwalder: Too Late for Unbending Ben to Yield," *Miami News*, September 24, 1970, 1D–2D.

10. Ronald Womack, interview with David Marc.

11. Clarence "Bucky" McGill, interview with David Marc.

12. Greg Allen, interview with David Marc.

13. Duane Walker, interview with David Marc.

14. The actual document sent to the coach is lost; no copy was made and Schwartzwalder did not return it to the members of the Syracuse Eight or place it among the papers he donated to the university. The complaints are paraphrased here based on the recollections of some of the original authors.

15. Abdullah Alif Muhammad, interview with David Marc.

16. Jim Boeheim, interview with David Marc.

17. Allen, interview.

18. Ibid.

19. McGill, interview.

20. "Godbolt Granted Scholarship to Syracuse University," *Bridgeport Sunday Post*, April 23, 1967, C-2.

21. McGill, interview.

22. Allen, interview.

23. McGill, interview.

24. The source of this and other biographical information concerning William Pelow is the obituary, "Dr. Pelow: Sports Medic, Nine Years at SU," *Syracuse Herald-Journal*, December 12, 1983, D4.

25. "Jules Reichel—1965." National Athletic Trainers' Association Hall of Fame website, accessed Sept. 5, 2014, http://www.nata.org/HallofFame/index.htm#35.

26. McGill, interview.

27. John Lobon, interview with David Marc.

28. Womack, interview.

29. Kevin McLoughlin, interview with David Marc.

30. "Negroes Boycott Syracuse Drills," *New York Times*, April, 22, 1970, 78.

31. Ibid.

32. Interestingly, the paper's apparent shift from "Negro" to "black" in the 1970s actually marked a return to the newspaper's preference for that term, which was part of its stylebook until 1930. According to the online Jim Crow Museum of Ferris State University in Michigan, W. E. B. Dubois lobbied the *Times* and other newspapers to use "Negro," preferring a capitalized proper noun to the commonly used generic terms "colored" and "black," which he felt were inaccurate. Forty years later, "Negro" was dropped in favor of "black." See "When Did the Word Negro Become Socially Unacceptable?" Jim Crow Museum, Ferris State University website, accessed Sept. 5, 2014, http://www.ferris.edu/News/jimcrow/question/oct10/index.htm.

33. Meeting with David Marc, March 2012.

34. "Blacks File Complaint of Discrimination," *Sarasota Journal*, August 21, 1970, 2c.

35. Ibid.

36. "Eight Blacks Fail to Appear: Syracuse Football Team Starts Practice," *Schenectady Gazette*, August 29, 1970.

37. "Jack Gaither Rattled Off Winning Seasons at Florida A&M," Fox Sports website, accessed Sept. 6, 2014, http://www.foxsports.com/college-football/story/jake-gaither-rattled-off-winning-seasons-at-florida-a-m-021414.

38. Samuel Freedman, *Breaking the Line: The Season in Black College Football that Transformed the Sport and Changed the Course of Civil Rights* (New York: Simon and Schuster, 2013), 255.

39. "Syracuse Gets Black Coach," *Spartanburg Herald-Journal*, July 25, 1970, 9.

40. "Black Syracuse Players File Charge with Amity Body," *Jet*, September 10, 1970, 56.

41. Muhammad, interview.

42. "All-Time Syracuse Football Coaching Staffs (Year-by-Year)," Syracuse University Athletics website, http://cuse.com/sports/2008/1/31/fbcoachstaffyear byyear.aspx.

43. Another source at the SU Athletics website presents "All-Time SU Football Coaches Roster" alphabetically (http://www.cuse.com/sports/2008/2/4/020408All -TimeFootballCoachesAlphabetical.aspx), listing Jones as "assistant freshman coach" for 1970 (the freshman football team ceased to exist after 1969) and then as "assistant coach" (1970–71).

44. Jared Diamond, "Nine Men Out: SU to Honor Black Players Saturday Who Boycotted 1970 Team Due to Racism," *Daily Orange*, Oct. 18, 2006.

45. "Blacks File Complaint."

5. End of an Error

1. Clarence "Bucky" McGill, interview with David Marc.

2. Greg Allen, interview with David Marc.

3. Jim Brown, press release, September 3, 1970.

4. "SU Snubs Six Black Varsity Grid Players," *Syracuse Post-Standard*, August 20, 1970, 19.

5. Joe Ehrmann, interview with David Marc.

6. Schwartzwalder refers to the reinstatement of seven rather than eight players because Richard Bulls had been a freshman the previous season, and not a member of the varsity.

7. Allen, interview.

8. It's worth noting that Griffin had played both halfback on offense and linebacker on defense at Easton High School in Pennsylvania, starring at both positions.

9. Robert Creamer, ed. "Scorecard: Orange and Black," *Sports Illustrated*, August 31, 1970, http://www.si.com/vault/1970/08/31/611215/scorecard.

10. Allen, interview.

11. Ehrmann, interview.

12. John Lobon, interview with David Marc.

13. John E. Corbally Jr., in a letter to Maurice N. Katz and Simon J. Katz of Springfield, Massachusetts, October 7, 1970.

14. Abdullah Alif Muhammad, interview with David Marc.

15. "Players Support Syracuse Coach," *New York Times*, August 28, 1970, 24.

16. The four white members of the football team who refused to sign the anti-Syracuse Eight "petition" were John F. Connelly, Nile Evans, Mark Wadach, and Stan Walters. Wadach was a multitalented athlete who was scrimmaging with the football team but made his name as a three-year starter on the Orange basketball

team. Walters, a left guard, had an eleven-year pro football career with Cincinnati and Philadelphia, eventually becoming an Eagles' broadcaster.

17. Don Pickard, "SU Football Boycott Threat Evaporates," *Syracuse Post-Standard*, September 23, 1970, 1.

18. Ibid., 22.

19. "Demonstration Forces Reinstatement of Athletes," *Jet*, Oct. 8, 1970, 51.

20. "Jim Brown Fails in Mediating Role: Lashes Syracuse Bias," *Jet*, September 17, 1970, 54–55.

21. John Robert Greene, *Syracuse University: The Eggers Years, 1969–1991* (Syracuse: Syracuse Univ. Press, 1998), 58.

22. William Morrissey (AP), "Syracuse Football Squabble Threatens Saturday's Game," *Wellsville* [NY] *Daily Reporter*, September 25, 1970, 10.

23. Jim Brown, interview with David Marc.

24. Arnie Burdick, "Problem All Ben's—Jim Brown," *Syracuse Herald-Journal*, September 3, 1970, 53.

25. According to Schwartzwalder's neighbor, Emmett Hoagland, "Ben was always making jokes about 'Polack this' and 'Jew that,' and so when I saw that in the paper ("the word 'bigoted' is not in my vocabulary"), I went over there with my dad and we kidded him about it," Hoagland said. "Then he got really mad and said, 'Goddamned reporters! I was trying to tell him that Brown was lying when he said I called my own players "bigots."'"

26. Phil Rizzuto, *It's Sports Time*, CBS Radio Network, Friday, September 25, 1970. Ben Schwartzwalder Papers, Syracuse University Archives.

27. Morrissey (AP), "Syracuse Football Squabble Threatens Saturday's Game," *Wellsville* [NY] *Daily Reporter,* September 25, 1970, 10.

28. Ibid.

29. Ibid.

30. Al Lawrence, "Quiet Prevails the Day After," *Syracuse Post-Standard*, September 28, 1970, 6.

31. Neil Amdur, "Kansas Conquers Syracuse," *New York Times*, September 27, 1970, S1.

32. "Police Disperse Brick-Throwing Mob at Syracuse University," *New York Times*, September 27, 1970, A14.

33. *Syracuse Post-Standard*, September 28, 1970, 6.

34. "The Morning's Mail," *Syracuse Post-Standard*, September 30, 1970, 4.

35. Greene, *Syracuse University: The Eggers Years*, 58.

36. Paul Riede, "Carl Paladino's Tale of Helping Defuse 1970 Syracuse University Student Strike Doesn't Ring True With Some," *Syracuse Post-Standard*, October 4, 2010, accessed September 6, 2014, http://www.syracuse.com/news/index.ssf/2010/10/carl_paladinos_tale_of_helping.html.

37. "Schwartzwalder Named Eastern Coach of Year," *Bangor Daily News*, December 1, 1970.

38. Bruno Sniders, "No Scars Left at Syracuse U" (Gannett News Service), *Plainfield* [NJ] *Courier-News*, August 28, 1971, 14.

6. Aftermath

1. "Report of Trustee, Faculty and Student Committee on Allegations of Racial Discrimination in the Football Program," Syracuse University (unpublished), 1970, 1.

2. Ibid., 31.

3. Ibid., 38.

4. Douglas S. Looney, "The Fearsome Foursome," *Sports Illustrated*, August 24, 1981, 37.

5. William Kates, "Thirty-six Years Later, School Honors Players' Anti-racism Stand," Associated Press, October 21, 2006.

6. Bob Kyle, "Syracuse President Discusses Black Boycotts," *Indiana Daily Student*, October 29, 1970, 9.

7. Robert McG. Thomas, Jr. "Ben Schwartzwalder Dies at 83; Revitalized Football at Syracuse," *New York Times*, April 29, 1993.

7. Legacies

1. The Coaches Poll, the other major barometer for determining national rankings, was more generous to Schwartzwalder, most likely due to his status as a revered colleague. But here too Syracuse did not finish a season in the top ten even once during the 1960s.

2. Penn State, which also posted an 8–2 record (including a victory over Syracuse) was the only team from the Northeast invited to play in a Division IA post-season game in 1967.

3. Art Monk, interview with David Marc.

4. James M. Mannheim, "Art Monk," *Gale Contemporary Black Biography* (1999). Retrieved from http://search.proquest.com/docview/196825192?account id=14214.

5. Monk, interview.

8. Gregory Allen

1. Don Pickard, "Allen Lost to SU," *Syracuse Post-Standard*, September 1, 1971, 31.

2. Charles V. Willie was the first African American professor on the Syracuse University faculty. After receiving a doctorate in sociology from Syracuse, he taught there until 1974, when he joined the faculty of Harvard University's School of Graduate Education.

9. Richard Tyrone Bulls (1951–2010)

1. "UB Drops Football," *Buffalo News*, January 18, 1971. The University of Buffalo revived its football program in 1977 and has been fielding a team ever since.

13. Abdullah Alif Muhammad

1. Mike Jarvis went on to a distinguished career as a college basketball coach. In eighteen seasons as head coach at Boston University (1985–90), George Washington (1990–98), St. John's University (1998–2003), and Florida Atlantic (2008–present), he amassed a record of 364–201. During the early 1980s he coached at Rindge, where his players included Patrick Ewing.

2. The Walter Brennan Award is named for the film and television actor, a 1915 graduate of Rindge.

14. John Lobon

1. The "blackballing" or "blacklisting" of Lobon, Allen, and other members of the Syracuse Eight from professional football was part of a general trend on the part of team owners, following the NFL-AFL merger, to clamp down on players perceived as militants or radicals, many of whom were African American. From 1960 to 1967, when the two leagues were in competition with each other for players, it was difficult if not impossible to enforce such a ban. But with the two leagues now sharing a common player draft, and the political atmosphere reaching a fever point, blacklisting was on the rise in professional football. In 1970, for example, Bernie Parrish and Walter Beach, two former NFL players with a history of social activism, told a Cleveland Grand Jury they believed they had been blacklisted for engaging in constitutionally protected speech. Parrish was writing a book on owner-player labor relations (*They Call It a Game*, 1971), in which he advocated transforming the NFL Players Association into a traditional labor union affiliated to the Teamsters. Beach, then attending law school in the off-season, had spoken publicly on racial discrimination and gambling in the league.

15. Duane "Spoon" Walker (1949–2010)

1. Allie Sherman, who graduated from Boys High School in 1939 at age sixteen, never played high school football; because of his age and size, his mother refused to sign a permission slip. Sherman did serve as captain of the Boys High handball team.

2. Tunnell started his college football career at the University of Toledo, but left in his sophomore year to serve in the military during World War II. After the war, he transferred to the University of Iowa, which had a reputation for the fair treatment of African American student athletes. Tunnel led the Hawkeyes in passing in 1946, completing 28 of 58 passes for 228 yards. Tunnell does not, however, qualify as the first black quarterback on a predominantly white college team; that distinction goes to Bernie Custis at Syracuse in 1948. Tunnell racked up his passing yards while playing left tailback for Iowa's single-wing offense, a formation that has no quarterback.

3. While it is difficult to document the Willie Smith story, as no statistics on defensive players were made public, this item appeared in the *Syracuse Post-Standard* (August 1, 1967, 25) in an article assessing the prospects of the Orange football team for the coming season: "Sophomores will hold the key to what degree of success the Orange enjoys . . . and two of the most highly regarded sophs are quarterback Rich Panczyszin and defensive tackle Will Smith. Both were instrumental in the Tangerines going undefeated last year." (The Syracuse freshman football team was informally known as the Tangerines.)

4. Walker points out that the demise of Willie Smith's football career in 1967 was the second of three consecutive seasons during which promising African American players were benched and otherwise harassed for interracial dating, much to the detriment of the team's performance. In 1966, Oley Allen, a halfback out of Cranberry, New Jersey, was touted by *Sports Illustrated* as the most promising sophomore running back in the country. He was assumed to be the heir-apparent to get the Number 44 jersey that had been worn by Jim Brown, Ernie Davis, and Floyd Little. Playing behind Little and Larry Csonka for Syracuse in 1966, Oley Allen made just 35 rushing attempts, but averaged more than 5 yards per carry. With Little graduating that spring, Allen looked forward to being paired with Csonka in 1967. But at some point in the off-season, the coaches learned that Allen, while keeping his dorm room, was living most of the time in an off-campus apartment with his girlfriend, who was white, and from his hometown. In a move designed to humiliate him, the Number 44 jersey was given to a (white) sophomore backup quarterback and Oley Allen was reassigned the Number 33. Walker, who was still in high school when this happened, says, "Willie Smith and John Brown

told me that that Number 44 was supposed to be a sign of pride for black players at Syracuse. They all got a message when Schwartzwalder suddenly gave it away to a white player that was just joining the varsity." Oley Allen was demoted on the halfback depth chart and exiled to the bench. During the 1967 season, his entire record consisted of 16 carries from scrimmage and seven kick returns. According to Walker, "the coaches destroyed Oley Allen's life over an issue that was none of their business. Bucky McGill puts it this way: "Oley lost his damn mind after that."

Dave Johnson, who caught the wrath of the Syracuse coaching staff in 1966 for interracial dating, described the way the matter was generally handled by the coaching staff: "Coach Bell was the messenger regarding the dating issue for me, and I'm sure he was for Willie Smith, too. My experience was that you were called into the coach's office and questioned about your dating relationship. But they weren't investigating anything. They already knew the name of the woman who was involved. In my case, they had already sent somebody to see her. It came down to this: If you told them it was none of their business what you did off the field and that you could date whoever you wanted, then your playing time would start to diminish. They never told you this would happen. They just did it to you and no reason was ever given. Once that process started, there was nothing you could do to regain playing time. The subject was never mentioned again" (interview with David Marc).

5. Dr. Willie Smith, known after his marriage as Dr. William Stevenson-Smith, died in 1992 at the age of forty-four. In addition to the MD degree he earned at Tufts University in 1974, he completed work on a doctorate at Temple University in 1986.

Bibliography

Books, Articles, and Theses

Bennett, Marla Anne. "Marginally Accepted: Policies and Practices Influencing the Enrollment of Black Students at Syracuse University from 1942 to 1969." Doctoral dissertation, Syracuse University, 1998. UMI 9904235.

Brokaw, Tom. *The Greatest Generation*. New York: Random House, 1998.

Bullock, Clifford A. "Fired by Conscience: The Black 14 Incident at the University of Wyoming and Black Protest in the Western Athletic Conference." Unpublished collection on Wyoming history, Department of History, University of Wyoming, n.d.

Carroll, John M. *Fritz Pollard: Pioneer in Racial Advancement*. Urbana: Univ. of Illinois Press, 1992.

Carroll, John. "Jim Brown at Syracuse." *College Football Historical Society* 19, no. 2 (February 2006). http://www.la84foundation.org/Sports Library/CFHSN/CFHSNv19/CFHSNv19n2a.pdf.

Clark, E. Culpepper, and Dan T. Carter. *The Schoolhouse Door: Segregation's Last Stand*. New York: Oxford Univ. Press, 1993.

Coates, James Roland Jr. "Gentlemen's Agreement: The 1937 Maryland/Syracuse Football Controversy." Master's thesis, University of Maryland, 1982.

Creamer, Robert, ed. "Scorecard: Orange and Black," *Sports Illustrated*, August 31, 1970. http://www.si.com/vault/1970/08/31/611215/scorecard.

Cyphers, Luke. "The Lost Hero: Wilmeth Sidat-Singh Was a Two-Sport Star at Syracuse and a Harlem Renaissance Man." *New York Daily News*, February 25, 2001. http://nydailynews.com/archives/sports/ lost -hero-wilmeth-sidat-singh-two-sport-star-syracuse-harlem-renaissance -man-article-1.906303.

Demas, Lane. *Integrating the Gridiron: Black Civil Rights and American College Football*. New Brunswick, NJ: Rutgers Univ. Press, 2010.

Edwards, Harry. *Revolt of the Black Athlete*. New York: Free Press, 1969.

————. *The Sociology of Sport*. Homewood, IL: Dorsey Press, 1973.

Ehrmann, Joe. *InsideOut Coaching: How Sports Can Transform Lives*. New York: Simon and Schuster, 2011.

Freedman, Samuel. *Breaking the Line: The Season in Black College Football that Transformed the Sport and Changed the Course of Civil Rights*. New York: Simon and Schuster, 2013.

Freeman, Mike. *Jim Brown: A Hero's Life*. San Francisco: HarperCollins, 2006.

Gallagher, Robert C. *Ernie Davis: The Elmira Express*. Silver Spring, MD: Bartleby Press, 1983.

Gitlin, Marty. *Jim Brown: Football Great and Actor*. Minneapolis: ABDO Publishing, 2014.

Glickman, Marty. *The Fastest Kid on the Block*. Syracuse: Syracuse Univ. Press, 1996.

Gould, Todd. *Pioneers of the Hardwood: Indiana and the Birth of Professional Basketball*. Bloomington: Univ. of Indiana Press, 1998.

Greene, John Robert. *Syracuse University: The Tolley Years, 1942–1969*. Syracuse: Syracuse Univ. Press, 1996.

————. *Syracuse University: The Eggers Years, 1969–1991*. Syracuse: Syracuse Univ. Press, 1998.

Grundy, Pamela. *Learning to Win: Sports, Education, and Social Change*. Chapel Hill: Univ. of North Carolina Press, 2001.

Hano, Arnold. "The Black Rebel Who 'Whitelists' the Olympics." *New York Times Magazine*, May 12, 1968.

Hoffer, Richard. *Something in the Air: American Passion and Defiance in the 1968 Mexico City Olympic Games*. New York: Free Press, 2009.

Hoffman, Melody K. "Syracuse University Recognizes 'Sacrifices' of Former Football Players." *Jet*, October 23, 2006, 51–52.

Jable, J. Thomas. "Jim Brown: Superlative Athlete, Screen Star, Social Activist." In *Out of the Shadows: A Biographical History of African American Athletes*, edited by David Kenneth Wiggins, 241–62. Fayetteville: Univ. of Arkansas Press, 2006.

Jay, Kathryn. *More than Just a Game: Sports in American Life Since 1945.* New York: Columbia Univ. Press, 2006.

Kirst, Sean. "Sidat-Singh, A Name SU Ignores." *Syracuse Post-Standard,* April 2, 2003, B1.

Koffman, Jack. "Competition Hot: Stone in Struggle to Catch Birth." *Ottawa Citizen,* July 28, 1955, 21.

Lacy, Sam. "Syracuse Acts on Race Issue." *Washington Afro American,* February 9, 1971, 13–15.

Lloyd, Earl and Sean Kirst. *Moonfixer: The Basketball Journey of Earl Lloyd.* Syracuse: Syracuse Univ. Press, 2010.

Looney, Douglas S. "The Fearsome Foursome." *Sports Illustrated,* August 24, 1981, 36–39.

Maiorana, Sal and Scott Pitoniak. *Slices of Orange.* Syracuse: Syracuse Univ. Press, 2005.

Marc, David. "Garland Jeffreys: Fearless Music," *Syracuse University Magazine* 28, no. 3 (Fall/Winter 2011): 56–57.

———. "Joe Ehrmann: Transformational Coach," *Syracuse University Magazine* 28, no. 3 (Fall/Winter 2011): 58.

———. "John Kellogg: Leadership Performances," *Syracuse University Magazine* 26, no. 3 (Fall/Winter 2009).

Martin, Charles H. *Benching Jim Crow: The Rise and Fall of the Color Line in Southern College Sports, 1890–1980.* Urbana: Univ. of Illinois Press, 2010.

———. "Integrating New Year's Day: The Racial Politics of College Bowl Games in the American South." *Journal of Sport History* 24, no. 3 (Fall 1997): 358–77.

Matthews, Vincent and Neil Amdur. *My Race Be Won.* New York: Charter House, 1974.

Miller, Patrick B. "Sport as 'Interracial Education': Popular Culture and Civil Rights Strategies during the 1930s and Beyond." In *The Civil Rights Movement Revisited: Critical Perspectives on the Struggle for Racial Equality in the United States,* edited by Patrick B. Miller, Therese Frey Stegffen, and Elisabeth Schäfer-Wünsche, 21–38. London: Lit Verlag Münster, 2001.

Morrissey, William. "Syracuse Football Squabble Threatens Saturday's Game." *Wellsville* [NY] *Daily Reporter,* September 25, 1970.

Nack, William. *My Turf: Horses, Boxers, Blood Money, and the Sporting Life*. Boston: Da Capo Press, 2003.

New York Times. "Alcindor Shuns Olympics." February 28, 1968. select .nytimes.com/gst/abstract.html?res=F40614FC3F5F127A93CAAB178 9D85F4C8685F9.

Putnam, Pat. "End of a Season at Syracuse." *Sports Illustrated*, September 28, 1970. http://www.si.com/vault/1970/09/28/611240/end-of-a-season -at-syracuse.

Rhoden, William C. "Syracuse Honors Nine Players Who Took a Stand." *New York Times*, October 22, 2006.

Scott, Robert J. and Myles A. Pocta. *Honor on the Line: The Fifth Down and the Spectacular 1940 College Football Season*. Bloomington, IN: iUniverse, 2012.

Smith, John Matthew. "'Breaking the Plane': Integration and Black Protest in Michigan State University Football during the 19060s." *Michigan Historical Review* 33, no. 2 (September 2007): 101–29.

Smith, Thomas G. *Showdown: JFK and the Integration of the Washington Redskins*. Boston: Beacon Press, 2011.

Sullivan, Will. "The Man Who Redefined the Game: Jim Brown," *U.S. News and World Report*, August 5, 2007.

Thorburn, Ryan. *Black 14: The Rise, Fall and Rebirth of Wyoming Football*. Boulder, CO: Burning Daylight, 2009.

Wiggins, David K., *Glory Bound: Black Athletes in a White America*. Syracuse: Syracuse Univ. Press, 1997.

———. "The Future of College Athletics Is at Stake: Black Athletes and Racial Turmoil on Three Predominantly White University Campuses, 1968–1972." *Journal of Sport History* 15, no. 3 (Fall 1988): 304–33.

Williams, John A. "Portrait of a City: Syracuse, the Old Hometown," circa 1964, published in *Syracuse University Library Associates Courier* 28, no. 1 (Spring 1993).

Willie, Charles Vert, *Effective Education: A Minority Policy Perspective*. Westport, CT: Greenwood Press, 1989.

Youmans, Gary and Maury Youmans. *'59: The Story of the 1959 Syracuse University National Championship Football Team*. Syracuse: Syracuse Univ. Press, 2003.

Collections and Archives

Ben Schwartzwalder Papers, University Archives, Syracuse University Libraries.

Lewis P. Andreas Papers, Syracuse University Staff Archives.

Interviews Conducted for This Book

Greg Allen, member of the Syracuse Eight

Melvin Besdin, Syracuse University basketball, class of 1954; real estate executive (ret.)

David Bloom, son of Dr. Meyer "Sol" Bloom

Jim Boeheim, Syracuse University basketball, class of 1966; head basketball coach, 1976–present

Manny Breland, Syracuse University basketball, class of 1957; teacher; Coordinator of Special Needs Education, Syracuse City School District (ret.)

Richard Bulls (1951–2010), member of the Syracuse Eight

Jack Cavanaugh, Syracuse University class of 1952; *New York Times* sportswriter (ret.)

Joe Ehrmann, Syracuse University football and lacrosse, class of 1973; NFL player, 1973–82; co-founder of Coach for America; author

William Haskins Jr., Syracuse University football and track, class of 1952; executive, National Urban League, Boys and Girls Clubs of America (ret.)

Garland Jeffreys, Syracuse University class of 1965; musician, recording artist

David L. Johnson, Syracuse University football, class of 1971; business executive

John P. Kellogg, Syracuse University class of 1973; attorney; faculty member, Berklee College of Music

Joseph Lampe, Syracuse University class of 1953; College of Law, 1955; attorney; Chair Emeritus, Syracuse University Board of Trustees.

John Lobon, member of the Syracuse Eight

Clarence "Bucky" McGill, member of the Syracuse Eight

Kevin McLoughlin, Syracuse University football, class of 1970; U.S. Forest Service (ret.)

Art Monk, Syracuse University football, class of 1980; NFL player (1980–95); founder, Art Monk Foundation; Syracuse University Trustee

Horace W. Morris (1928–2011), Syracuse University football, class of 1949; executive, United Way of New York

Abdullah Alif Muhammad, member of the Syracuse Eight

Allen R. Sullivan, Syracuse University, PhD, 1970; teacher, school administrator, Executive Director for Student Development and Student Advocacy, Dallas Independent School District (ret.) Duane "Spoon" Walker (1949–2010), member of the Syracuse Eight

Ronald Womack, member of the Syracuse Eight

Index

Italic page number denotes illustrations and tables.

Known principally for his writing on television, film, and popular culture, editor and ghost writer DAVID MARC is the author of *Demographic Vistas: Television in American Culture*, and *Our Movie Houses*, with Norman O. Keim, named 2008 "book of the year" by the Theatre Historical Society of America. His feature articles, essays, and reviews have been published in *The Atlantic Monthly*, *The Village Voice*, and *Television Quarterly*. He has contributed chapters to more than a dozen critical anthologies, including *Mad Men: Dream Come True TV* (edited by Gary Edgerton, 2011). A graduate of Binghamton University, Marc holds a doctorate in American studies from the University of Iowa. He has taught at Brown, Brandeis, Cal Tech, USC, UCLA, UC-San Diego, and Syracuse University, and has been a writer for *Syracuse University Magazine*.